ANCIENT CULTURES OF CONCEIT

ANCIENT CULTURES OF CONCEIT

CONCEIT

BRITISH UNIVERSITY FICTION
IN THE POST-WAR YEARS

IAN CARTER

ROUTLEDGE

London and New York

First published 1990
by Routledge
11 New Fetter Lane, London EC4P 4EE

Simultaneously published in the USA and Canada by Routledge
a division of Routledge, Chapman and Hall, Inc.
29 West 35th Street, New York, NY 10010

©1990 Ian Carter

Typeset by LaserScript Limited, Mitcham, Surrey

Printed and bound in Great Britain by
Mackays of Chatham PLC, Chatham, Kent

British Library Cataloguing in Publication Data

Carter, Ian, 1943–
Ancient cultures of conceit: British University
fiction in the post war years.
1. Fiction in English, 1945– Special subjects
universities critical studies
I. Title
823'.914'09355

Library of Congress Cataloging in Publication Data

Carter, Ian.
Ancient cultures of conceit : British university fiction in the post war
years / Ian Carter.
p. cm.
Includes bibliographical references.
1. English fiction–20th century–History and criticism.
2. College stories, English–History and criticism. 3. College stories,
English–Sociological aspects. 4. Universities and colleges in literature.
5. Educational sociology–Great Britain. 6. Education, Higher, in
literature. I. Title.
PR888.U5C3 1990
823'.91409355–dc20
89–10942
CIP

ISBN 0-415-03154-0
0-415-04842-7 (pbk)

For K.G.C. and R.R.C.

No wonder the ancient cultures of conceit
In his technique of unsettlement foresaw
The fall of princes, the collapse of
Their lucrative patterns of frustration.
(W. H. Auden, *In Memory of Sigmund Freud*, 1939)

CONTENTS

ACKNOWLEDGEMENTS

Debts accumulate when writing any book. When the book has been gestating for many years, and the ground covered is so far from the author's home range, then debts pile up much faster. Beti Roberts was a splendid unofficial research assistant in Swansea public library's mouldering heaps of crime novels. I discussed university novels with Debra Parker over an academic year. Her advice is reflected throughout this book, but particularly in Chapter 7. I discussed university novels with Richard Sheppard over delectable pints of warm, flat beer. From a very different disciplinary background, he persuaded me that my argument was not wholly trivial, and curbed my tendency to wander injudiciously into languages other than English. (I beat him with Welsh, though.) For other advice, help, and suggestions I thank Vivienne Gray, A.H. Halsey, Mike Hanne, Dai Hawkins, Carolyn Heilbrun, Alun Howkins, Olive Johnson, Alan Judd, Ken MacKinnon, Andrew Mcpherson, Nick Perry, John Reid, Andrew Rutherford, Tom Sharpe, Kendrick Smithyman, John Stagg, J.I.M. Stewart, Norman and Tina Stockman, Nicholas Tarling, Keith Thomas, Glanmor Williams, and Roger Oppenheim's shade. Much of this book was written while I was a visiting professor in the Anthropology and Sociology Department of University College, Swansea. I thank Professors Bill Williams and Chris Harris, and their staff, for their hospitality. None of these people bears any responsibility for the manifold faults of this book. It is a poor thing, but mine own.

I thank copyright holders for permission to quote copyright material from: K. Amis, *Lucky Jim*; D. Anderson, J. Lait, and D.

Marsland, *Breaking the Spell of the Welfare State*; J.R.L. Anderson, *Death in a High Latitude*; R.D. Anderson, *Education and Opportunity in Victorian Scotland*; E. Atiyah, *Black Vanguard*; W.H. Auden, *W.H. Auden*; J.P.V.D. Balsdon, *Freshman's Folly, The Day They Burned Miss Termag*; R. Barnard, *Death of an Old Goat*; 'L. Bellingham', *Oxford: the Novel*; M. Bradbury, *Cuts, Eating People Is Wrong, Stepping Westward, The History Man*; P. Burnhill and A.F. McPherson, 'The Scottish university and under-graduate expectations', *New Universities Quarterly*, 1983; G. Butler, *A Coffin for Pandora, Coffin in Oxford*; A.S. Byatt, *Still Life*; V.C. Clinton-Baddeley, *Death's Bright Dart*; B. Cook, *Disorderly Elements*; 'W. Cooper', *The Struggles of Albert Woods*; D.K. Cornelius and E.K. Vincent (eds), *Cultures in Conflict*; C.B. Cox and R. Boyson (eds), *Black Paper 1977*; C.B. Cox and A.E. Dyson (eds), *Black Paper Two, Fight for Education: a Black Paper, The Black Papers on Education*; 'E. Crispin', *The Glimpses of the Moon, The Moving Toyshop*; 'J. Davey', *Murder in Paradise*; G.E. Davie, *The Crisis of the Democratic Intellect*; A. Davies, *A Very Peculiar Practice, A Very Peculiar Practice: the New Frontier*; L. Day, *The Looker-In*; C. Dexter, *The Riddle of the Third Mile, The Secret of Annexe 3, The Silent World of Nicholas Quinn*; D. Fiske, *Academic Murder*; M. Forster, *Dames' Delight*; A. Fraser, *Oxford Blood*; D. Gethin, *Dane's Testament*; P. Honan, *Matthew Arnold: a Life*; F. Hoyle, *Ossian's Ride*; F. and G. Hoyle, *The Molecule Men, and the Monster of Loch Ness*; 'M. Innes', *Appleby at Allington, Appleby on Ararat, Appleby's Answer, Appleby's End, A Private View, Death at the President's Lodging, Going it Alone, Hamlet, Revenge!, Old Hall, New Hall, Operation Pax, Stop Press, There Came Both Mist And Snow, The Secret Vanguard, The Weight of the Evidence, What Happened at Hazelwood*; P.D. James, *An Unsuitable Job for a Woman*; M.S. Jameson, *A Cup of Tea for Mr Thorgill*; J. Kennaway, *The Mind Benders*; A. Kennington, *Pastures New*; P. Larkin, *Jill*; F.R. Leavis, *Education and the University, English Literature in Our Time and the University, Two Cultures?*; 'A. Lejeune', *Professor in Peril*; C.S. Lewis, *That Hideous Strength*; D. Lodge, *Changing Places, Nice Work, Small World, The British Museum is Falling Down*; A. Lurie, *Love and Friendship, The War Between the Tates*; L. McIntosh, *Oxford Folly*; S.P.B. Mais, *Who Dies?*; J. Mann, *The Only Security*; J.C. Masterman, *An Oxford Tragedy, To Teach the Senators Wisdom*; W.G.C. Morgan, *An Oxford Romance*; V.G. Myer, *Culture Shock*; F. Parkin, *The Mind and Body Shop*; J.H. Plumb (ed.), *Crisis in the Humanities*; R. Postgate, *The Ledger is Kept*; A. Price, *Colonel Butler's Wolf, Soldier No More*; J.B.

Priestley, *Out of Town*; M. Proctor, *The English University Novel*; B. Pym, *An Academic Question, Crampton Hodnet, Less Than Angels*; F. Raphael, *The Glittering Prizes*; S. Raven, *Places Where They Sing*; J. Rex, 'British Sociology 1960–1980', *Social Forces*, 1983; R. Robinson, *Landscape with Dead Dons*; T. Robinson, *When Scholars Fall*; T. Sharpe, *Porterhouse Blue*; H. Shaw, *Death of a Don*; W. Sheed, *A Middle-Class Education*; M.L. Smith, *No Easy Answer*; C.P. Snow, *The Affair, The Light and the Dark, The Masters, The Two Cultures and the Scientific Revolution*; P. Spencer, *Full Term*; J.I.M. Stewart, *A Memorial Service, A Palace of Art, Full Term, My Aunt Christina and Other Stories, Mungo's Dream, The Aylwins, The Gaudy, The Guardians, The Madonna of the Astrolabe, The Man Who Won the Pools, The Naylors, Vanderlyn's Kingdom, Young Pattullo*; *Times Higher Education Supplement*; R. Trickett, *The Course of Love*; R. Usborne, *Wodehouse at Work to the End*; C.E. Vulliamy, *Tea at the Abbey*; G. Watson, 'Fictions of Academe', *Encounter*, 1978; R. Williams, *Culture and Society*; P.G. Wodehouse, *The Man Upstairs, and Other Stories*; 'M. Yorke', *Grave Matters*.

Part one

NOT WITH A WIMP, BUT A BANGER

Let us begin, as the philosophers say, with a thought experiment. Mutually assured destruction proves to have been aptly named. Nuclear winter is as formidable as predicted. Death lies deep and crisp and even. *Homo sapiens* – a hollow joke, that – is obliterated.

Earth's big bang generates a radiation burst that is monitored elsewhere in the universe. The inhabitants of one planet – its name need not concern us – mount an investigative expedition. That expedition finds ruin everywhere. It enjoys a single success. A small van is discovered, immured in a collapsed road tunnel. It is extracted, and loaded aboard a space craft.

Our inquisitive aliens know nothing about the van. We know a little more. We know that it is a small travelling library owned by Gwynedd County Council. We know that it was trapped when a first strike attack on RAF Valley blocked both ends of the tunnel. We know that the attack came on a summer's morning, as the van was trundling towards that stretch of north Wales between Tremadoc and Ffestiniog. We know – does not everybody? – that in this tract of country at that time of year hill sheep farmers, the dominant social group at other seasons, were outnumbered by vacationing university teachers. We know, finally, that on the fatal morning a combination of this clientele's predilections and the random processes of lending and borrowing had filled the van with fiction, and with a particular mix of fiction. No westerns, no Mills and Boon. Many novels of manners, even more comic novels, multitudinous detective novels. By one of those extraordinary strokes of luck without which no story would be worth telling, the van contained a copy of every post-war British university novel, and nothing else.

Now the question. What can we expect the aliens to learn from this material? We shall have to fit them with deep structures sufficiently similar to our own for them to be able to translate from English (and, in a few cases, from Welsh) to their own language. That is no more than fair; and without it they, and we, would be lost.

Thus equipped, we may trust our aliens to reach two conclusions. First, that all the books claimed to be fiction, not to be 'true'. Second, that a significant part of each book's action was centred in a university, even though attention might move elsewhere. We do not need them to know – or even ponder – what a university might be. They merely need to understand that this was a particular and well-recognized social institution.

But let us now provide them with one more human artefact; Halsey and Trow's (1971) classification of British universities. Had they known rather more about British universities, then this classification would puzzle our aliens. Why, for example, make Heriot Watt and Strathclyde 'Scottish' universities rather than 'ex-CATs'? Why are new universities exclusively 'English', thus excluding Stirling? Why separate the universities of London and Wales from major and minor redbricks? Like Barthes' cod Chinese bestiary, this set of categories makes sense only when read from within the culture that produced it. Pity the alien. But ours are tough folk. Assuming that the classification meant something to those who constructed it, they locate and count novels' university settings. Table 1 summarizes the results.

Table 1 British university novels' settings, 1945–88

Major redbrick	8
London	6
Minor redbrick	22
Wales	4
Scotland	4
New English	11
Ex-CATs	4
Oxford and Cambridge	145
Total	204

Note: Since some fictions take significant account of more than one kind of university, the total in this table exceeds the number of novels and short stories.

4

Armed with this information, our aliens draw their third conclusion. The British university system, they decide, contained many different kinds of institutions, but one – Oxford and Cambridge – was vastly larger than all others combined since it figured in over 70 per cent of the novels. Oxford alone must have been monstrously large, since the 119 novels set in that single place far outnumber those set in all other universities.

Aliens are useful folk. We can set them down before a heap of evidence, provide them with logical canons of deduction, and watch them trundle away to disastrously mistaken conclusions. We know that there were sixteen mainland British universities in 1945, forty-eight in 1985. We know that in 1945 Oxford and Cambridge contained no more than 14 per cent of British university students, and that by 1985 the figure had fallen below 8 per cent. Thus we can appreciate what our aliens cannot: the difference between presence and visibility (Oakley 1974). We recognize that British university novels make no attempt to describe the whole system. We understand that we face a discourse, a machine that controls what we see by generating rules for including some things and excluding others.

Let us now leave the aliens, and watch the discourse in action. Like most of the cases in Table 1, 'Anthony Lejeune's' *Professor in Peril* (1987) is centred in Oxford. Lejeune gives us a routine spy thriller, with the KGB seeking to plant yet another fake defector on British intelligence. But this one is a Russian classicist. Hence the flower of the British intelligence services needs to call in an equivalent British classicist to check the Russian's academic credentials at a conference in Rio de Janeiro. The lot falls on James Glowrey: a middle-aged bachelor, classics professor at Oxford, fellow of an unnamed college. He narrates the story as it moves from London to Rio, then to up-country Brazil and the southern states of the USA, before concluding in Oxford.

Glowrey has high Tory social attitudes: 'The Duke of Wellington was quite right in fearing that railways would encourage the wrong people to travel. Aeroplanes encourage them to travel further' (Lejeune 1987: 227). He declares himself gregarious: 'I enjoyed the life of the college and the club.' He regrets the admission of women to Oxford men's colleges: 'I always did say that was a mistake' (1987: 157, 235). Within the college world, he admires those who seek to keep alive an early-nineteenth-century sense of Oxford:

> I'm fond of Giles. He's idle and jovial, his erudition floating lightly on a sea of port; an epitome of the old, unworldly, celibate Oxford which the modern zealots – including Emily Bryant – have been trying, for at least a generation, to stamp out.
>
> (Lejeune 1987: 242)

Bryant is the enemy. This is true in a narrow sense: she is the deeply buried Russian spy whose unmasking drives the plot. But she is also the enemy in a much wider sense. Glowrey controls the novel through his first-person narrative. Bryant is constructed negatively, displaying the obverse of Glowrey's virtues. She is female, he male. She is 'a plain dowdy woman'; he, we must take it, is urbanely handsome. She 'was a classic type [of spy]; clever but unloved and unlovable, therefore vulnerable' (Lejeune 1987: 240–1). Sexually attractive and experienced, therefore invincible, he ends the book looking forward to matrimony with the suitably deferential gangster's moll who he collected, chivalrously, in Rio. Bryant is content to sit on a university committee which Glowrey had refused to join 'on grounds both of tedium and of disapproval, since it was one of the many designed by reformist liberals to make Oxford, socially, more like a redbrick university' (1987: 237).

We see that Glowrey's high Toryism extends to his politics. He keeps a bottle of South African sherry in his rooms, 'purely to annoy liberal visitors'. He identifies with the Cavaliers in the English civil war, the confederacy in the American.

> Both represented, if nothing else, a lost civilisation, crushed by advancing modernity: colour and courtesy against the levellers' drabness.
>
> (Lejeune 1987: 192)

Bryant is a leveller. Cornered, she spits her negative political testament at Glowrey, her antithesis: 'You represent everything I detest in Oxford and this society. You're exactly why I've done what I've done' (1987: 245).

'In Oxford and this society'. What is going on here? Clearly rather more than meets the eye. We have a spy thriller in which good struggles against evil on two continents, but in which the

6

struggle eventually is sheeted home to Oxford. Oxford is treated not simply as a provincial city, not simply as the site of an ancient university. It stands for other things.

The spy thriller is an insider's genre: the reader is an outsider to whom is shown more and more of the picture, often at the rate at which the narrator comes to see it. That picture, on the British side, is constructed around a web of semi-private institutions: gentlemen's clubs, public schools, learned societies, Oxford and Cambridge colleges. Other institutions – regiments, civil service departments – are part of the state, but they are presented as beyond public accountability, socially closed worlds connected through ties of common origin, common experience, and common perspective to the club, school, and college. This, it is claimed, is the network that is in power, no matter which political party is in government. Given that, it is no surprise that the spy thriller should be a politically conservative genre.

Lejeune gives us a text so conservative that it leaps backwards across the morally tortured liberal conservatism of le Carré – my country right, but only just – to the untroubled pre-war jingoism of Sapper and Dornford Yates with their latent homophilic clubmanship. A Tory even in his classics, Glowrey declares that

I do not love the company of my professional colleagues, who take their subjects at once too seriously and too lightly; too seriously in their zeal for unimportant technicalities, and too lightly in that they don't really listen to the authors. Xenophon would feel much more at home among the young Guards officers, and with the hunting and fishing conversation at Pratt's Club in London than in the company of modern scholars.

(Lejeune 1987: 36)

A particular view of what classics should comprise connects the worlds of club, regiment, and scholarship. On this basis Lejeune constructs a more comprehensive list of what is to be admired and defended in Oxford: social privilege, masculine privilege, deep-blue conservative ideas, scholarship as *belles-lettres*. This amalgam sets the discourse in which deviation is to be judged. Women university teachers, textual critics, political liberals: all are damned. Emily Bryant is a KGB mole, and hence is opposed to Glowrey. University liberals associate with Bryant. My enemy's friend becomes my enemy: liberals become as threatening to Oxford's good governance as a Russian spy. Bryant and the liberals seek to open Oxford to students from a wider range of social background. Since these people are in favour, the proposal must be resisted. If the clock cannot be turned back, then at least Oxford must be preserved in its present form. Why?

Consider the British delegates at the Rio conference. 'There were three of us from Oxford, one from Cambridge, and a couple from provincial universities' (Lejeune 1987: 239). Note that the subtly conflated distinctions in Halsey and Trow's classification have been collapsed to a simple dichotomy. We are given precise information about the number of delegates from Oxford and Cambridge, imprecise information about those from elsewhere. All other universities are lumped in a category called 'provincial'. This, too, is revealing. Physically Oxford and Cambridge are provincial towns, well removed from the capital. But culturally, Lejeune asserts, they are part of the metropolis. Hence Bryant's opposition to what Glowrey stands for 'in Oxford and this society'. Oxford stands for metropolitan virtues, 'Society' within British society. To attack Oxford is to attack those who control Britain. The discourse conflates the security of this governing group's position with the stability of the nation. To defend one is to defend the other.

We have spent some time on *Professor in Peril.* It is not that this novel is typical in all respects: its reactionary politics set it apart from some – but by no means all – British university fiction. Nor is it overloaded with literary merit. Rather its very lack of imagination makes the discourse stand out more clearly here than in more ambitious, more ambiguous, texts. We see that the complicated divisions between different kinds of British universities are reduced to a stark opposition: Oxbridge against not-Oxbridge. But we also see that Oxbridge exists in literary space, with a contingent relationship to the physical world. Just as 'Rummidge is an imaginary city, with imaginary universities and imaginary factories, inhabited by imaginary people, which occupies, for the purposes of fiction, the space where Birmingham is to be found on maps of the so-called "real world"' (Lodge 1988: author's note), so university novels' Oxbridge and not-Oxbridge are literary constructs. But Lodge's knowing reference to 'the so-called "real world"' warns us that reality is a slippery term. We often find commentators implying that novels are a simple description of reality. A Scottish university principal declares that 'This great, cosy world of self-satisfied and self-satisfying dons is laughed at in *Porterhouse Blue*, which was extremely funny because it was largely true' (*THES* 27 May 1988). A newspaper account of alleged professorial plagiarism begins: 'During the last few weeks . . . a tale of academic skullduggery has been unfolding slowly and one suspects even that wily student of dons and college politics, C.P. Snow, would have found it too improbable for fiction.' A newspaper story about university research begins by recalling *Lucky Jim*, in which 'Kingsley Amis felicitously described much university scholarship as "Throwing pseudo-light on non-problems"'. The fact that these last two reports came from the Australian *Bulletin* (1 October 1985) and the *New Zealand Times* (27 October 1985) shows that the discourse of British university fiction has a flourishing export trade.

But if reality is multiple and contested, as post-structuralism would have us believe, then we must abandon the common-sense assumption that novels reflect the real world: there is no uncomplicated real world to be reflected. Rather, fiction constructs accounts of the world which it then seeks to pass off as real. Accounts are interested statements, assertions that this is to be admired, that challenged: they are not simple description. A range of studies, from the UGC's research selectivity exercise (*THES* 30 May 1986; 6 June 1986) through the *Times Higher Education Supplement*'s peer reviews (*THES* 3 December 1982; 5 August 1983; 20 January 1984; 8 February 1985; 13 December 1985; 23 January 1987; 24 July 1987) to A.H. Halsey's survey of donnish opinion, has shown that Oxford and Cambridge stand pre-eminent in British academic prestige (Halsey 1982a). Just like the novels. Partly – but only partly – this has to do with Oxford and Cambridge's important role as nurseries of university teachers. Just – we shall see – like the novelists. But novels conceal the fact that statements about academic prestige are essentially contested: 'One problem for a "provincial" in writing about "Oxbridge" is to judge just how disrespectful he ought to be,' said W.J.M. Mackenzie (1960–1: 337): 'There is practically no significant general statement about Oxbridge that we can make without adding its opposite.' Novels do not indicate the complexity of rankings, with some not-Oxbridge universities overtopping Oxbridge in some subjects. They do not show us the fine gradation of prestige among not-Oxbridge places.

Fiction replaces a continuum with a dichotomy. And if novels constitute rather than reflect the world, then fiction can have real effects. A literary place can develop spurious facticity, can come to appear just as real as a 'real' place. Their reality warranted, literary accounts then can influence policy discussions.

But events can develop in ways that novels would not lead us to expect. Oxford University's Congregation voted by 738 votes to 319 not to offer an honorary degree to the Oxford-educated Margaret Thatcher, thus breaking a tradition that stretched back through the aeons of time to 1946. The *Times Higher Education Supplement*'s leader writer made this vote

> a powerful signal to Downing Street that enough is enough as far as educational cuts are concerned and that Oxford dons really do care about less fortunate colleagues in Salford, Aston, Bradford and other universities as well as about cuts in colleges, schools and nurseries.
>
> (*THES* 1 February 1985)

This was a result and an interpretation that the inveterate university novel-reader would not have predicted. Real Oxford and Cambridge university teachers are a far more mixed bunch than novelists would have us believe, far more varied in their attitudes to social closure through education. Novels narrow them down in the interest not of truth, but of discourse.

This book examines the British university novel as discourse. That is, it examines what passes for knowledge about universities in British fiction. In later chapters we shall examine the discourse in motion. We shall see in greater detail what it includes and what it excludes. We shall see who are the citadel's defenders, and who the besieging barbarian hordes. We shall then be able to see how this has articulated with the post-war experience of the British university system. Finally, we shall be able to see whether, and how far, suppressed alternative discourses might give us a different purchase on the sorry current condition of state higher education policy in Britain. I make no claim to provide an authoritative account of what British university fiction is about: readings are illimitable. Rather, I claim that combining the ideas in Matthew Arnold's *Culture and Anarchy* (1869) with Max Weber's notion of social closure (Parkin 1979: 44–118; 1982: 100–2) allows us to construct a coherent account of what British university fiction is, in all its ambiguities, and how it has been used.

Clark Kerr is reported to have claimed that the only thing holding together the modern university is a central heating plant (or, in a variant reading, a concern for car parking). Droll, but wrong. There is one other unifying feature. All could have the same motto graven over their doors: 'Things are more complicated than they seem.' It is the exploration of, the delight in, complexity that sets the university apart from other educational bodies. 'You've come – back, is it not? – to one of the more subtle parts of England', Giles Gott tells John Appleby in a distinguished college mystery novel (M. Innes 1936: 159).

Hence my title. 'Ancient cultures of conceit' does not sound friendly. But I do not intend to follow the Thatcher government's example and shovel contempt on British universities and their inhabitants, further reducing their once-high international reputation. Each word in my title is pregnant with ambiguity. Ancient can mean simply old; but an obsolete usage makes it mean a standard-bearer. Some British universities are old in that they are long-established, but all are organized around social practices which imply that they were operating when Noah was a lad. Novels provide judiciously heightened evidence. Rachel Ambrose, a marginal women's college in a disguised Cambridge, received its first government grant in the mid-1960s. The college immediately instituted dining nights (Myer 1988: 7), in emulation of proper Cambridge colleges. Calleshire is a weakly collegiate redbrick university which expanded in the 1960s. Two new colleges were built. The first, Cremond, bears the family name of the earls of Ornum. Almstone, the second, bears the family name of the dukes of Calleshire (Aird 1977: 26–7). The new Watermouth University has its own ceremonial robes, designed by Mary Quant (Bradbury 1975: 107). John James Lapford, first vice-chancellor of a college of advanced technology rapidly promoted to university status, is discovered checking his Public Orator's vestments: an 'enormous purple velvet cap', a robe 'purple and pink and heavy with gilt' (Priestley 1968a: 23–4). In all these cases we see tradition being invented (Hobsbawm and Ranger 1983). In the 1960s brand new universities were located in places and organized their teaching in a manner that recalled the ancient English universities rather than

the redbrick models that Wilson's guttering white-hot technological revolution might have led an observer to expect. In Sussex,
for instance, lectures were designed to take second place to
seminars, and the university was organized in schools rather than
departments: both factors were intended to create that disciplinary
interchange thought to be typical of Oxford Greats, and to free
junior staff from not-Oxbridge professorial tyranny (Corbett
1964). New universities became absorbed in an older discourse, in
which the university was standard bearer for civilized values. Two
definitions of 'ancient' collide, merge, splinter.

We can play the same game with our other two terms. Culture is
one of the most ambiguous words in the language. Setting aside
the radically different set of meanings clustered around anthropological usage (except to note that novels construct for us a
consistent image of two different ways of life in Oxbridge and
not-Oxbridge universities), culture can mean the controlled
growth of organisms in a prepared medium. It can also mean
cultivation, in an agricultural sense. British university fiction puns
these meanings to produce a third: in many novels of undergraduate experience organisms (students) enjoy – or fail to enjoy
– a controlled growth of cultivation (civilization) in a prepared
medium (the university). These novels, and many others, identify
civilized culture as the central value justifying universities'
existence. In return, those places are seen as culture's ultimate
refuge. The long covert history of pondering the cultural role of
the university explains why we consider only novels concerned
with universities, why we spend no time on fictional accounts of
other kinds of higher and further education; colleges of education
(Hill 1971), agricultural colleges (G. Mitchell 1958), colleges of
technology (Sharpe 1976). Even within universities, we spend no
time on medical education: the 'doctor in the house' novel
(Gordon 1952) dances to an altogether different tune. We do
consider Jacobson's *Coming From Behind* (1983), hailed as the first
'rotting poly novel,' but only for its marginal comments on
Cambridge and Sydney Universities. Finally, the dictionary tells us
that conceit can mean affectation and pretension, but it can also
mean thought (as process or outcome), or a literary form; 'a
fanciful, ingenious, or witty notion or expression'. Conceit as
affectation or literary form, or even as thought, is never absent for
long from a British university novel.

This book studies post-war British university fiction in a web of meanings constructed by the ambiguities in these three terms: 'ancient', 'cultures', and 'conceit'. This is more than simple word-spinning. Our web can catch features of British universities' recent experience that other filters would pass. For universities *are* complicated places. They are complicated in function, in their unique mix of education, scholarship, and research. They are complicated in constitution; nominally self-governing institutions, in Britain usually (but not invariably) founded by Royal charter, that now derive a high proportion of capital and income from a state captured by Ostragoths. They have diverse formal structures. Most are unitary, but others (London, Wales) are federal. These two, together with Cambridge, Durham, Kent, Lancaster, Oxford, St Andrews and York, show us a wide range of college-based universities.

'The author must not interpret,' Umberto Eco (1984: 8) tells us. 'But he may tell us why and how he wrote the book.' How I wrote this book is of little interest: just the usual story of blood, sweat, toil, and tears. The 'why' is more significant. I wrote this book through curiosity at what British university novels were about. Its origins lie in 1975. Head-down teaching sociology in Aberdeen University, I suddenly found a string of friends from other departments sidling up and sniggering that I ought to read Malcolm Bradbury's *The History Man* (1975), recently arrived in the university library. At last my name rose to the top of Kings' Library's reserve list for the book – this *was* Aberdeen; one could not contemplate buying a hardback novel – and I took *The History Man* home. I read it with increasing outrage and contempt. Bradbury equivocates over what he takes the novel's stance to be. On the one hand, he confirms an interviewer's sense of an underlying hostility to sociology (Haffenden 1985: 26, 47). He has also claimed that he was surprised to see the book interpreted as an attack on sociology, but the real surprise lies in his surprise. Christopher Hampton's television adaptation was even less restrained in its hostility.

Once I had surmounted my initial outrage, three questions interested me. First, what was the implication of reviewers taking Bradbury's book to be a simple reflection of what went on in a particular discipline? For the *Financial Times* Bradbury had provided 'a peculiarly ruthless dissection of the pretensions of sociological cant'. Second, what was the effect of reviewers' taking *The History Man* to be a description of what went on in certain places? 'At last we have . . . a splendidly ironic cold eye cast on life as it is in our new trendy universities,' said the *Daily Telegraph*. As Raymond Williams (1987) noted in a late essay, 'trivial fictions, in the comic novels of academia, have been received by many as sober documentation of some authentic inner story'. These questions became more urgent in 1981, when BBC2 played the television adaptation of *The History Man* against Granada's adaptation of Evelyn Waugh's *Brideshead Revisited* (1945) at the precise time when the fine detail of the first savage round of university cuts was being determined in Whitehall. Nor was this an isolated episode. While the University Grants Committee's research selectivity exercise was being prepared, television viewers were watching Andrew Davies's *A Very Peculiar Practice* (1986). While Kenneth Baker's GERBIL (a radical Right education bill) was gnawing its way through Parliament, viewers could choose between television adaptations of Tom Sharpe's *Porterhouse Blue* (1974), David Lodge's *Small World* (1984), and Andrew Davies's *A Very Peculiar Practice: The New Frontier* (1988). As the policy thrust for student grants to be replaced by loans hotted up in 1988, the BBC repeated *A Very Peculiar Practice*. No doubt the timing of all these broadcasts was determined by programming values rather than political values, but we are entitled to consider what effect these accounts of British university life might have on policy-makers, and on public reception of the Thatcher government's emasculation of British higher education. No definitive answers are possible, but the least that can be said is that they did little to ease the generally hostile contemporary political and public attitudes to British universities: attitudes partly formed and consistently fostered by British university fiction's dominant discourse.

This leads to my third question. Where did Bradbury's novel come from? Clearly his argument had its own history. Even I, an inveterate university novel not-reader, was aware of some earlier books: Snow's *The Masters* (1951), Waugh's *Brideshead Revisited*, Beerbohm's *Zuleika Dobson* (1911). Books talk to books. What had earlier books told *The History Man*? To put the point more portentously, what were the intellectual conditions of its production? I started ploughing through every British university novel that I could exhume, in order to find out. My current list (see the Appendix) contains 196 fictions published since 1945, together with earlier work by authors who published after that year. (The regularity with which new titles float out from bibliographies, street barrows, and friends' bookshelves suggests that there are more than this to find, but let others find them now.) Wading through this lot, I soon began to get the feeling that E.M. Forster claimed came from reading *War and Peace*: great bells began ringing in my head. I would pick up a novel newly discovered in library stack or decayed secondhand bookshop. It could belong to one of many genres: comedy of manners, thriller, whodunit, romance. After a couple of pages I would discover the awful truth. *I had read it before*. After a couple of years, I had read them all before. Despite their apparent diversity, almost all British university novels play modest variations on one of three linked stories: how an undergraduate at Oxford (usually) or Cambridge came to wisdom; how a don at Oxford (usually) or Cambridge was stabbed in the back physically or professionally, sometimes surviving to rule his college; and how rotten life was as student or teacher outside Oxford and Cambridge. By this time *The History Man* no longer surprised me: it had become no more than an unusually forcefully expressed Type Three novel. Reading university novels became steadily easier, though steadily less interesting. It also became steadily more exasperating. Here was I, a graduate of an ex-CAT, a new English and an ancient Scottish university, being invited to venerate an academic hierarchy topped by a serenely magnificent and indispensable Oxford and Cambridge. I had managed very well for twenty-five years as student and university teacher while never entering a Cambridge college, and only visiting the trade-unions-sponsored Ruskin College in – but emphatically not of – Oxford. For all the sense that university novels' underlying assumptions made to me, I might have been a visitor from outer space.

One reason why the dominant discourse of British university fiction seemed so alien was that I was educated as a sociologist. This had two important effects. On the one hand, it encouraged me not to take English experience as the *sine qua non* of human experience, and not to genuflect automatically to hierarchy. We shall see in later chapters that these attitudes disqualify anybody from being taken seriously in British university fiction. On the other hand, by the 1960s 'even that mild and generally conformist discipline, sociology, [had] acquired a kind of diabolism' (R. Williams 1987). To be a sociologist was to be an alien in British academic culture.

One reason why reading university novels came to be so boring was their obsession with content rather than form. If universities are temples of thought, of conceit, then one would expect authors to delight in playing games with the manner in which they present their work. Many books refer back to earlier university novels, as we shall see. Few go further. Oddly the otherwise prosaic C.P. Snow suffered a rush of formal blood in *The Light and the Dark* (1947). His manic depression means that the weather in Roy Calvert's soul swings between light and dark, but the growing 1930s' fascist threat provides a deeper Manichaean echo.

Only David Lodge goes further than this. In *The British Museum is Falling Down* (1965) we trail Adam Appleby for a day in his dismal life as a postgraduate student in and around the British Museum Reading Room. Slowly the truth dawns: Appleby's day in Bloomsbury is a pastiche of Bloomsday. Lodge uses Joyce's *Ulysses*, itself a reworking of Homer, to organize the plot. His next university novel, *Changing Places* (1975) shows Lodge's skill as a structuralist literary critic. From the opening pages, when Philip Swallow's west-bound airliner passes Morris Zapp's east-bound plane, this tale of difference between British redbrick and American state university mores is controlled by structural balance between the two protagonists. As in any structuralist argument, the individual actors are mere puppets, tugged around by iron wires of necessity. Balance determines who does what to whom, and when. So it goes, until the last chapter. Once again we have two aircraft. This time they are converging on New York. One carries Philip Swallow and Désirée Zapp, the other Morris Zapp and Hilary Swallow. The four are flying to a meeting where they will decide who should live with whom. The structural parallels come together, generating an air-miss over Manhattan. This scene, and the hotel scene that follows, are written not as a connected narrative like the rest of the book, but as a shooting script for a film. Philip Swallow ends the hotel scene, and the novel, with a speech about how one knows that one is coming to the end of a book by realizing how few pages there are left. He ponders the problems that this gives the novelist. We leave the four characters in the hotel bedroom with their relationships still not clarified, and with the author facing the camera in his Swallow-persona. Lodge's cinematic conceit breaks the determinist frame of what has gone before, clearing a small space for personal choice among structural factors.

The marvellous *Small World* (1984) extends and inverts *Changing Places*. Lodge gives us the first British post-structuralist university novel: now everything is possible, constraint is absent. The radical relativism of a post-structuralist method puts anything that one can think on the agenda, with no criterion for distinguishing 'good' from 'bad'. Lodge's organizing device – Bloomsday in *The British Museum is Falling Down*, structural balance in *Changing Places* – here is the notion of the quest. The point about quests is that they never end. Persse (equals Percival, equals Parsifal, equals Perseus, equals Pierce) McGarrigle searches for his beloved, his sexual grail. But his search entwines with others' search for the UNESCO chair of Literary Criticism, a post which carries the world's highest salary for a literary critic, and no teaching. A post whose capture will confirm the primacy of one form of criticism among the many whose practitioners contend for the honour: British *belles lettres* and liberal humanism, structuralism, reception theory, Althusserian structural Marxism, and post-structuralism. The two themes, the personal and the disciplinary, come together at the Modern Language Association annual conference in New York, but nothing is settled. Nothing can be settled: as the now post-structuralist Morris Zapp's lapel badge tells us, 'Every decoding is another encoding'. The quests continue.

In *Small World* as in Lodge's earlier books, much of the work is done by the way words are organized; to separate form from content crushes the text. It is a formidable achievement, rarely attempted by other authors. Andrew Sinclair's *My Friend Judas* (1959), with its larding of beat language on a straight novel of undergraduate experience, is a pale reflection. Even Bradbury's use of a historical present voice (a long way after Damon Runyon) in *The History Man* seems very tame by comparison. Valerie Grosvenor Myer tries for post-structuralist playfulness in *Culture Shock* (1988); but her novel collapses in the absence of those firm organizing devices that support *Small World*'s narrative while maintaining the illusion of unconstraint. Given the slight talent enjoyed by so many British university novelists, lack of formal ambition is to be applauded. Consider one case in which self-denial was overcome. In the foreword to his justly forgotten work, W.G.C. Morgan (1948: 10–11) told us that

> The reader during the perusal of AN OXFORD ROMANCE is requested to remember that he is not reading a short story, a novelette or a novel. . . . On the contrary, he is 'reading' a film.
>
> AN OXFORD ROMANCE is the first of a series of productions. Others to be published in rotation are
>
> NIGGER BLONDE, a photodrama set in Richmond-Twickenham and N. Wales.
>
> PEARLS AND PENITENTS, a Cinematic Melodrama in two parts:
>
> First film, Setting: Ostende and Paris.
>
> Second film, Setting: Paris, Hongkong, Macao, Paris.
>
> MENDEL'S LAW, a Photodrama set in rural England, etc, etc.

If *An Oxford Romance* is a true reflection of the quality of these coming attractions then we should give grateful thanks that they never became more than faces on the cutting-room floor.

British university novels are genre novels. But making sense of this genre requires a clear frame of reference, a set of criteria for deciding what is important in a book. Where should one go for help? Pretty obviously, to literary criticism. This is a useful source of other novels to read, but less enlightening in other ways. Mortimer Proctor's (1957) book-length study of English university fiction stops at 1945. In his review of Proctor, Anthony Quinton (1958) seeks for reasons why most Oxford novels are so awful, concluding that insuperable obstacles prevent undergraduates, dons, and outsiders from getting (or, in the case of dons, publishing) a true sense of the place. A nice line for a philosopher, prescribing catatonia by exhausting the logically possible sources of action. Quinton's argument is unintentionally revealing, however. 'A novel about a cathedral is not seriously defaced by its author's mixing up the times of compline and vespers,' he tells us (1958: 214). 'But Oxford detail is too important and too well known to many people.' There are many things that could be said about this statement. The least offensive is to declare it a valuable piece of evidence about the way in which some academic Oxonians think about their university. George Watson (1978) usefully notes that university fiction is an Anglo-American phenomenon, largely unknown in Europe. He joins Quinton in taking British examples of that fiction to be a crude reflection of the institutions in which they purport to be set. Novels offer, he asserts, 'a sizeable charge against the institutions'. They prick three bubbles. The first is 'the sin of Pygmalion'; the attempt to make university students resemble their teachers. The second is hypocrisy. The third is fake-righteousness.

> A sage cannot afford to be wrong. And our universities – or at least their most vocal and highly publicised elements – were publicly wrong in the 1960s about public events. There can be little appeal in history against that collective hysteria that was once called the New Left.
>
> (Watson 1978: 46)

Any pretence of literary criticism gives way to vituperation. Cambridge English's new Right faction speaks here, bitter and self-righteous, in an appropriate place: the pages of *Encounter*. J.P. Kenyon (1980) denied Watson's argument point by point in a later issue of *Encounter*, but he then was sidetracked from wondering why there were so many British university novels into asking why there were so few British business novels. Another place provided a more constructive setting. British universities' trade journal, the *Times Higher Education Supplement*, has paid close attention to fiction: interviews with novelists like Bradbury (14 November 1975, 9 January 1981) and Jacobson (12 August 1983), and criticism (Elkin 1976). In an article first published in *THES* then recycled elsewhere John Schellenberger (1981; 1982b; 1982–3) distinguishes four types of modern British university novel: the university-comic, rooted in nineteenth-century Oxford under-graduate models; a more serious variant of this, 'an earnest and painstaking account of Oxford as an educational experience'; the college detective novel; and the novel of redbrick disillu-sionment. These are useful categories (though not, I think, the most useful), but it is possible to argue that continuities between novels located in Schellenberger's several pigeon-holes are as significant as their surface differences. Malcolm Bradbury shows why this should be so in another *THES* piece. 'The university', he tells us, 'seemed a strong metaphoric setting for the pursuit of wider preoccupations, intellectual and aesthetic' (Bradbury 1984: 13). He is writing about *The History Man*, but his argument applies much more generally. The shift from mimesis to metaphor opens up useful territory.

The British university as metaphor. But for what? Proctor had grounded his account of nineteenth-century university fiction in the liberal educational philosophy of J.H. Newman and Matthew Arnold. In the most impressive piece of all literary criticism directed at British university fiction Peter Widdowson (1984) used Arnold to pin down the fictional and critical practice of Malcolm Bradbury and David Lodge. In my view he overstates his case – the differences between Bradbury and Lodge are more significant than he allows (Haffenden 1985: 167) – but Arnold's ideas do give us a key for opening up British university fiction's dominant discourse. We turn that key in Chapter 3. Before that, we look at the work of the most distinguished of all modern British university novelists. It is oddly fitting that he should be so little recognized.

Part two

Chapter Two

THE EXEMPLAR

Ask any fifty literary critics, gleaned at random from the pavements of a university town, which writer best exemplifies British university fiction since 1945. Seventeen will name Kingsley Amis, seventeen C.P. Snow. The remaining sixteen will name Malcolm Bradbury. Challenged to justify this, they will point to literary criticism: a raft on Amis (Boyle and Brown 1966–7; Fallis 1977; Hutchings 1977; McDermott 1985; Swinden 1984: 180–209; K. Wilson 1982), a respectable amount on Snow (Ramanathan 1978; Turck 1967; Vogel 1963), another raft on Bradbury (Banks 1985; Cohen 1977; Friedmann 1986; Reckwitz 1987; Todd 1981; Widdowson 1984). All this would puzzle our aliens. They would point out that Amis has written only two university novels, one set in a minor redbrick and one in Oxford; that Snow wrote only four, three set in Cambridge and one in a new university. They would point out that Bradbury has written only three, with minor redbrick and new university settings. To the crudely literal minds with which we have equipped our aliens, one should start with the author who has written most books about the most popular university. They would identify two leading candidates who have written principally about Oxford: Michael Innes with his seven books, and J.I.M. Stewart with thirteen novels and six short stories. Tell them that the former has attracted no critical attention whatsoever, the latter only one article – in German (Schumann 1983) – and they would be puzzled about critical priorities. But tell them that Innes and Stewart are the same person, the former a pseudonym of the latter, and they would have no doubt about the writer with whom we should start.

Not all aliens will approve this judgement, for Stewart once set a monstrous calumny on their putative cousins. Professor

Pluckrose is found squashed in the Wool Court of Nesfield University, apparently by a falling meteorite. Who could be responsible? John Appleby – Innes's 'great detective' – conjures up one of literature's least likely sets of suspects:

> The Martians, . . . stolid and phlegmatic by their dull canals: why should they take to pounding Pluckrose with their planetary artillery? Ask Orson Welles.
>
> (M. Innes 1944: 6)

Stewart drifted into university fiction. In his seventh novel, *Appleby on Ararat* (1941), he has John Appleby ponder his previous triumphs:

> This was not the way to solve a mystery. It was not thus that he had plumbed the mystery of Dr Umpleby and the bones, of the stylish homicides at Scamnum Court, of the daft laird of Erchany; it was not thus that he had exposed the Friends of the Venerable Bede or preserved ten persons from the blackest suspicion by recollecting a line in The Ancient Mariner.
>
> (M. Innes 1941: 48)

The references are to his creator's first five novels, in their correct order: *Death at the President's Lodging* (1936), *Hamlet, Revenge!* (1937), *Lament for a Maker* (1938), *Stop Press* (1939), and *There Came Both Mist and Snow* (1940a). A hundred pages later, we find a reference to the sixth novel, *The Secret Vanguard* (1940b).

Death at the President's Lodging is set in a fictitious Oxford college, St Anthony's. *Stop Press* is rooted in an unnamed Oxford college, though much of the action takes place elsewhere. This location is important for some of Stewart's purposes in these books, but the college is less central to his intentions here than in many of his later books. He is concerned with three things in these seven early books. The first is to entertain a wide audience. The second is to put his training as a literary historian and critic at the service of his pseudonymous practice as a writer of 'light fiction'. The third is to play games with two genres: the detective novel and the thriller. He succeeds in all three ambitions.

In Julian Symon's words (1985: 115), 'the Innes novels were instantly acclaimed as something new in detective fiction'. *Death at the President's Lodging* – 'that queer, creaking case' (M. Innes 1948:

56) – first appeared in the magnetic yellow wrapper of Victor Gollancz's crime list and Stewart has remained faithful to Gollancz for hardback publication. This must have been mutually profitable, for every public library has its shelf, often sadly depleted through borrowing, of Innes books in their successive hardback editions. Many novels have been published in paperback, most notably by Penguin but also under other imprints. Innes/Stewart has enjoyed unusually wide popular success.

The first seven novels are stuffed with literary allusions. These allusions are not mere dressing; much of the novel's work goes on through them. Let us consider a couple of examples. *Hamlet, Revenge!* concerns a play within a play. No prizes for guessing where that idea came from. Other references tumble out: to other bits of *Hamlet*, other bits of Shakespeare; other Jacobean dramatists; Jane Austen (*Mansfield Park*, for an attitude to country-house theatricals). And, for the first of many times in Stewart's work, to Hardy:

> The near-midsummer dusk is deepening on Horton Hill. The sheep are shadowy on its slopes; to the north the softly-rolling downland is sharpened into silhouette; and below, Scamnum is grown mysterious. Its hundred points of light are a great city from the air. Or its vague pale bulk is the sprawl of all Europe as viewed from an unearthly height at the opening of *The Dynasts*. And here, as there, there are spirits. The spirits sinister and ironic look down on Scamnum Court these nights.
>
> (M. Innes 1937: 22)

We move from an implicit evocation of the opening pages of *The Return of the Native* to an open reference to *The Dynasts*. The view from Horton Hill, like the prospect of Egdon Heath, is of a rural southern England under threat of doom. Scamnum Court stands for an urbane Europe awaiting the bomber that, it was believed, always would get through. England faces Hitler as England had faced Bonaparte. The literary references make political points.

In *Lament for a Maker* we move from England to Scotland. Here the world is made book, since allusions govern both form and content. The plot is woven round Dunbar's grim medieval monologue *Lament for the Makaris*. The narrative is carried in seven voices. A Calvinist sutor, Ewen Bell, gives us the first and last sections. Here Stewart tries – with mixed success, it must be admitted – for the heightened Mearns Lallans of Lewis Grassic Gibbon's *A Scots Quair*, the prose masterpiece of the left nationalist Scottish literary renaissance. The second section, in which Noel Gylby writes to his fiancée, puts twentieth-century content into a Richardsonian epistolary framework. Algo Wedderburn, Writer to the Signet, gives us a pastiche of Stevenson's *Weir of Hermiston* in the third section. The fifth is a diary. Ian Guthrie – note the reference back to Gibbon – mixes Joseph Conrad with Tom Collins in his appalled account of the Australian bush. The fourth and sixth sections are in John Appleby's voice, and bring us back to the Golden Age detective novel's conventions. In this book Stewart uses resources developed by Gibbon, MacDiarmid, and others to deny their vision of a Scotland regenerated through a socialist nationalism: a Scottish murder is rooted in Australian events.

One could analyse the other early novels in this way; but there is little point. Let us simply note in passing that *Stop Press* has literary connections principally to Pope, *There Came Both Mist and Snow* to Coleridge, *The Secret Vanguard* to Buchan, and *Appleby on Ararat* to Ballantyne's *Coral Island* and Wyss's *Swiss Family Robinson*.

One novel stands out. In *Death at the President's Lodging* explicit literary allusions are far less common than in the six succeeding novels.

> Deighton-Clerk, thus appealed to, looked first puzzled and then startled. 'Mr Haveland no doubt means,' he said, 'that anthropology is a strong subject with us at St Anthony's. Haveland is an anthropologist himself. Titlow's classical archaeology has got mixed up – please excuse the expression, Titlow! – with anthropology of late. And Pownall's ancient history and Campbell's ethnology have linked up with the subject too. The linking-up was fostered by the late President. Dr Umpleby himself came to anthropology through comparative philology, as did his pupil, Ransome, who is now abroad.'
>
> (M. Innes 1936: 51–2)

Here a classics-derived anthropology, an anthropology of a decidedly antique cast to modern eyes, organizes the plot.

St Anthony's contains only one litterateur, but he deserves our attention. Giles Gott is a bibliographer by profession, but he writes celebrated detective novels under the pseudonym Gilbert Pentreith. In *Death at the President's Lodging* Dr Gott seems to have only one novel to his credit: *Murder at the Zoo*. We meet him a year later in *Hamlet, Revenge!* A lot has happened in twelve short months. He seems to have been stripped of his doctoral degree, but in compensation he has been elected a Fellow of the British Academy. Still a Fellow of St Anthony's, he now is Hanmer Reader in Elizabethan Bibliography at Oxford. He has written three more novels: *Murder Among the Stalactites, Poison Paddock*, and *The Case of the Temperamental Dentist*. He leans towards the psychological school of thriller writing. We are invited to admire 'the elaborate analysis of the gorilla-mind in *Murder at the Zoo*' (M. Innes 1937: 187), though the Aberdeen savant, Malloch, brings Scottish hard-headedness to bear:

> 'I readily believe that the creature could be trained to fire the fatal shot. But the training of it by means of the series of sugar revolvers to swallow the real revolver? I asked Mortenthaler – you know his *Intelligence in the Higher Mammalia*? – and he seemed to think . . .'
>   It was Gott's turn to groan.
>
> (M. Innes 1937: 51–2)

Stewart is punning his own practice as university teacher and detective story writer in the figure of Gott. But that is not why he exists. To borrow a phrase, one could say that if Gott did not exist then Stewart would have had to invent him. He permits his creator to play tricks with genre. This possibility is never far from Stewart's mind. In the first edition of *Bloody Murder* (1972: 127) Julian Symons distinguishes Stewart's detective novels sharply from his thrillers; but this is to do violence to the evidence. Very often a plot ambles backwards and forwards across the boundary between the two genres. In *Hamlet, Revenge!* he does something much more ambitious.

Gott first appears halfway through *Death at the President's Lodging*. His own part in various obfuscations forgiven, he becomes Watson to Appleby's Holmes in this orthodox murder mystery. But this Watson is no fool. Stewart divides his great detective. Gott works on intuition, supplementing Appleby's cool, analytical mind. The same holds in the next novel. The central puzzle in

Hamlet, Revenge! is whether the fatal shooting of the Lord Chancellor behind the arras (he plays Polonius in a private performance of *Hamlet*) is to be understood through the conventions of a murder mystery, or those of a thriller. Stewart runs the two possibilities in tandem. Clues could point one way or the other. He plays with the genres for a couple of hundred pages, then gives us a spectacular denouement. In the standard final chapter of a whodunit Gott solves the mystery as straightforward murder, building a convincing case around a particular set of villains. But this is not the last chapter; that is still to come. In it Appleby solves the puzzle as a spy thriller, with an entirely separate set of villains. We leave Scamnum Court with a sense that genre can be bent and extended by those with adequate wit and technique; that there are more things in heaven and earth than are dreamt of in Dorothy Sayers' philosophy.

Genres are twisted, interlarded; but in the early novels it is detective fiction that is the dominant form. Hence their settings. *The Secret Vanguard* is a fairly straightforward Buchanesque thriller (with an appropriate Scottish setting) and need not detain us. The settings for the other six novels are more significant. *Death at the President's Lodging* takes us to an Oxford college, *Hamlet, Revenge!* to a very grand aristocratic mansion. *Lament for a Maker* finds us in a Scottish tower house, *Stop Press* in two middling-large southern English country houses. *There Came Both Mist and Snow* takes us to a Yorkshire mansion. The three parts of *Appleby on Ararat* are set in a makeshift lifeboat, on an apparently deserted Pacific island, and in a small *émigré* colony on the island. What do these settings have in common? The answer is constraint: they all have firm physical boundaries which limit the cast of characters, and what those characters can do. As Umberto Eco tells us (1984: 25), it is necessary to create constraints, in order to create freely.

Stewart plays with the notion of constraint. Like all good detective story writers, he is fascinated with locked room puzzles. *Hamlet, Revenge!* gives us locked rooms as Chinese boxes. The Lord Chancellor is shot in the rear stage of a recreated Shakespearian stage: a curtained enclosure with passages on three sides and the front stage on the fourth. The Shakespearian stage is set on the stage of Scamnum Court's private theatre. That theatre is locked, and physically separate from the rest of the mansion. The mansion's walls separate house from park. The park's walls form a last line of defence. All these lines are defended when the murder is done. Appleby's triumph is to show how each was breached in the interest of passing a document to a foreign power.

St Anthony's College, Oxford has firm boundaries. In this it resembles the settings for the other early novels. But there is a sense in which it seems to differ radically from them. *Death at the President's Lodging* is unique among Stewart's novels in its lack of explicit literary reference – Gott's *Murder at the Zoo* excepted. We might take this to follow from the fact that this is Stewart's first novel. Certainly it has the unevenness common in a first novel. Perhaps Stewart, finding his voice, had not yet realized the possibilities of literary references providing a set of clues through which the alert reader might disentangle his characteristically knotted plots? An attractive idea, but wrong. *Death at the President's Lodging* is literary: but it is set so firmly within its frame of references that one does not realize the fact. It is a genre novel, an Oxford murder, lying in a stream of similar work (Broome 1929; Morrah 1933; Cole and Cole 1937; 1938; 1943; Crispin 1944; 1946; Sayers 1935). It looks back most immediately to J. C. Masterman's *An Oxford Tragedy* (1933). Symons makes the similarity no more than 'the same kind of "don's delight" book, marked by the same kind of urbanity' (Symons 1972: 126). This is too simple. Masterman's novel, to which we will have cause to return, extended the genre by giving us an Oxford book in which undergraduates are no more than spear-carriers: attention is focused on their teachers. Masterman roots Shirley's death in complications arising from obscure antipathies among a moderately large group of fellows. This is a college murder in a much fuller sense than had been usual. In *Death at the President's Lodging* Stewart takes Masterman's extension and pushes it much further. St Anthony's has no more than a dozen fellows. The young are intelligent and cunning, most of the old merely cunning. Appleby uncovers two conspiracies that intersected to produce the president's murder and its accompanying wild confusion. One plot among three younger fellows, Gott included, was to burgle the president's safe in order to recapture research material stolen by Umpleby from his young co-worker. The second plot was murderous. An older fellow, more than slightly mad, killed Umpleby in the hope of succeeding to his office. He planted the corpse in circumstances that would direct suspicion to another fellow. This man found the corpse and rumbled the intention but not the author. He trundled the body around the darkened college in a wheelbarrow, unwittingly connecting the second plot with the first. So it goes on. Harmless old Professor Curtis, locked in Orchard Ground and unable to return to his rooms, watched with increasing bemusement and outrage as a procession of his colleagues rendered themselves accessories after the fact of murder by dragging and barrowing Umpleby's remains around St Anthony's. At a college meeting Appleby untangles what happened, and a crazy brew of misapplied suspicion spills around the table. Haveland may have struck the fatal blow, but all the fellows of St Anthony's killed Umpleby. Nor did the president deserve not to die. Stewart give us the classic college murder, often imitated since but never equalled. That done, he never again works within that genre's limits. Death stalks Oxford colleges in several later novels, but never simply in the Golden Age detective story form. Henceforth he mixes genres, plays with forms.

J.I.M. Stewart was born in 1906, the son of the Director of Education for Edinburgh City. He went to Edinburgh Academy, and then to Oriel College, Oxford. In 1928 he took a first-class degree in English Language and Literature. After some further time in Oxford he was appointed Lecturer in English Literature at Leeds University in 1930. Five years later he became Jury Professor of English at Adelaide University. He returned to Britain after ten years, to a lecturing post at Queen's University, Belfast. In 1949 he was elected a Student (equivalent to Fellow in other colleges) of Christ Church, Oxford. There he stayed until he retired in 1973. From 1969 to 1973 he was Reader in English Literature at Oxford.

From 1935 to 1945 Stewart sat under the sweltering skies of South Australia, teaching literature and writing pseudonymous light fiction. One section of *Lament for a Maker* and the whole of *Appleby on Ararat* apart, those novels took no account of where he was. He wrote thrillers, including *The Daffodil Affair* (1942). He wrote those novels of constraint that we considered earlier, to which should be added *The Weight of the Evidence* (1944). The settings for these books were places in which he had lived before going to Australia: Scotland (*Lament for a Maker, The Secret Vanguard*); Oxford and its environs (*Death at the President's Lodging, Hamlet, Revenge!, Stop Press*); and the West Riding (*There Came Both Mist and Snow, The Daffodil Affair, The Weight of the Evidence*). His next three novels, published while he taught in Belfast, had English settings. The one after that, *The Journeying Boy* (1949), combined Hardy with Somerville and Ross in a thriller that, alone among Stewart's work, has an Irish setting. He records slogans painted on rocks alongside Ulster's railways: Life Is Short; Death Is Coming; Eternity – Where? 'Belfast, grimly utilitarian and shrouded in rain . . . suggested . . . a various detritus from the less appealing parts of Glasgow' (M. Innes 1949: 131). Here, for the first time in Britain, Stewart writes about the city and country in which he was living and working: but there is no missing the sense of imminent and unregretted departure.

Operation Pax appeared in 1951. If *The Journeying Boy* had been a means of bidding farewell to unloved Belfast then this, his next book, was a celebration of his delighted return to Oxford. Superficially not much has changed since *Stop Press*. John Appleby is still investigating dark deeds, though he now has risen from Detective Inspector to Assistant Commissioner at Scotland Yard. We still are patrolling the boundary between the detective novel and the spy thriller. We still have Stewart's light, farceur style. We still have a gallery of comic grotesques, most notably the enormously fat and enormously cultivated scientist, Bultitude. But Oxford is conjured much more concretely in *Operation Pax*. We are toured around the city: to married dons' villas in north Oxford; to the vaults of the Bodleian Library; to several colleges, real and imagined. These colleges are ranked hierarchically:

'This is St Gregory's,' he said. 'Never been in it. Have you – before today? Low college.'
'We can't all go to Balliol.'
'True – true.'

(M. Innes, 1951: 284)

Stewart claims a place in this hierarchy for the college which he has just joined:

It was six minutes after nine o'clock. Christ Church, following its immemorial vesperine custom, was in process of asserting its just hegemony of the lesser academic establishments clustered around it by the simple expedient of uttering a hundred-and-one magisterial peals on an enormous bell.

(M. Innes, 1951: 124)

31

In 1954 Stewart published his first novel under his own name, *Mark Lambert's Supper*. Since then roughly half his output has been ascribed to Michael Innes, half to J.I.M. Stewart. Blurbs suggest that the distinction is one of quality: Innes writes the light detective fiction, Stewart the serious novels. There is some truth in this, but the distinction has a curious consequence. From *Death at the President's Lodging* to *Operation Pax* Stewart often had used Oxford as the ground for his whimsically farcical fictions. Only in *A Family Affair* (1969) and *Appleby's Answer* (1973) has he done so since. The later Innes books have many threads leading to Oxford (or, more rarely, to Cambridge): one could say that the routine stamping ground of the light fiction is the Oxbridge-going classes. But we never find ourselves in Oxford for any length of time in these books. The serious fiction published under Stewart's own name makes a strong contrast. Not all of it is set in Oxford: there is a sustained stream of sub-Jamesian work – *Avery's Mission* (1971) provides an example – in which the Oxford connections, while present, are as tenuous as in the Innes books. But in 1954 he started to produce a flow of serious work in which Oxford University is not the setting but the subject of the fiction. In these novels Stewart gives us an extended cogitation on what Oxford is for, and how changing circumstances bear on the university and its constituent colleges. *Mark Lambert's Supper* (1954) combines a Jamesian theme with sardonic contemplation of life in the women's colleges. *The Man Who Won the Pools* (1961) concerns the relationship between working-class Oxford and academic Oxford. *The Last Tresillians* (1963) is about several things, but one of them is how colleges managed the expansion of the Robbins era. *The Aylwins* (1966) is about academic fraud and collegiate electoral politics. *Vanderlyn's Kingdom* (1967) considers the need for, and possible loss from, constitutional reform at Oxford. This is Stewart's most openly didactic university novel, at least until the recent *The Naylors*. We then come to the *Staircase in Surrey* sequence: *The Gaudy* (1974), *Young Pattullo* (1975), *A Memorial Service* (1976), *The Madonna of the Astrolabe* (1977), and *Full Term* (1978). These five novels, of distinctly varied quality, move backwards and forwards between 1945 and the mid-1970s in order to examine how Oxford has changed over a generation, and to draw up a balance of the place's virtues and demerits. It is no surprise if the *Staircase in Surrey* sequence should give Oxford a relatively clean bill of health, written as it was in the years immediately following Stewart's retirement from his Studentship and his Readership. What is more surprising is that his most recent Oxford novel, *The Naylors* (1985), should reverse a good few of the generous judgements in the earlier work.

In fictional terms Oxford is the exemplary modern British university. J.I.M. Stewart gives us a starting-point for considering representations of major redbricks in *The Weight of the Evidence* (M. Innes 1944), and of new universities in *Old Hall, New Hall* (M. Innes 1956b): but above all he is the exemplary modern Oxford novelist. He employs the self-deprecating irony characteristic of Oxford's public face: in a rare self-portrait, Quail 'gave lunch to his Christ Church friend, an elderly English tutor of mild temper and no conversation' (J.I.M. Stewart 1955: 213). He gets first, and usually best, to themes which other authors then discuss. As Philip Larkin (1983: 53) said of Michael Innes,

> I don't know why there has never been a serious study of him: he's a beautifully sophisticated writer, very funny and, now and then, very moving.

That is true; but it also is true that for those interested in post-war British university fiction Innes, and his *alter ego* Stewart, is at once the indispensable starting-point and the high point of the entire literature.

Chapter Three

KEEP AND OUTWORKS

J.I.M. Stewart is the master, but his work is merely the most lustrous thread in a web of writing. That web contains few patterns. Without doing too much violence to their integrity we can place these 196 books in a limited set of categories: detective novel, thriller, science fiction, novel of manners, romance, comic novel. Together they constitute a separate genre, the modern British university novel. When Professor Simkiss mentions 'what you call "campus fiction"' (J.I.M. Stewart 1986: 142) we understand immediately what he means.

The existence of the genre is evident from the dense cross-referencing between book and book, writer and writer. Some authors make open connections. '"What do you think of Anus?"' asks a lugubrious foreign postgraduate student, '"The novelist, Kingsley Anus"' (Lodge 1965: 129). A minor redbrick, anxious to follow the ethos of Thatcher's enterprise culture, seeks endowment for senior academic positions: 'the Westland Chair of Anglo- American Relations, the Kingsley Amis Chair of Women's Studies, and the Durex Chair of French Letters' (Bradbury 1987: 41). Earlier, Bradbury (1976: 143–52) had given us an imaginary conversation between Amis's Jim Dixon and C.P. Snow's Lewis Eliot. J.I.M. Stewart makes a passing reference to Snow (1974: 106) and to J.C. Masterman (1986: 143). Jacobson (1983: 34) genuflects to an erection called Bradbury Lodge, Myer (1988: 17) to Brodge. Ron Rust vows to write the definitive campus novel: 'Nobody's done this one right before. Amis, Bradbury, Lodge, Sharpe . . . that other sod . . . what are they, frightened of telling the truth, or something?' (A. Davies 1986: 43; original punctuation). Dr

Browning invites us to consider how much detection fiction '"has been written by Oxford graduates – Dorothy Sayers, Edmund Crispin, Michael Innes, C. Day Lewis, J.C. Masterman and so on. Not only are they graduates," his voice became low and dramatic, "many of them are at this moment senior teaching members of the University"' (T. Robinson 1961: 13). So it goes on.

More frequently, books talk to books without mentioning names. C.S. Lewis's *That Hideous Strength* (1945) inspired J.I.M. Stewart's *The Naylors* (1985) and Andrew Davies's *A Very Peculiar Practice: The New Frontier* (1988). Lewis's collegiate Edgestow University is echoed in slightly less Oxbridge Calleshire (Aird 1977) and Buriton (Mann 1975). C. P. Snow's *The Masters* (1951) and *The Affair* (1960) provided the basis for a crop of novels about academic intrigue. The best wrought is J.I.M. Stewart's *The Aylwins* (1966), the most vicious Tom Sharpe's *Porterhouse Blue* (1974). The most surprising is Barbara Pym's *An Academic Question* (1986), a doomed attempt at an unfamiliar form. More influential even than Snow, however, is J.I.M. Stewart himself. University-based passages from his whodunits attracted comment and imitation from a host of admirers. Bruce Montgomery divided Gervase Crispin, a character in *Hamlet Revenge!*, to produce parts of both his own *nom de plume* – 'Edmund Crispin' – and the name for his detective, Gervase Fen. Who was Edmund Fen, one wonders. Whole sections from *Stop Press* were echoed in Crispin's *The Case of the Gilded Fly* (1944). Robert Robinson's *Landscape with Dead Dons* (1956) displayed close reading of Stewart on every page. Robinson copied his master's light farceur style, his occasional brutal irony. He even gave us an episode in the Bodleian Library's stacks; a straight crib from *Operation Pax*. The fellows of Warlock College, an unlovely bunch, recall the equally unlovely fellows of St Anthony's (M. Innes 1936); the death of the unloved master, Manchip, that of the equally unloved Umpleby. Clapp, a lecturer in military history and fellow of Warlock, speaks an archaic aristocratic English: '"Hijus prospect, fillin' the place with Russians"' (R. Robinson 1956: 28). Where have we heard these tones before? In *The Weight of the Evidence*, in the mouth of that declined gentleman ('"Supportin' myself like a little school teacher"') Lasscock, Senior Lecturer in English at Nesfield University: '"What I've never liked about this place is the mice. Hijjus noise they make in the wainscots – quite hijjus"' (M. Innes 1944: 77). Timothy Robinson (1961: 64–5) has his Balliol-educated Scotland Yard detective enlarge on the special character of crime in his old university.

> 'Ah well, Oxford murders are a special instance of the importance of being well read. We classify them under a separate heading in the Force, you know. Oxford murders are literary murders. To deal with them you need to have literary policemen. Take the Assistant Commissioner, for instance. I've no doubt that he would be able to place this rhyme of yours in no time.'

The unnamed Assistant Commissioner is the St Anthony's-educated John Appleby: as the Michael Innes canon unfolds we watch Appleby rise in the Metropolitan Police from humble dick to enlightened but beknighted Commissioner. Elsewhere, baby Link is saved from a fanatical psychologist by the Oxford-educated detective Richard Ringwood, another Appleby clone (Farrer 1955). Stewart returns the favour rather later: in *Appleby and the Ospreys* (M. Innes 1986) John Appleby solves his last country-house crime in association with Detective Inspector Ringwood.

The last example of obeisance to Stewart's excellence comes from a surprising pen:

> He was master of Appleby forgot just what Cambridge college, a power in the land at something called Greek Epigraphy, and given, every decade or so, to uttering some deep mystery in the tradition of Douglas and Margaret Cole or Ronnie Knox. Appleby *had* once read a novel by Hussey. It had been called *The Seventeenth Suspect.*
>
> (M. Innes 1973: 37)

In order to avoid confusion between British and American usages, *Death at the President's Lodging* was published in the United States as *Seven Suspects*. Of course John Appleby had read *The Seventeenth Suspect*: he was that (slightly metamorphosed) book's least tarnished leading character. In the person of Hussey Michael Innes gets an admiring nod from the author best placed to judge his excellence: himself. The pattern of reference and allusion has recurved into a perfect circle.

This chapter and the next examine the main features of the British university novel as genre. In Chapter 4 we consider what the novels urge us to defend. Here, as a prelude to that, we consider novels' accounts of universities' physical and social structure. We begin with names.

In few Oxbridge novels is the location of the university disguised. The first of these is *Death at the President's Lodging*. St Anthony's College forms part of a composite Oxbridge university located at a junction midway along the meanderingly direct railway line betweeen Oxford and Cambridge. This places it at Bletchley, on the main line that was built as the London and Birmingham Railway. Hence the significance of this university's location. Looking south, its inhabitants would face towards the huge, federal London University. Looking north, they would face the major redbrick Birmingham University. Thirty years after Umpleby's murder Milton Keynes, the new city that has swallowed Bletchley, would be the site for the new Open University. St Anthony's stands at a crossroads: Oxbridge to east and west, different kinds of not-Oxbridge to north and south. But long before the Open University was founded Stewart admitted that St Anthony's really was in Oxford (M. Innes 1937: 42; 1982: 154–5). *That Hideous Strength* (Lewis 1945) is set in Edgestow, another composite Oxbridge; a small, ancient English university with only three colleges. Francis Lyall's *A Death in Time* contains a character who has risen from promising beginnings as a concentration camp guard to be professor of economics and fellow of Palmer College at Bicaster University. The name – two fortresses – would tell us that this is a composite Oxbridge, even if Benedict were not suspected of recruiting Britain's future leaders to be KGB sleepers (Lyall 1987: 193). In Vulliamy's *Don Among the Dead Men* (1952) Oxford is lightly disguised as the ancient Ockham University. Liddell's *The Last Enchantments* (1948) covers Oxford with a yet gauzier disguise as Christminster: we are even given a less than subtle reference to Jude Fawley. Valerie Grosvenor Myer's *Culture Shock* (1988) is also set in the collegiate Christminster University. This name, and the fact that one college is called St Jude's, might persuade us that we are in Oxford: but Myer's Christminster, with its flourishing high-tech science park and an English faculty that suffered – or enjoyed – internecine warfare in the early 1980s, is a lightly disguised Cambridge.

37

If there is little need to disguise a setting in Oxford or Cambridge University, then authors can be less sanguine about identifying those universities' constituent colleges. Names can be tricky, as Stewart discovered. His first novel, we have seen, was set in St Anthony's College; a name borrowed from Adam Broome's *The Oxford Murders* (1929). No problem, until Oxford University permitted the foundation of St Antony's College in 1940.

Writers handle this difficulty in two ways. The first is not to name colleges, except to identify the affiliation of the odd visitor dining in hall. This is a common strategy. It is Snow's tactic in his Cambridge books, for example. His early lesson learnt, it is Stewart's tactic in most of his Oxford work from *Stop Press* onwards. The second approach is to dream up a new name, and hope that the university does not adopt it for a new foundation. Thus we are given three sets of fictive Oxford colleges. The first set conjures ecclesiastic connections, reminding the reader that Oxford's roots are monastic: All Saints' (Lodge 1984), Bede (M. Innes 1951), Canterbury (Avery 1957, 1960; Hsuing 1952), Cherubim (Balsdon 1952), Episcopus (Wain 1988), Holywell (MacInnes 1948), Judas (J.I.M. Stewart 1986: 118), Latimer (Fleming 1965), Pentecost (Farrer 1957; Sayers 1958a), St Agatha's (G. Butler 1960), St Aldgate's (Hsuing 1952), St Anthony's (M. Innes 1936), St Asaph's (Kennington 1948), St Cecilia's (J.I.M. Stewart 1954), St Christopher's (Balsdon 1952; Crispin 1944, 1946, 1947), St Denis' (Farrer 1957), St Elizabeth's Hall (Kennington 1948), St Frideswide's (McIntosh 1956), St George's (Balsdon 1952, 1961), St Gregory's (M. Innes 1951), St Helena's (Balsdon 1961), St Hereward's (Balsdon 1961), St James' (Postgate 1953), St Joseph's (Hartley 1946), St Jude's (Balsdon 1952; Mais 1949), St Lucy's (Fraser 1985), St Margaret's (Mosley 1965), St Mark's (Cole and Cole 1937; Liddell 1948; Mosley 1965; Yorke 1973, 1976), St Mary's (Davey 1982; Hsuing 1952; McIntosh 1956), St Michael's (J. Gray 1947), St Monica's (Liddell 1948), St Old's (Spencer 1961), St Olav's (Vulliamy 1952), St Philip's (Cole and Cole 1943), St Rachel's (A. Waugh 1963), St Saviour's (T. Robinson 1961), St Sepulchre's (McIntosh 1956), St Simon's (Cole and Cole 1938), St Theobald's (A.E.W. Thomas 1969), St Thomas' (M. Innes 1940a; Masterman 1933, 1952, 1957), St Wergildas' (Hale 1955), St Winifred's (Morgan 1948), Temple (Kennington 1948), Walpurgis Hall (R. Robinson 1956), and Warlock (R. Robinson 1956). The second group asserts monarchical or aristocratic links: Beaufort (Morrah 1933; Shaw 1981), Clarendon (W. Cooper 1966), Comyns (Amis 1978), Godolphin Hall (A. Waugh 1963), Hereford (Balsdon 1952), King Alfred's (J.R.L. Anderson 1981), King's (Price 1972), Leycester (Hocking 1957), Lonsdale (Dexter 1975, 1977, 1983), Prince's (Morgan 1948), Randolph (Pym 1985), and Rochester (Fraser 1985). The third set is miscellaneous, with a tendency to the topographical: Clapham (Vulliamy 1952), Gaveston (G. Butler 1960), Martlesham Hall (Vulliamy 1952), Maryol (Murray 1945), Sapientia (Balsdon 1961), Shrewsbury (Sayers 1935), Sturdley (Sheed 1967), and Weller Hall (Vulliamy 1952). The thinner crop of fictional Cambridge colleges gives us Carol (Gloag 1980), Fisher (Rees 1945), Lancaster (Rees 1945; Raven 1966, 1970, 1976), Malapert (Jacobson 1986), Mary (Sinclair 1959), Paracelsus (Carr 1951), Ryland's (Price 1981), St Jude's (Fiske 1980; Myer 1988), St Margaret's (B. Cooper 1963), St Michael's and All Angels (Byatt 1985), St Nicholas' - also called St Anastasius and the Magnificent Virgin Edwina (Clinton-Baddeley 1967) – and Sheepshanks (Fiske 1980). Note the different tone of these Cambridge names: rather more secular than in Oxford, with fewer claims to aristocratic connection.

We see that novelists may not want us to know which college we are examining, but they all want us to know that we are in Oxford or Cambridge. This provides a striking contrast with novels about other places. Once again a common tactic is to maintain a discreet silence, though we can be given a spectacularly vague name like The Northern University (Mann 1975) or University College (D. Williams 1977). More precise names almost invariably are attached to fictitious universities: Aberlady, Bannerman, Pitstone and Trail (Lyall 1987), Ashfield (Gethin 1986), Banley (Goller 1979), Bantwich (Candy 1971), Beechnall (Middleton 1987), Branchfield (Devine 1969), Bridport (G. Butler 1960), Brockshire (Priestley 1968a, 1968b), Buriton (Mann 1973, 1975), Calleshire (Aird 1977), Cumbria (Price 1972), Darlington (Lodge 1984), Eastringham (Trickett 1954), Ferraby (Mann 1974), Follymead (Peters 1967), Gowerburgh (Campbell 1945), Grimsby (R. Barnard 1979), Halifax (White 1971), Hardgate (Devine 1966), Lincoln (Ruell 1974), Lowlands (A. Davies 1986, 1988), Mansterbridge (Vulliamy 1961), Midport (Melville 1970), Nesfield (M. Innes 1944; J.I.M. Stewart 1981: 21), North Staffordshire (R. Robertson 1956),

Polford (J. Bell 1972), Quetley and Ruffbridge (Ashford 1972),
Rummidge (Lodge 1975, 1984, 1988), Stamford (Cole and Cole
1942), Staunton (Raphael 1976), Suffolk (Lodge 1988), Trendon
(Connington 1947), Watermouth (Bradbury 1975), Wessex (Price
1976), Westlands (Hosegood 1973), Westminster (D. Muir 1948),
and Wolverhampton (Raven 1960). The only exception is fictions
set in disguised nooks and crannies of that rambling Byzantium,
London University (Lodge 1965; Nash 1962; Pym 1955, 1982;
Rendell 1976; J.I.M. Stewart 1981: 130–54; Storey 1972).

We see something significant. Writers are content that we
should recognize Oxford or Cambridge. Within those universities
it is the college that is disguised. Elsewhere it is the university that
is disguised. The college is the focus in the Oxbridge novel, the
university in the not-Oxbridge novel. Since the Oxbridge novel
sets the discourse, other kinds of university are measured against a
college yardstick. We see this happening in accounts of
institutions' buildings. Architecture is never simply there, the
physical backdrop to events. Buildings encode meanings;
descriptions of buildings seek to guide the reader's sympathies.

In Oxford and Cambridge men's colleges we are shown places
anciently established. The reader enters through the obligatory
great gate guarded by a stock character: the Head Porter who
never forgets a face. In front there stretches a variable number of
linked lawned squares. These are called quadrangles in Oxford
and courts in Cambridge. The reader is conducted through the
buildings ranged around these lawns: to the rooms of undergraduates and postgraduates, and their teachers, opening off
staircases which punctuate the ranges at regular intervals; to the
college hall, the chapel, the library; to the port-lubricated,
unbuttoned comfort of the senior common room (combination
room in Cambridge) in which so much of British academic novels'
action takes place. Not infrequently we are taken inside the
master's lodging, sometimes to examine the corpse; less
commonly (Sharpe 1974 and Wain 1988 are the outstanding
examples) we see the college's real foundations, its kitchen and
boiler room.

The college's architecture has ancient roots, but the buildings
have been modified down the years. St Nicholas', Cambridge,
bears the marks of its origins. This place was once a monastery.

The older buildings are therefore grouped in the monastic way – the Refectory, now the Hall, the Dormitory, now the Library, the Abbott's Lodging, now the Master's Lodge, and the Chapel, all squared round the Cloisters. The courts beyond have been built at different periods since, from the seventeenth century court . . . to the ghastly Victorian additions.

(Clinton-Baddeley 1967: 15)

When Noddy Warlock, a disastrously incompetent Restoration Chancellor of the Exchequer, came to found his new Oxford college he decreed an architecture fake-monastic in its roots, but with a yet more marked variety.

Warlock is a standing monument to the entire history of architecture. What Noddy forgot, later generations added. For every Saxon doorway there is a Norman tower, for every Doric column, there is a Corinthian, an Ionian, a Composite, and a Tuscan. Pediments and cornices peep out round flying buttresses, and are lost amid the roundheaded arches, the quoins, the baroque jambs, the voussoirs, and the Mohammedan domes. Battlements are flung about the roofs like confetti, and in the Summerhouse quad there is a pagoda.

For cloisters, Warlock is the first in the world: Mrs Radcliffe . . . is said to have seen the Summerhouse Cloisters and to have started on *Udolpho* the same afternoon. Frescoes and statuary jostle for place among the eaves and gables, and gargoyles grimace from architrave and entablature. The stylistic assortment had become so various by the nineteenth century that Sir George Gilbert Scott chucked in the towel, and went away to build the Albert Memorial.

(R. Robinson 1956: 24–5)

This description is played for laughs, but it is no more than a heightened version of other novelists' college architecture. Common to all is a covert sense that this building and rebuilding, decay and adaptation, has produced a humane setting for humane study; that learning fits the college like an old suit of thornproof tweeds.

There are some ruptures in this massive continuity. Tastes

change, most notably about the virtues of Victorian architecture. Until the full flood of Betjemanesque romanticism washed over them in the 1970s, colleges' Victorian accretions were roundly condemned.

> 'Gosh, I wish I'd had a chance to study in one of these wonderful old buildings,' said McCabe [a journalist], in routine veneration of the asymmetrical and presumptuous pinnacles of the Victorian facade.
> 'Oh, but this isn't old,' said Madelaine, 'it's the most ghastly piece of Gothic revival in the whole of Oxford.'
>
> (McIntosh, 1956: 67)

A competition to design a new chapel for St George's, Oxford, ended in deadlock among three eminent Victorian architects. The solution was to pool their work. The result was odd.

> Of his own design, Mr Butterfield was most in love with a red brick campanile, adapted to suit the Gothic style (without bells, of course); Mr Waterhouse fancied his nave (in stone), and Mr Scott his apse. The building was executed and was full of curiosity, in particular because the apse was designed to suit a building far lower than the nave which had been taken from Mr Waterhouse's plan.
>
> (Balsdon 1952: 12–13)

The polychrome facade of Keble College's Victorian buildings raises an automatic snicker, as do the villas built by the first generation of married college fellows. Hence the description of a 'terrible North Oxford house, built . . . when Keble College's lavatory bricks were still the rage' (Kennaway 1963: 40). J.I.M. Stewart pokes gentle fun at north Oxford villas:

> The house in Norham Gardens was large and lofty. It rose massively through the gathering fog in a confusion of variegated brickwork and carved stone to a turret the purely medieval suggestion of which was impaired by its having been made the terminus of a spiral iron fire-escape. The windows, all of them lurking like small wary eyes beneath pointed arches and between columns crowned with conscientiously diversified capitals, were so numerous and so irregularly disposed that a profusion of exterior plumbing subsequently

added to the fabric was obliged to crawl with a tortuous
obliqueness over its surface. The whole structure, designed
to evoke in cultivated Victorians nostalgic thoughts of
Murano or the Grand Canal, in fact achieved a different
marine suggestion, that of some vast, barnacle-encrusted
object in the clutches of an answeringly gigantic octopus.

(J.I.M. Stewart 1955: 40)

Thirty years on, Colin Dexter looks at the same district of
Ruskin-inspired Venetian Gothic houses; but he looks through
transformed eyes. Some may find them 'severe and humourless,'
he tells us,

But such an assessment would be misleading: attractive bands
of orange brick serve to soften the ecclesiastical discipline of
these great houses, and over the arches the pointed contours
are re-emphasised by patterns of orange and purple.

(Dexter 1986: 12)

The difference between these last two passages reflects a British,
as well as an Oxbridge, revaluation of Victorian architecture; but
revaluation is negative as well as positive. Keble College and north
Oxford come to look attractive by contrast with modern buildings.
Thus a new appreciation of Victorian Oxbridge is partly a response
to the building programmes rendered necessary by the university
expansion that gathered pace from the late 1950s. In Oxford,
Beaufort has 'the Brandon Building, a recently built residential
block, the one piece of modern architecture in the college' (Shaw
1981: 66). Rochester has 'the library, a recent gift of a rich Turk,
[which] reposed beyond the Hawksmoor quadrangle, all glass and
steel, looking like some vast beached ship or ark' (Fraser 1985: 58).
St Mark's has 'a new building in a corner of the college grounds.
Dr Wilmot deplored the modern architecture of its design' (Yorke
1973: 19). Luke Tresillian's tutor 'disapproves of the new fashion
for all-glass buildings in Oxford because it impedes
undergraduates in two of their most important activities:
love-making and saying their prayers' (J.I.M. Stewart 1963: 324).
His college is split politically by a proposal to construct 'a
grotesque squashed corkscrew of a picture gallery . . . within the
shadow of the college's principal pride: Nicholas Hawksmoor's
slender neo-Gothic tower' (J.I.M. Stewart 1963: 285, 266).

Cambridge University Library's tower is the university's

> notoriously phallic symbol . . . . It is regrettable that
> Cambridge's chief library possesses no antique nook, no
> venerable cranny where the learned may contemplate the
> erudition of past ages in a setting suitably archaic. Instead,
> the graceless brick edifice which so brazenly rears its obscene
> tower to dominate the Cambridge skyline provides for the
> purpose a room more fit for the filing of forms by drab and
> faceless minor civil servants than the faun-filled researches of
> classicists or the gilded and jewelled imaginings of medieval
> scholars.
>
> (Fiske 1980: 209)

Lancaster College, Cambridge, has constructed a small student
hostel in the Fellows' Garden as 'a tactful concession to the times'
(Raven 1970: 24): the college splits on a much more radical
proposal to build two large hostels in Scholar's Meadow. The
inmates will not have college servants. The hostels will be cleaned,
food purchased and cooked, by all students on a rota system. Food
will be eaten not in Lancaster's noble hall, but in a new Student
Co-operative Cafeteria (Raven 1970: 99).

'I loathe almost every new building in Oxford.' Ultra-Tory
though he is, in this Glowrey (Lejeune 1987: 235) speaks for all.
'The greater part of Oxford', the leftist Storm Jameson tells us,

> is detestable and hideous. No town, no city containing, as
> Oxford does, buildings of incomparable loveliness has been
> more heartlessly disfigured. A small kernel, partly medieval,
> corroded by shops, cars, buses, like a stream choked by
> ordures, is embedded, suffocating in a flux of mediocre
> streets.
>
> (Jameson 1957: 9)

'Perhaps it is to be expected that a public privileged with the daily
sight of so many old and noble buildings should feel a natural
prejudice against the reinforced concrete of the curious post-war
structures,' Colin Dexter (1977: 91) muses, 'or perhaps all modern
architects are mad.' Only one novel resists this uncharitable
conclusion. *Memoirs of a New Man* pokes no more than gentle fun
at Clarendon College's Scandinavian architecture and fittings.
This is a postgraduate college built for scientists, 'a Chinese copy

of Churchill College [Cambridge]' (W. Cooper 1966: 60). Its self-service cafeteria may make this college different from others in Oxford, but we are shown a place whose form fits its function. In other places new buildings are at best tolerated, at worst excoriated. Beaufort undergraduates vote with their feet, greatly preferring rooms in the medieval Lancaster Hall to those in the brand-new Brandon Building (Shaw 1981: 66).

In novelists' accounts the architecture of redbrick universities never catches the humane heterogeneity of the Oxbridge college. The effect may be sought, but it is not achieved. The point can be made delicately: at Ashfield University 'The buildings were a careful architectural blend of the old and the new. The original was an exact copy of an Oxford or Cambridge college, complete with quadrangle and a small fountain in the middle. The fountain didn't work' (Gethin 1986: 43). Rather earlier, a group of friends walk towards the minor redbrick Eastringham University. 'The air of melancholy that pervaded the place kept them silent as they approached the main buildings, castellated and splendidly Gothic, and, at a distance, seemingly deserted . . . Everything was enclosed and monumental, the trees and the buildings combined in a display of damp mysterious unreality' (Trickett 1954: 21). The last phrase undercuts any possibility that we might admire this place, but we are still some distance from J.I.M. Stewart's excoriation of not-Oxbridge university life through a withering description of not-Oxbridge architecture. John Appleby, called to the major redbrick Nesfield University to investigate Professor Pluckrose's apparent meteoric pounding, is provided with a 'tank-like' room for an office.

> The place was some species of board-room; presumably the professors of the university, as also the council of local notabilities by whom they were controlled, held their deliberations here. Large and square and high and gloomy, with walls of oily brown paint relieved by inconsequent outcrops of bare stone, it would have, if disfurnished, much the appearance of a sanitarily conceived receptacle for polar bears or hippopotami in a nineteenth century zoological park. Gothic windows, anxious to present a symmetrical effect when viewed from without, had disposed themselves into a bewildering chaos when viewed, as now, from within;

rafters, obedient to the necessities of some warren of rooms and corridors superimposed, edged themselves into positions suggestive of an obscure system of antipathies and affinities above.

(M. Innes 1944: 8–9)

This is sham-Oxbridge in not-Oxbridge. The external Gothic is carried through without regard to the building's internal arrangements. The result is grotesque, a warren of rooms upstairs, a gloomy tank below. The result is inhumane, since architectural pretensions outweigh the needs of the building's inhabitants. Inappropriate ambition characterizes all public buildings in Frank Deasy's northern city. Above rows of terraced housing,

the city rises to a skyline sparsely topped by works of greater architectural pretension: the dome of the Town Hall, the two nineteenth century cathedrals, the Victorian Gothic tower of the old University buildings and the hulking cliffs of the new.

(J.I.M. Stewart 1966: 9)

Branchfield is a 'miserable town with its third-rate university'. 'People sometimes called it "the little Oxford" – mostly people who didn't know Oxford... The buildings gave the impression of having been scattered at random over the campus' (Devine 1969: 7, 33–4). This jumble, altogether lacking Oxbridge's humane variety, is also to be found in another minor redbrick. The university's heart is a manor house:

various Acts of Parliament still gave protection to its rotting beams and scorched thatch. A Victorian extension had been built at one side and an Edwardian extension on the other, both of which were dwarfed by the cantilevered concrete block of the main building.

(Parkin 1987: 17)

The purpose-built accommodation at the major redbrick Rummidge University is false in a different way. The university's staff exchange scheme with the American State University of Euphoria is grounded in the accident that

the architects of both campuses independently hit on the same idea for the chief feature of their designs, namely, a replica of the leaning tower of Pisa, built of white stone and twice the original size at Euphoric State and of red brick and to scale at Rummidge, but restored to the perpendicular in both instances.

(Lodge 1975: 13)

One of Rummidge's student halls of residence was 'hastily erected in 1969, at the height of the boom in higher education'. Ten years later, it is a wreck: cracked and pitted walls, stained and broken furniture, sagging beds. 'Every room had a washbasin, though not every washbasin had a plug, or every plug a chain. Some taps could not be turned on, and some could not be turned off' (Lodge 1984: 3). Roche's memory of post-war student days in Manchester evokes even grimmer comparisons: 'those ghastly bomb-swept open spaces around the University and the History Faculty, which were dismal even when it was dry, like a piece of East Berlin authentically reproduced in England, no expense spared' (Price 1981: 130). Within somewhere very like Manchester's mock-Gothic buildings

Something like a hallowed silence reigned. A few dirty pigeons cooed malevolently at him from the sagging gutterings, and from the stone head of the statue of the founding Victorian philanthropist that rose up like a ghost in the middle of the court. The bell in the broken clock tower bronchitically croaked out the turning hour. Someone without musical ability was practising the bassoon. A few notices flapped on a board, announcing essay competitions on whether there should be a third sex or pointing directions to where one could give blood.

(Bradbury 1987: 59)

Things are no better when the not-Oxbridge university has recycled buildings. Adam Appleby's English department is housed in a former warehouse. The next, identical, warehouse holds the department of civil engineering (Lodge 1965: 73). The shape of the bottle gives no clue to its contents. Colin Clout is writing a novel called *The Examination*, based on his experience of a university housed in a disgraced mansion. The only character, C, struggles to make sense of minor redbrick life. 'There would be intermittent doubt about the place being a university at all, and not, say, a maternity hospital or the municipal abattoir' (M. Innes 1956b: 45). This explicit evocation of Kafka is echoed more distantly in Bradbury's account of another minor redbrick:

> It was frequently mistaken for the railway station and was in fact closely modelled on St Pancras. The pile had, in fact, a curious history. When, in a riot of Victorian self-help, the town had finally decided that it wanted a university, it had provided it with all that vision, that capacity for making do, that *practicality* which had been the basis of the town's business success. Its founders had obtained its cloistered halls for next to nothing. The town lunatic asylum was proving too small to accommodate those unable to stand up to the rigours of the new world, and a larger building was planned. It was not big enough for an asylum, then; but it was big enough for a university college. . . . There were still bars over the windows; there was nowhere you could hang yourself. The place sat . . . on Institution Road, between the reception centre and the geriatric hospital.
>
> (Bradbury 1959: 24)

New foundations do not solve old problems. Stewart's 'unremarkable . . . makeshift university' (M. Innes 1956b: 13), in which Colin Clout struggles to bring *The Examination* to life, sits on the boundary between minor redbrick and new university forms. Like many new places that were to follow, it began life in a mansion around which buildings would be constructed as time and money permitted.

> The rather grandly bleak Georgian facades of Old Hall possessed, in their barely controlled disrepair, the rubbed abraded appearance of something done on canvas to an improbably stupendous scale. The sprawl of army huts, Nissen and Spider, on the one flank, and the raw brick boxes housing laboratories and workshops on the other, didn't look like anything that a responsible human being would pitch down beside an eighteenth-century mansion in a seventeenth-century park.
>
> (M. Innes 1956b: 9)

Instead of Oxbridge's humane continuity, here we have

irresponsible rupture, dis-order. Janet Dempsey refused to follow her husband to architectural inhumanity in Darlington University's early days:

> 'Well the campus is a bit bleak in winter, outside the town, you know, on the edge of the moors, and mostly prefabricated huts in those days, it's better now, we've got rid of the sheep and our Metallurgy building won a prize recently.'

(Lodge 1984: 6)

The same negative judgement comes through other accounts of ex-CAT and new university campuses as mud-engulfed building sites (Byatt 1985: 273; Priestley 1968a: 22–3).

Watermouth's campus is a permanent building site as 'the Kaakinen-style university, and its pious modernismus and concrete mass' (Bradbury 1975: 49) is constructed. Kaakinen is a Finnish architect, we are told; but his name comes from the Greek *kakos* meaning dirt or shit. The building programme exemplifies England's social history. From aristocratic origins in the Elizabethan Watermouth Hall, the campus bourgeoisie rises with buildings for Humanities and Natural Sciences. Industrialization brings the Business Building and the Engineering Building. 'The era of the crowd and the factory' is exemplified by Social Sciences' glass tower. A multidenominational chapel is constructed and 'named, to avoid offence, the Contemplation Centre' (Bradbury 1975: 64). Howard Kirk enters his office in the inhumanly angular social science building. 'It is a simple rectangle, with unpainted breeze-block walls, described in the brochure as proof of Kaakinen's frank honesty. The rooms at Watermouth are all like this, stark, simple, repetitious.' From his window Howard stares at 'the high phallus, eolipilic in shape, of the boilerhouse chimney, the absolute focus, the point of maximum architectural eminence, of the entire university, its substitute for a tower or a spire or a campanile' (Bradbury 1975: 62). In the midst of this brave new university he is startled to hear the atavistic chiming of Watermouth Hall's eighteenth-century stable clock (Bradbury 1975: 66), lost echo of Oxbridge civility.

Watermouth's is the classic fictional new university campus. Other books embroider details. Denying Kaakinen's vision, in some places continuities are sought with Oxbridge. This merely produces incongruity: 'We walked on,' says Caro Grimstone of an ex-CAT, 'through the complex of modern buildings that looked as if they might have been made from a child's box of bricks with a few neo-Gothic pinnacles jutting up at the corners' (Pym 1986: 33). Like Watermouth, instead of a chapel this place has a meeting-house shared by all faiths: 'the authorities had hardly liked to provide nothing at all' (Pym 1986: 34). For the churchy Barbara Pym this is devastating criticism. Rather later, in church, Caro is startled to hear a prayer inviting God to

> 'enlighten with thy spirit all places of education and learn-ing', seeing my own university with its undenominational meeting house, the dead pigeon lying in the water and the obscenity scrawled on the piece of modern sculpture. One would have thought that enlightenment could hardly go further than that.'
>
> (Pym 1986: 121)

The completed campus of Sussex University appears to be the most humane new place, 'tastefully harmonised buildings in the modernist-Palladian style, arranged in elegant perspective at the foot of the South Downs'. Yet this, too, is illusion.

> Toiling up the slope from Falmer railway station, you had the Kafkaesque sensation of walking into an endlessly deep stage set where apparently three-dimensional objects turned out to be painted flats, and reality receded as fast as you pursued it.
>
> (Lodge 1988: 24)

In new universities as in redbricks, choosing not to make pale copies of Oxbridge colleges does not mean that new humane patterns will be discovered. The Vice-Chancellor of Staunton University walks his new Professor of Interdisciplinary Studies around the campus, 'the "factory" as he put it'.

> Everything was new and had about it the strict elegance of the architect's drawings, except that there was none of the Italian sunshine which had lent the fountains in the broad *piazza* a charm their driven spray did not possess on a raw East Anglian afternoon.
>
> (Raphael 1976: 205)

From a distance Lowlands University's campus is a 'fortified rabbit-warren' (A. Davies 1986: 31), though here, too, the architect was trying for a glancing reference to Italian hill towns. The student hostels are 'a sophisticated rendering in concrete of the cave-dwellings of Altona'; the winding staircases in those hostels are a 'witty translation in concrete from some French dungeon' (A. Davies 1986: 23–4). The Medical Centre's corridors are Kaakinen-brutalist: 'tastefully exposed concrete, low ceiling, strip lighting, no pictures' (A. Davies 1986: 14).

At Lowlands staff and students have to endure the distance between architectural whimsy and grim reality. Exposed walkways flood, making the university notable for trench foot.

> Let me tell you about this terrible place, Stephen. They call it a new university, but it's twenty years old now. . . . Concrete's crumbling, all those bloody silly flat roofs leak, tiles falling off walls on to people's heads, we've got a repair budget four times the total salary bill.
>
> (A. Davies 1986: 17)

Nesfield, miraculously transposed from major redbrick to new university, 'although barely twenty years old, was distinguishably coming out in sympathetic cracks and flakings' (J.I.M. Stewart 1986: 149). In Oxbridge time mellows, blends. In Nesfield and Lowlands time exposes the inherent inhumanity and impracticality of the university's architecture.

It might be thought that this sharp contrast between Oxbridge and not-Oxbridge would evaporate when we turn from buildings to their inhabitants. What brings coachloads of tourists to the English ancient universities is the antiquity not of their statutes but their erections. 'Only the large number of moderately ancient and for the most part architecturally unimaginative buildings,' says J.I.M. Stewart (1985: 28) of Oxford, 'distinguished the place from any other English city of equivalent size.' Since the inhabitants of all British universities may be lumped under the three headings of academic staff, students, and non-academic staff one might expect that there would be few contrasts here between different kinds of universities. One would be disappointed. Once again we find a sharp distinction drawn between arrangements in Oxford and Cambridge and those elsewhere; a distinction in which the former provides the measure against which the latter is to be judged.

For the most cogent summary of the differences between the circumstances of academic staff in Oxbridge and not-Oxbridge one turns – inevitably it must now seem – to J.I.M. Stewart. In his early major redbrick novel, *The Weight of the Evidence*, he lightly points the contrasts.

> The provincial universities of England, although often abundantly medieval in point of architectural inconvenience, have little of the organisation characteristic of traditional places of learning. The staff – a word which at Oxford or Cambridge might be used of persons employed in a hotel – is not accommodated in spacious common rooms and cosy suites. Sometimes it is provided with a cellar in which the extravagant may drink coffee-essence at eleven o'clock; sometimes there is also an attic with chairs, where meetings may be held; a midday meal is obtainable by those who will grab from a counter with one hand and from a cutlery basket with another. The scholars live in remote suburbs, often surrounded by two, three, or even four children and a wife; they 'come in' three times a week (giving it out to be four) or four times a week (giving it out to be five).
>
> (M. Innes 1944: 5)

This passage establishes a set of oppositions between Oxbridge and not-Oxbridge universities. The former are metropolitan, the latter provincial; the former are traditional, the latter unhallowed by time; the former provide comfortable conditions for their bachelor teachers, the latter reward their married teachers with a grudging discomfort; eating arrangements are civilized in the former, barbarous in the latter; the former display a rich communal life, the latter are nine to five (or, in Nesfield, nine to ten) teaching factories. We need not take Stewart, writing this passage in South Australia, to be giving us social realism: enforced celibacy for fellows of Oxford and Cambridge colleges died in the nineteenth century, for instance. What he gives us is typifications of academic life in what he claims are two very different kinds of universities.

Stewart makes explicit what others take for granted. Hence the reader who wades through post-war British university novels by the score looking for accounts of academics' lives must be impressed by the stability of the discourse. As we saw earlier, Lejeune's

Professor in Peril (1987) employs precisely the same set of contrasts that Stewart had used in 1944. Other novels show marginal change; notably some set in new universities. In general, however, the contrast with accounts of Oxbridge academic life remains stark. Used to American conditions, Morris Zapp is impressed by the modest privilege of staff offices and common rooms in Rummidge (Lodge 1975: 52). Few others are impressed. An Eastringham University historian's room 'was dingy and had the musty smell of disuse' (Trickett 1954: 23). Staff in another minor redbrick work in 'quarters having the appearance of lumber-rooms hastily three-parts cleared', eat in 'the refectory, some sort of hanger that might have been reared to accommodate the last of the big dirigibles' (M. Innes 1956b: 24, 36). In Watermouth's integrated cafeteria staff and students eat under Kaakinen's 'domed plexiglass and flexiglass. . . . The great fancy room towers above them, a thing here of stark places, there of wild Scandi-navian frenzies' (Bradbury 1975: 147). We have come a long way from descriptions of candle-lit college halls and of port, nuts, and leather club chairs in senior common rooms.

What lies behind these contrasts between Oxbridge and not-Oxbridge is the unique constitutional formation of Oxford and Cambridge universities. Many novelists feel constrained to explain something of this to their readers, but none has done so better than J.C. Masterman. He wrote of Oxford in the early 1950s, but our purposes allow us to take him to have been writing of the whole post-war period, and of both ancient English universities. As Henry James said, 'when I say Oxford, I mean Cambridge' (quoted in Sparrow 1969b: 177): or, as paraphrased by Bruce Montgomery, 'Oxford – nursery of blooming youth. No, that was Cambridge, but it makes no odds' (Crispin 1946: 13).

Most generally, Masterman tells us (1952: 59), 'Oxford is both a residential university and one in which the undergraduates are members not only of the University but also of the various Colleges which make up the University'. The tasks of the university are remarkably modest: it 'provides examinations, it confers degrees, and it exercises a somewhat loose and precarious discipline' (1952: 61). One should add that it employs professors, readers, and lecturers, and operates university-wide libraries and scientific laboratories. Other things that would be done by the university elsewhere are done in Oxbridge by the college.

> Each college is, in fact, a microcosm of the University itself. A College is autonomous, governed by its own statutes, and responsible to no one but its corporators and its Visitor for its internal administration and policy. Each College has its own Head and Fellows, its own revenues, its own kitchen and Hall and Chapel, its own teaching and bursary staff. It is, in fact, a self-governing community, of which the Head and Fellows form the governing body. Most important of all, a College has an unfettered choice in the selection of its own members – a man may pass Responsions or its equivalent and then become eligible to enter the University, but he cannot act-ually matriculate until he has found a College to present him.
>
> (Masterman 1952: 224)

Each college has officers elected by – and, headship sometimes apart, elected from – the body of fellows: its head, whether called master, provost, president or whatever; a dean to manage discipline; a senior tutor to organize teaching; a bursar to handle the money. Headship apart, novels tell us that occupation of these elected positions carries little kudos. Among the fellows, J.I.M. Stewart (1966: 17) tells us, 'there is very little of hierarchy, and as a consequence the whole place is rather like a South American army as popularly conceived. Nearly everybody is a general, and a colonel's rank is the lowest that can be found.' Nor is it differences of rank alone that are levelled: 'There were octogenarians in our [senior] common room and there were youths in their earliest twenties. Within certain limits of discretion we all played at being contemporaries – a convention which worked well' (J.I.M. Stewart 1977: 32).

This generous play-acting, the reduction of difference in senior common rooms, is not found outside Oxford and Cambridge. English provincial universities, J.I.M. Stewart tells us (1983: 54), are 'stiffly hierarchical': a judgement that he and others extend to all not-Oxbridge universities. Formally the institution is controlled by a court combining a few senior academics with 'the local notabilities who boss the University' (M. Innes 1956b: 181). Sitting on the court provides a harmless hobby for the local landed grandee at Nesfield (M. Innes 1944), a grazing ground for local business men and superannuated Oxbridge dons in an ex-CAT (Snow 1968).

Academic decisions lie in the hands of a senate. The senate meeting is to the not-Oxbridge novel what the college meeting is to its Oxbridge peer; but the tone is quite different. In the latter, a fellow's subject becomes significant only if expert comment is required. Otherwise fellows argue as generalists, using wide knowledge to make disinterested cases. In the not-Oxbridge senate, by contrast, nothing is disinterested. Members argue their departments' corner under the less than benevolent chairmanship of the vice-chancellor (principal in some places), real – and despotic – monarch of all he surveys.

Vice-chancellors get a bad press. Nesfield's Sir David Evans, a comical Welsh philosopher, 'exhuded so pungent a benevolence that the effect was rather that of coming unawares on a skunk' (M.Innes 1944: 37). The principal of a minor redbrick, 'a small ventricose man with a polished, rosy bald head, gave one of his laughs. These strongly recalled the peals of horrid mirth so often audible in films about murder in castles' (Amis 1954: 212). Brockshire, 'this jumped-up-CAT university' (Priestley 1968a: 18), is ruled by Jayjay Lapford, the county's former director of education turned vice-chancellor. A palpable fraud, he welcomes poseurs to his campus once he discovers that they bring research money. Arnold Shaw is a competent historian of chemistry, but an arrogantly inflexible vice-chancellor (Snow 1968). Ernest Hemmingway is equally arrogant but excessively flexible (A. Davies 1986): both he and Shaw richly deserve their eventual sackings. Hemmingway's successor at Lowlands is an American technocrat apostrophized by one of his inferiors as 'the prince of darkness' (A. Davies 1988). An unnamed new university's vice-chancellor bawls out his Eton and Oxford philosophy professor with all the authority derived from his Diploma in Laundry Administration from the Pontypridd College of Commerce (Parkin 1987: 14). John Appleby's axiom holds for all fictional not-Oxbridge universities: 'a Vice-Chancellor, *ipso facto*, cannot be a good man' (M. Innes 1944: 35).

Below the vice-chancellor sit the professors, dominating their departments. As they are ruled from above, so they rule those below. Rummidge English staff cannot welcome an American visitor until their professor has returned from holiday: 'It was as if some obscure taboo had restrained them from introducing themselves before their chief had formally received him into the tribe' (Lodge 1975: 76). At a Pig Market for new students, 'pens, pounds, or booths had been set up for the several Faculties and Departments, and the professors and their dependent hierarchies were settling in to do business' (M. Innes 1956b: 48). It is not good policy to democratize these autocracies: the meetings of Watermouth's sociology department, held in the Durkheim Room, are interminably extended as students and junior staff exploit constitutional niceties for illiberal purposes (Bradbury 1975: 152–61).

Professors are shown as figures terrifying to students (Walker 1959); to their junior staff they are merely oppressive. Neddy Welch is a nonentity. 'How had he become Professor of History, even at a place like this? By published work? No. By extra good teaching? No in italics' (Amis 1954: 8). This does not prevent Welch from exploiting Jim Dixon: using him as a research assistant; passing the burden of the eventually cataclysmic formal lecture on Merrie England. The professor of English in a London college ignores his junior academic staff. At a party,

> as was his custom on such occasions, the Head of Department sat in a corner of the room with his back to the company, drinking with his constant companions, the two technicians who operated the professor's pride and joy, a computer for making concordances.
>
> (Lodge 1965: 134)

Beechnall University's professor of English bullies and terrorizes his staff, identifying each person's weakness in order to exploit it (Middleton 1987: 10–11).

Novelists writing about scholars' lives in Oxbridge colleges are fascinated above all by the virtues and difficulties of living a collegiate life. C.P. Snow is an optimist: his university novels show a Cambridge college struggling successfully to maintain amity while electing two new heads. In *The Masters* (1951) the head of Lewis Eliot's college lies dying in the late 1930s. The college's thirteen fellows manoeuvre in anticipation of the coming election. Two leading candidates emerge: Jago, a humanist, and Crawford, a scientist. Eliot commits himself to Jago and works for his election. This outcome seems secure until Crawford's anti-fascist politics tip the balance in his favour. Eliot regrets the result, but is not desolated. In the early chapters he strongly opposes Crawford's

56

candidature, but the latter's principled behaviour in the manoeuv-
rings, and the reasoned arguments of his supporters, persuade
Eliot that he will make a good master. The election is close, seven
votes to six: but by the date of the election there is the makings of
a consensus that Crawford will do. The college has talked its way to
an outcome that nearly everybody can accept. Collegiality has
produced the right result. *The Affair* (Snow 1960) takes up the story
some twenty years later. A new master is needed to replace
Crawford, whose term of office has been successful not least
because of loyal support from Arthur Brown, Jago's campaign
manager in the earlier contest. Now Brown himself is a candidate,
representing the humanities against the distinguished scientist
Francis Getliffe. It is a bitter election, complicated by an accusation
of academic fraud against a fellow; but, once more, the college
comes to the right decision.

In *The Aylwins* J.I.M. Stewart plays games with Snow's plot from
The Affair. Once again we have a novel concerned with academic
fraud and electoral politics; this time in Oxford, in an 'obscure and
seedy college' (J.I.M. Stewart 1966: 61). Once again fraud's stigma
is denied successfully. But this election is a good deal more complicated. The old provost lies dying from kidney failure. The fellows
machinate in anticipation of his demise. The leading contender is
Arthur Aylwin; but he also is a leading candidate for a professorial
chair that is on the stocks. He can have only one, and his choice
will mark him as a 'college man' or a 'university man'. He chooses
the former, letting it be known – even before the chair has been
established – that he would decline the position if it were offered
to him. This tactical masterstroke assures him the succession to the
headship: but the dying provost causes a dialysis machine to be
installed in his lodging's apple-room, and thus 'cheated the
Spectre. The Last Enemy. Death' (J.I.M. Stewart 1966: 189).

Stewart gives the plot a twist worthy of Michael Innes, that
notable farceur; but while celebrating collegiality he also claims to
reveal to the reader much more about academic life in Oxford
than Snow had revealed for Cambridge. We are shown that fellows
enjoy a choice between building a career through college or
university channels. We are shown an aristocratic rather than
bureaucratic appointment procedure for university posts, in which
the decision is sewn up before the job is advertised. Stewart returns
to this matter in *The Gaudy* (1974). Duncan Pattullo, a successful

playwright, returns to his old Oxford college. He thinks that he is there solely for a reunion, but he is disabused. The university is meditating the establishment of a Readership in European Drama. Would he take the position, with its attached fellowship of his old college, if it were offered? He would, and Pattullo is launched on his career as insider/outsider observer of Oxford *mores* in the *Staircase in Surrey* novel sequence. We have much the same plot in Dan Davin's *Brides of Price* (1972), as an expatriate New Zealand anthropologist shuttles between Oxford and Auckland while trying to decide whether he should allow his name to be floated for succession to an Oxford chair. Not much has changed in the generation since Lewis Eliot 'wanted to rest a little':

> Some of my influential friends made enquiries, and soon Francis Getliffe told me there might be an opening in his college for an academic lawyer. At last, after a long delay, the offer was officially made, I accepted it, and was elected.
>
> (Snow 1947: 11)

'What lured me now,' says Pattullo of his decision to return to Oxford, 'was the idea of life within a society: a stable and closely-knit society – changing indeed, decade by decade or lustre by lustre as old men went and young men came, but preserving a constant sense of permanent and impersonal purposes' (J.I.M. Stewart 1974: 143). We are back with massive continuity, the transmission and slow modification of shared understandings over generations. We have a measured celebration of collegiality.

But some do not celebrate. If *The Aylwins* is one extension from Snow's *The Masters* and *The Affair*, then *Porterhouse Blue* is a second; a scarifying novel in which Tom Sharpe settles scores with that Cambridge University where he had been an undergraduate. The setting establishes the novel's tone. Porterhouse, like some other Cambridge colleges but few in Oxford, has modest investments,

> and to this impecuniosity it owes its enduring reputation as the most socially exclusive college in Cambridge. If Porterhouse is poor, its undergraduates are rich. Where other colleges seek academic excellence in their freshmen, Porterhouse more democratically ignores the inequalities of intellect and concentrates upon the evidence of wealth.
>
> (Sharpe 1974: 9–10)

This is a college known for rowing, rock-bottom academic standards, and a proud cuisine.

We arrive shortly after yet another election for a head of house. The new master is Sir Godber Evans, a failed social democratic Cabinet minister put out to grass. He returns to Porterhouse, where he was an undergraduate, only because other electoral procedures have failed. College statutes specify that Porterhouse's master is elected for life, and that the dying master has the prescriptive right to name his successor. Unfortunately Evans's predecessor died too quickly – from a Porterhouse Blue, a stroke brought on by over-eating – to exercise this prerogative. The second procedure has the fellows electing their new master, but deeply embedded hatreds within the fellowship produce deadlock. Failing these two methods, election is by Royal – which means governing party – nomination. Thus Evans is installed by a process he deprecates in the mastership of a college which he hated as a youth, and which stands for everything he opposed in his political career. Goaded by his harridan wife, he resolves to reform the place. Entry is to be open only to candidates with academic qualifications. Women undergraduates will be admitted. Most radically of all, '"the practice of dining in Hall will be abolished. A self-service canteen run by an outside catering firm will be established in the Hall. There will be no High Table. All forms of academic segregation will disappear"' (Sharpe 1974: 72).

These proposals horrify the fellows, but they are powerless in the face of Evans's threat to expose their exploitation of collegiate autonomy in Cambridge: the systematic sale of entry to the university, their connivance in the head porter's lucrative trade in ringers for university examinations. They hang together, because otherwise they will hang separately. Evans's triumph seems assured. In Chapter 19 the fellows contemplate the loss of all that Porterhouse had stood for:

> For five hundred years they and their predecessors had ordained at least some portion of the elite that had ruled the nation. It had been through the sieve of their indulgent bigotry that young men had squeezed to become judges and lawyers, politicians and soldiers, men of affairs, all of them imbued with a corporate complacency and an intellectual

scepticism that dessicated change. They were the guardians
of political inertia and their role was done.

(Sharpe 1974: 201)

Not quite. Eight pages later, Sir Godber Evans is dead, slain by the
head porter, Skullion. Evans's deathbed naming of his murderer is
taken to be the master's prescriptive nomination of his successor.
Meanwhile, Skullion has suffered a Porterhouse Blue. With a
paralysed master, the fellows return to the good old days: to
over-eating, bickering, watching young men row.

Snow and Sharpe set the boundaries for the discussion of
collegiality; the one wholly positive, the other entirely negative.
Others operate in the space between these positions. Simon
Raven's (1970) anathema on Cambridge radicalism is close to
Sharpe (though the latter's politics are more ambiguous), but not
all fellows of Lancaster College succumb to evil and corruption.
Like Porterhouse, however, Lancaster's fellowship is riven beyond
the possibility of repair through customary methods. It takes an
apocalypse – a Jacobin attack on the college chapel and the
sacrifice of lives in defence of the chapel's treasures – to bring the
fellows to their collective senses. There are other examples of
death exposing flaws in collegiality. The numerous college
murders routinely are revealed to be rooted in more or less
obscure antipathies among fellows, though the motive for murder
may vary: personal ambition (Dexter 1983; Fiske 1980; M. Innes
1936; Vulliamy 1952), defence of wartime crime (Clinton-
Baddeley 1967; Farrer 1957), defence of fraud (R. Robinson
1956), filling the college's coffers (Spencer 1961), political
conviction (T. Robinson 1961; Shaw 1981), or sex (Masterman
1933; Raven 1960). Characteristically the slip-shod Dorothy Sayers
(1958a) does not bother to provide a motive for the Master of
Pentecost's murder by a dotty classicist.

Yet the finest account of collegiality's ambiguous delights is in
none of these places. We find it in four bravura pages about port-
drinking in the senior common room of an unnamed small
Oxford college before the Second World War. These pages culminate in a wicked celebration of the antipathies among four men:

Winter was glad to see Mummery being directed to the little
table. [Winter] found himself directed to the middle-sized
table along with the Master, Dr Bussenschutt. A moment

later they were joined by Benton, the senior tutor.... No arrangement, Winter reflected, could have been more dismal. Benton believed that Bussenschutt drank. Bussenschutt knew this. Bussenschutt affected to know that Benton had an out-of-the-way vulgar accent, and he was in the habit of consulting undergraduates from remote parts of the country in an effort to identify it. This Benton knew. Bussenschutt had once heard Benton say that Winter thought that Bussenschutt was the very type of the scholar who has never mastered his Latin grammar; and this had confirmed Bussenschutt in his conviction that Winter was, intellectually at the least, dishonest. Winter and Benton disliked each other, as a matter of mere instinct. And on mere instinct they both disliked Mummery, whose table was now levitating stealthily nearer. Mummery, in a moment of some unrestraint, had once apostrophised Bussenschutt as a hoary-headed and toothless baboon and Bussenschutt, declaring that nothing could be more unacademic than such language, had preached a powerful sermon against Mummery on the text *The name of the wicked shall rot*. It was the business of all four men to work closely together on the production of a learned journal called *Comity*.

(M. Innes 1939: 30–1)

Comity is defined as courtesy, civility, urbanity; kindly and considerate behaviour towards others. In the contrast between their journal's title, encapsulating Snow's attitude to collegiality, and these four men's behaviour to each other Stewart captures what other novelists grasp at: a sense of the mingled joy and terror of living in other fellows' pockets.

There are compensations. At an unnamed college's high table, groaning with pretentious food and drink, two men talk:

On these occasions he used to put on what I called his C.P. Snow manner.

'One wonders,' he said, 'whether today's fellows appreciate the good living this ancient university provides. We're the last of a dying generation, Martin, we're the last.'

It occurred to me as I looked round that today's fellows were well aware of their advantages.

(Smith 1962: 38–9)

61

Nor, we are told, was the end of such comfort imminent. Twenty years later, Jemima Shore has a friend in Oxford; 'Jamie Grand, currently visiting professor at a new college founded by a shy millionaire apparently entirely for Jamie's delectation since it provided vast funds for lavish dons' dining, but none for the sordid everyday needs of undergraduates' (Fraser 1985: 82).

If, as some novelists tell us, the dark side of collegiate living is a major demerit of Oxbridge, then this might be one feature in which the not-Oxbridge university scores. Looking at 'the new clean functional senior common room and refectory which had arisen so surprisingly, tacked on to the nineteenth century building that had housed the old technical college', Caro Grimstone wonders about the future of an ex-CAT. 'There should be no malice or evil here.... These buildings must surely provide the setting for a fresh start where the old intrigues and petty academic irritations could be forgotten' (Pym 1986: 27). Caro is disabused, of course. Intrigue, jealousy and gossip flourish as rankly in this institution as in Oxford. The form is modified – prevailing internal hierarchies influence who insults who to whom – but the content is no better than in Oxbridge. '"A hole like this is largely bicker, bicker, bicker"' Timmy Church tells John Appleby (M. Innes 1944: 33). The author had informed us rather earlier that although academic staff at places like Nesfield 'cannot bring with them from Oxford and Cambridge the immemorial organisation of a learned society, they can and often do bring the somewhat attenuated charities which such societies produce' (M. Innes 1944: 6). But life in not-Oxbridge can be so boring that rancour's excitement would be welcome. Recollecting the brief sputter of 1960s' student protest at a minor redbrick, one character tells another that '"It was a dull hole then as it's a dull hole now"' (Middleton 1987: 43).

British university fiction before 1945, Mortimer Proctor (1957) tells us, focused almost exclusively on student experience. Despite the dramatic post-war shift to a concentration on the experience of their teachers, an attenuated stream of novels continues to examine student life. First-hand narratives show a range of responses. Duncan Pattullo, arriving in Oxford as an undergraduate refugee from middle-class Edinburgh, 'fell absolutely in love with it – ... it represented a whole dimension of things I hadn't dreamed existed' (J.I.M. Stewart 1976: 62). Ann Livingstone is similarly entranced by the city, before being disgusted at her women's college:

> Oxford, washed and shining, broke on her like a miracle. Blue and gold like the illustrations in a Book of Hours, burning with light, every detailed marvel duplicated in the gleaming wet streets. It looked freshly created, sticky with varnish, just now descended from heaven, each spiky turret still hung round with a garland of guardian angels.
>
> (Day 1961: 111)

John Kemp, by contrast, arriving in wartime Oxford from Huddlesfield – a Lancashire manufacturing town that a fellow undergraduate claims always to have believed to be a music-hall joke rather than a real settlement – was devastated by the place. Desperately lonely, he created an imaginary friend, Jill, as a psychic prop (Larkin 1946). Cadogan, contemplating a return to Oxford, combines these attitudes. "'I hated it when I was up there as an undergraduate: I found it mean, childish, petty and immature. But I shall forget all that. I shall return with an eyeful of retrospective dampness and a mouth sentimentally agape'" (Crispin 1946: 13).

The Oxford passages of Evelyn Waugh's *Brideshead Revisited* (1945) give us the classic account of a mouth sentimentally agape. Charles Ryder and Sebastian Flyte are members of a *jeunesse dorée*; drinking, climbing into college after hours, doing no work, despising and patronizing the oily don Samgrass. A few novels follow this lead. Curtis Morgan's *An Oxford Romance* is an extraordinary relic; set between 1938 and 1941, it out-Waugh's Evelyn with its pickled Victorian undergraduate Oxford.

> 'Talking of "The House,"' he added, referring to Christchurch [sic] College, 'I met Lord Landstorm on the train. He and his mother live in the next parish to the pater's. . . . He's a member of the Bullingdon, don't you know, the *ne plus ultra* social club of Oxford, very horsey, what, what.'
>
> (Morgan 1948: 14, 32)

Auberon Waugh's *Path of Dalliance* (1963) is a picaresque novel of undergraduate manners in his father's mode: the comparison with the opening chapters of Evelyn Waugh's *Decline and Fall* (1928) is instructive. The son shares his father's snobbery, his Catholicism, and his dramatically reactionary politics. What he does not share, sadly, is Evelyn's exquisite style and comic eye. In *Path of Dalliance* the laboured pursuit of comic effects leads only to an embarrassing archness. The Oxford passages in George Goodman's *A Time for Paris* (1958) have a Yank-in-Yurp dazzled by aristocratic under-graduate manners. Wilfred Sheed's *A Middle-Class Education* (1967) tells us in its title what we are to expect of the book. This is Brideshead Down-Market; aristocratic manners in a *petit bourgeois* setting, undergraduate idling in a college as obscure as Flyte's is prestigious. Antonia Fraser's *Oxford Blood* gives us Brideshead Resurgent, an ambiguously supportive account of undergraduate life among 'gilded rubbish' (Fraser 1985: 79).

Nineteenth-century novelists had used four categories to describe Oxford undergraduate culture: aristocratic bloodies, sporting hearties, weedy – and, it was hinted, sexually unsound – aesthetes, and dim reading men. Post-war novels continue to use these categories; though just after the war demobilized servicemen form a temporary fifth column (Kennington 1948: 21-3). Antonia Fraser (1985) anatomizes 1980s bloodies. J.I.M. Stewart declines to join her in celebrating these anachronistic folk. Two young college fellows find themselves trapped one night.

> The whole quad was ringing to the clamour of a savage tribe: trampling feet, the blast of a hunting horn, hallooing voices giving uninhibited utterance to the cries of the chase. And through an archway came the occasion of all this: a group of young men in full evening-dress, their tail-coats brilliantly faced with scarlet and blue, as if they were a rout of angry penguins incongruously splashed with the colours of birds of paradise. They belonged to the most admired of Oxford's undergraduate clubs. Shefford and his friend came to a halt in their dignified stroll, terrified and appalled.
>
> 'I think,' Shefford managed to say, 'we might slip up this staircase.' They dived into a saving near-darkness, and remained in craven silence until the sound of blood-lust died away. Presidents and Deans, Proctors and Vice-Chancellors have blanched before it, so no doubt they were to be held excused. 'They'd think nothing of chucking a couple of young ushers into the fountain,' Shefford said. 'Gavin, just think of being a bloody fox.'

'It's incredible.' Even Naylor's calm was shaken. 'It's straight out of the middle ages and Evelyn Waugh.'

(J.I.M. Stewart 1967: 49)

Hearties play minor walk-on parts, often as the mindless shock-troops of more cunning but less muscled undergraduates. Aesthetes are still to be found: Mark Varley is surprised in a college's darkened Fellows' Garden, doing performance sculpture as a nude Cupid (J.I.M. Stewart 1967). Reading men still lurk in libraries. Sturdley's one example is hounded from bay to bay of the college library by a mob of indolent undergraduates employing the place alternately as the site for a card school and as an indoor cricket pitch (Sheed 1967: 17–20). Bobby Appleby, John's son, is a complex hybrid, combining the scrum-half berth for Oxford and England with a promising career as an anti-novelist after Robbe-Grillet (M. Innes 1970) and membership of an exclusive dining club (M. Innes 1969).

Other novels bring new form and content. In *My Friend Judas* (1959) Andrew Sinclair punned Jude Fawley with the lost disciple to give us Cambridge's beat novel, a book in which adolescent sex is much more central than any adventitious formal education: Judy/Jude/Judas is a female undergraduate. Sex is prominent again in Julian Mitchell's *Imaginary Toys* (1961), a realist novel with major characters standing for important groupings in Oxford's student body. The Victorian novel of undergraduate experience still provides some kind of model here, but the experiences are much more varied. Content is shaking loose from form. The farthest point of this road is marked by Leo Bellingham's *Oxford: The Novel* (1981). Here undergraduates move between men's and women's colleges without thinking about the fact. They are much less constrained than had been previous generations in who can do what to whom, where, and when; and they take this freedom for granted. Bellingham gives us Oxford as just another university, Oxford undergraduates as no more than students enjoying a common relaxation of elderly supervision over the young. Yet even here the bones of the old Oxford obtrude as the vacation arrives:

In Brasenose, which was Andrew's college, the graduate students who had seemingly spent the previous eight weeks hibernating in the Inorganic Chemistry Laboratory suddenly

65

reappeared in hall, in small reconnoitring groups at lunch-
time but in platoon strength at 6.30 dinner, and composed
almost the entire assembly at meals. The atmosphere was
quite different from that of meals during Full Term. Instead
of the babble of well-bred voices, the accents of Middlesbrough and Barrow-in-Furness competed with those of
Madras and Milwaukee. There was no more general laughter,
throwing of bread, ostentatious ordering of vast silver tank-
ards of beer; only muted conversation about technical
subjects.

(Bellingham 1981: 95)

Members of suppressed, derided subcultures edge back to the
light. But the categories of the Victorian novel have been transformed. These pariahs are not aesthetes or reading men: they are
provincials, foreigners, scientists, postgraduates. Pancho Jaego
rolls all these disabilities into a single bundle (Lait 1970). A physics
doctoral student at Cambridge, his name, his subject, his Swedish
wife, his northern coalmining background, compound his
alienness. Yet most of this is redundant. Lait's plot merely requires
that Pancho should have the technical skill to fluke a break-
through in electronic surveillance. His superfatted marginality
comes not from plot demands but from the book's Cambridge
setting. His surname recalls Jago, the unsuccessful candidate in
Snow's *The Masters*.

There is no tradition of writing about students in not-Oxbridge
universities. Only two novels follow the nineteenth-century model,
centred on undergraduate experience. William Cooper's *Young
People* (1958) follows a group of students in a twenty-year-old minor
redbrick between 1929 and 1932. Much is familiar – modest
carousing, fumbling sexual experiments, climactic examinations.
But there are differences. A group of students is rusticated for
drinking alcohol on college premises, offending the university's
ruling Methodist ethos. The vice-chancellor celebrates achieve-
ments that would be pitiful in an Oxbridge novel: '"This year has
been a truly remarkable year for our men. Gunning is our first man
to get into the ICS"' (W. Cooper 1958: 92). Keith Walker's *Running
on the Spot* (1959) forms the other ambiguous exception to the
Oxbridge rule. The only modern Scottish university novel, it is set
in an unnamed but unmistakable St Andrews. The central chara-

cter is English, like so many post-war St Andrews students, and he returns to London after graduating. St Andrews is an ancient university, and one with a vestigial collegial system. Walker notes some Scottish specificities – the predominance of lectures over tutorials, the stratification between Ordinary and Honours classes, the god-professor – but his novel sits comfortably as an Oxford undergraduate novel in strange parts. Cooper and Walker apart, novelists scarcely notice not-Oxbridge students except in relation to academic staff. Reflecting William Cooper's (1958: 106) account of two students forming 'a little society of their own, a little island of horse-riders in a sea of inferior persons', Colin Clout tells Olivia Jory that a minor redbrick's park is used by 'the smart set' for horse-riding.

> 'What do you mean by the smart set?'
> 'Does it sound so funny? There are some students, you see, who are the children of very prosperous local business people. They send their hopeful young here out of a strong sense of regional piety – but give them three times as much money as anybody else. It's highly democratic.'
>
> (M. Innes 1956b: 22)

Students are mere spear-carriers in not-Oxbridge novels. When they appear, it is to establish dilemmas for staff. Should one sleep with students? This problem is presented to not-Oxbridge male academics only by female students. While novels tell us that homophilia is an amusing eccentricity in Oxford (particularly) and Cambridge, in not-Oxbridge novels – J.R. Hulland's *Student Body* (1986) apart – homophilia is treated as perversion, homosexuality as unthinkably filthy. How can one make contact with foreign students? How does one handle proletarian students if one is a liberal (Bradbury 1959), conservative students if one is a Marxist (Bradbury 1975), or assured students if one is a confused misfit (Amis 1954)? These are the problems which face fictional not-Oxbridge staff encountering individual fictional students. But the emphasis on larger-scale teaching settings in not-Oxbridge, on the lecture and seminar rather than the tutorial, means that most staff see students in rather large groups.

This staff perspective is one reason why not-Oxbridge students tend to be displayed in the mass. In a major redbrick,

An electric bell of ingeniously piercing quality shrilled
overhead. Doors banged. Students filled the corridors. Girls
hurried past, bespectacled, notebooked, serious; girls
loitered past, nudging, giggling, powdering; men skylarked,
shouted, bit into sandwiches. Down the five ill-disposed wings
of Nesfield University, vaulted, machine-carved, echoing and
damp, surged conflicting columns of adolescent humanity, a
rout of jostling automative sponges hurried from pool to
pool of a knowledge codified, timetabled, and approved.

(M. Innes 1944: 7)

Forty years later we find ourselves in a new university.

They were standing outside the pub on the piazza on the first
day of term, watching the seething throngs of posers and
wankers crisscrossing the square, screaming at each other
and embracing, giving each other hardeye, moving
purposefully towards places they looked confident of being
able to find, and generally behaving as if they knew what was
what.

(A. Davies 1986: 47)

The place has changed, the language has changed. What has not
changed is a sense of massed students, ignorant armies that clash
by night.

If students do no more than carry spears in not-Oxbridge
novels, then non-academic staff are insignificant both inside and
outside Oxbridge. In Oxbridge an under-porter may be murdered
(Rees 1945); but only in Dorothy Sayers's *Gaudy Night* (1935) does
a servant commit murder, thus offending a basic Golden Age
detective convention. Generally Oxbridge college servants are like
their cousins in the country houses that share such close structural
and social similarities with fictional colleges; less venal than
invisible. A gyp (a personal servant working on a particular
Cambridge staircase) might have to be sacked for pushing beyond
the customarily recognized boundaries of petty larceny (Snow
1947: 193–8). Bedmakers might discover a corpse (Rees 1945).
These apart, servants are just servants, organized in their own
hierarchies under head porter, butler and chef, and taken for
granted. Only one novel recognizes that a college's Head will have
a female secretary. It was written by a woman (Farrer 1957).

68

A servant called Plot holds together an otherwise almost plotless novel, the last in J.I.M. Stewart's *Staircase in Surrey* sequence. In *Full Term* (1978) Plot bears college tradition, linking the generations of young and old men that he had served on his staircase. Four years earlier, Tom Sharpe had taken this line much further in *Porterhouse Blue*, a book about a college (a 'house') ruled by the porter. Sharpe disrupts the usual discourse by making the head porter, Skullion, the novel's moral focus. It is he, not the Master and fellows of Porterhouse, who stands for continuity: his inadvertent murder of Sir Godber Evans saves the place from social democracy, his shares (bequeathed to him by a former Master) restore the college fortunes. Around Skullion we see other servants. Cheffy's proud cholesterol-stuffed cuisine is threatened by Evans's proposals for self-service catering. Mrs Biggs, the bedder on Zipser's staircase, dies a martyr to his acute sexual frustration when, late one night, she creeps back to Zipser's room and lights the gas fire before slipping under his bedcovers, unaware that the unhappy youth had spent the previous evening filling the flue behind the fire with gas-filled condoms. At least they go out with a bang.

Non-academic staff are sighted even less commonly in not-Oxbridge universities. Morris Zapp has comical misunderstandings with the secretaries in Rummidge's English department (Lodge 1975); Howard Kirk manipulates the secretaries in Watermouth's sociology department for his own machiavellian purposes (Bradbury 1975). But these secretaries are merely part of the campus furniture. The only member of non-academic staff who comes to the front stage – and that briefly – is the head porter of a minor redbrick. 'Nobody', we are told, 'could advance the hypothesis that Gedge was perhaps really the Vice-Chancellor or the Reader in Biometrics. Gedge was plainly too important to be either' (M. Innes 1956b: 44). As with Keith Walker's Scottish undergraduate novel, here we have a standard figure lent to not-Oxbridge. Gedge is a stock college head porter, brother to Parsons of St Christopher's, Oxford: 'a large formidable man with horn-rimmed glasses, a marked propensity for bullying, and the unshakeable conviction that in the college hierarchy he stood above the law, the prophets, the dons, and the President himself' (Crispin 1946: 45).

Like the Wodehouse butler that he also resembles, Gedge's stately motion around his campus lends tone to the establishment.

But even he cannot disguise the fact that he works in a minor redbrick rather than, say, Blandings Castle or Magdalen College. Novels tell us that in some things not-Oxbridge universities are no better than Oxbridge, but that in most things they are worse. They give us a consistent description of a ranked set of institutions. Oxford and Cambridge float serenely above lesser universities. Eastringham University's Oxbridge-educated vice-chancellor makes small talk to the Oxbridge-educated Stephen Henderson after Eastringham's carol service: '"Yes, it's a fine church. . . . Not Kings' certainly, but a good second best." They exchanged the gratified looks of men who have moved from the superlative to the sufficient, but have retained the advantages of both' (Trickett 1954: 98–9). Duncan Pattullo's Uncle Rory

> spoke of 'the two universities' as he might have spoken of 'the two sexes'. That Oxford and Cambridge played their prescriptive roles without any supporting cast, however dim, would scarcely have occurred to him. He had lived for the greater part of his life in Scotland. Niched somewhere in his head must have been knowledge of the existence of universities at St Andrews, Glasgow, Aberdeen, and Edinburgh. But that the first three of these had been in business since the fifteenth century and that the fourth was a going concern within the lifetime of Shakespeare was probably information with which the particular slant of his antiquarian interests had failed to acquaint him.
>
> (J.I.M. Stewart 1975: 60)

An unruly Cambridge undergraduate is threatened with transfer to Liverpool (Raven 1980: 13). A romantic novelist accuses her friend, a crime novelist specializing in ecclesiastical subjects – '*Murder in the Cathedral, her* work of that title, not the late Mr T.S. Eliot's' - of having a friend who 'coaches his charges for admission to strange new universities' (M. Innes 1973: 28). The doomed Zipser's last weeks of life were made hell by Skullion, because the Cambridge porter believed that a Durham-educated postgraduate could not be a gentleman (Sharpe 1974). Olivia Jory, a scion of the family that once owned Old Hall, is not impressed with '"your absurd university"' that now occupies the hall, with '"your scruffy students"' (M. Innes 1956b: 183, 194). A Sturdley College alumnus bemoans

'a habit that I have come across since returning to Oxford for a few days. I have heard references to "second-year" men and "third-year" men. This is all very well in the provincial universities . . .'
'And in the bloody colonies, what?' said Gosworth.
'But not good enough for Oxford. Not good enough by half. We are *undergraduates* at Oxford.'

(Sheed 1967: 121)

Within Oxford and Cambridge, colleges are ranked in an intricate hierarchy combining academic prestige, sporting prowess and social cachet. Thewless coaches boys towards 'Magdalen or Christ Church' [Oxford], King's or Trinity [Cambridge]: those farthest goals' (M. Innes 1949: 5). Oxford undergraduates isolate 'the Big Four – Balliol, New College, Magdalen and Christ Church' (McIntosh 1956: 149). At the end of the Second World War Duncan Pattullo leaves behind an austere world to sit a scholarship examination in a socially forbidding college:

So I found myself scribbling furiously amid surroundings which showed to my provincial sense as oppressively august, and as quite without that hint of the modestly domestic which I detected during my more or less furtive prowlings, each afternoon, through the quadrangles of Oriel, Jesus, St Edmund Hall, and similar foundations of what might be called the middling sort. I had been tumbled, I told myself, into a haunt of the most shattering privilege.

(J.I.M. Stewart 1975: 8)

Peter Garlick discovers that Bill English is an undergraduate at Magdalen College. '"Ah, Magdalen." To the real Godolphin man, he might as well have been at Cambridge or Keele' (A. Waugh 1963: 43). At the other end of the hierarchy, 'It was nice to know that there were places like Sturdley, even in Oxford. It did wonders for one's confidence. It made Christ Church seem even possible' (Sheed 1967: 11). The hierarchy is defined and defended with brutal wit:

71

'Your refusal to face facts reminds me of the two Christ
Church men. One bet the other five pounds that there was
no such college as Wadham.'

'Who won?' asked Undigo, solemnly.

(R. Robinson 1956: 26)

I am grateful to Richard Sheppard for pointing out the political
dimension to this insult: aristocratic Christ Church denigrating
demotically leftist Wadham.

Hierarchy controls judgements about teaching staff. A BBC
scriptwriter recalls a chance acquaintance: '"Some loony historian
from one of those dud universities in the Midlands. A professor he
was . . ." The bearded man laughed. "You should have seen him. I
wouldn't have given him a job as a cleaner"' (Deighton 1981: 236;
original punctuation). One Oxford academic mentions to another
his chance of a job at Bridport: '"Oh, *there*. They have a vested
interest in mediocrity there"' (G. Butler 1960: 109). Still in Oxford,

Calder at fifty had the tastes of a refined undergraduate,
which was something that he had never been. But then he
had been educated in Belfast, not at Oxford, and that is the
sort of thing an ambitious academic well remembers, even
when he has reached the stage of a Knighthood and an
original Picasso.

(Kennaway 1963: 19)

Edgar Simmonds has been winkled from a Cambridge fellowship
to take the economics chair at redbrick Hardgate. His Cambridge
friends tell him that he has made a retrograde step (Devine 1966:
10). David Audley is to be rewarded for his services to the state's
security agencies. A Cambridge fellowship might be arranged. 'I
suppose Oxford would do as well. He'd probably turn up his nose
at a redbrick place' (Price 1981: 70). Francis Gethin – a remote
kinsman of Snow's Francis Getliffe? – is a junior lecturer in
Nesfield University. 'He just couldn't believe that Winchester and
Oxford had vanished from his ken and that here he was in this
absurd place.' Nor does he think that things will improve for his
colleague and himself '"when we've become professors in some
awful hole in Wales or the Middle East"' (J.I.M. Stewart 1981: 21,
23). The don on the top of the Headington omnibus is recommended to an Oxfordshire pub: 'If you are lucky, you will find no

similarly knowing colleague there; only an alien and abstracted *savant* from the academic deserts of Birmingham or Hull, come to meditate the remoter implications of the quartic curve' (M. Innes 1936: 123). Since Roland Redpath 'was about to be appointed to a Chair at Cambridge . . . no house in a provincial wilderness would be required' (J.I.M. Stewart 1981: 128). Wyman faces the reverse prospect when his pregnant paramour suggests that he should find an academic job outside Oxford and Cambridge, now that he had been sacked from MI6 and his Oxford honorary fellowship had fallen victim to expenditure cuts:

> 'You think I should work in some redbrick, do you?' Wyman snorted. 'A tremendous idea. I can just picture myself sitting happily in a plastic-and-chrome lecturers' common room in some squalid provincial city, exchanging pleasantries with sociologists with halitosis, structuralists with dyed hair and earrings, and the entire panoply of middle class Marxists. A fitting end to a distinguished academic career, don't you think?'
>
> (Cook 1985: 146)

One might expect to find this deluge of vituperation resisted, to find novels celebrating – let us say – provincial sturdiness against – let us say – Oxbridge foppishness. The absence of such counter-arguments is a striking feature of British university fiction. Instead one finds an acceptance of hierarchy, even when that consigns author, character or institution to a degraded position.

> Dixon realised that their progress, deliberate and to all appearances thoughtful, must seem rather donnish to passing students. He and Welch might well be talking about history, and in the way history might be talked about in Oxford and Cambridge quadrangles. At moments like this Dixon came near to wishing that they really were.
>
> (Amis 1954: 8)

'"You'd think Peter was ex-Oxbridge, wouldn't you?"' asks a redbrick postgraduate. '"But he's just a little ex-provincial like the rest of us"' (Hulland 1986: 51). Octavius Chevally 'has hopes of a junior lecturership in the history of art in some outlandish provincial university' (J.I.M. Stewart 1972: 194). '"You might just as well have gone to the London School of Economics with Doris"' an aunt tells her niece in wartime. '"They've been evacuated to Cambridge now, so you would have been at a Major 'Varsity in any case"' (P. Harrison 1946: 273). An anthropologist made redundant from a new university meets the doctor who ran that university's medical centre: '"Toytown", the doctor said. "You were at Toytown. We were there at the same time"' (Parkin 1985: 75). Another anthropologist's mother-in-law believed that 'There was something not quite right, not exactly what one would have wished for, about an academic post at a new university that had once been a technical college' (Pym 1986: 19). Robert Raven muses on the modern equivalent of his kinsman's wasted life as an amateur sculptor: '"Today Theodore would be a professor of economics in some hole in Wales"' (M. Innes 1945: 80). Mrs Peppercorn

> understood that the university in which the doctor's son taught had not the prestige of Cambridge or Oxford. But the doctor's son was an Oxford man, and as that was almost as good as being a Cambridge man he was probably regarded as conferring distinction on the institution for which he laboured.
>
> (J.I.M. Stewart 1983: 41)

That this perception was well-founded is attested by the reaction at Nesfield to the news that Francis Gethin was moving on. 'Since his destination . . . was Cambridge, his going was regarded with some awe by a good many junior members of what this provincial university called its staff' (J.I.M. Stewart 1981: 60–1).

Deferring to Oxbridge, the not-Oxbridge university is shown to be obsessed with the position which it takes in the following pack. Rummidge

> had never been an institution of more than middling size and reputation, and it had lately suffered the mortifying fate of most English universities of its type (civic redbrick): having competed strenuously for fifty years with two universities chiefly valued for being old, it was, at the moment of drawing level, rudely overtaken in popularity and prestige by a batch of universities chiefly valued for being new.
>
> (Lodge 1975: 9)

This passage is a time capsule. Ten years after it was published the notion that the novelty of British new universities could count in their favour would seem perverse. But Lodge's assertion that in 1969 the hierarchy among universities was relatively flat is striking. Nowhere else in British university fiction does one get that sense. Much more characteristic is Treece's tortured contemplation, in a minor redbrick's staff common room, of interlinked hierarchies:

> Of all the problems that nibbled at Treece's mind and brought him to anxiety, there were none sharper than his worries over status. The catechism began simply, what, in this day and age, was the status of a professor in English society, and what rewards and esteem may he expect? Secondly, and to add another dimension, what was the status of a professor *in the humanities*, in England, in this day and age? Third, what, then, was the status of a professor in the humanities *at a small university in the provinces*, in England, in the present age?
>
> (Bradbury 1959: 45; original emphases).

To be in the humanities is good. To be a professor is good. To be in a small university in the provinces is bad, evidence that one is second-rate. For to be first-rate, by definition, one has to be at Oxford or Cambridge.

Why is this true by definition? What is the hidden machinery for creating and maintaining a privileged flow of cultural capital to and through Oxbridge over four decades during which, on measures of quantity and (less uncontroversially) on measures of quality, not-Oxbridge British university life had improved dramatically? To put the question differently, whose interests are served by having a discourse which takes Oxbridge hegemony for granted? To begin to approach these questions we need to be thoroughly Thatcherite, and consider some Victorian values. The next chapter takes up this task.

75

Chapter Four

CULTURE AND ANARCHY

Two college fellows perambulate Oxford in the early 1970s. They come upon a student demonstration blocking the streets. Duncan Pattullo guides Arnold Lempriere, his elderly colleague and remote kinsman, through the revolting young. They gather that the demonstration is 'in the interest of establishing a kind of super-cafeteria – declared by the insurgent forces to be essential to their well-being, and believed by many of their seniors to be in fact a demand for the building of a miniature Kremlin on the Isis' (J.I.M. Stewart 1976: 128). As if he were one of our useful aliens, what might we expect the aged Lempriere to make of all this? Would he be one of the alarmed seniors, following that middle-aged fogey Simon Raven (1970) in seeing student agitation and the threat of self-service catering as a Jacobin apocalypse? Not a bit of it.

> 'Plenty of riots in medieval Oxford,' he said. 'Knives as well as staves at times, and no end of broken sconces. Probably not much vice in them, all the same. Still, a mob's a mob, and there's not much to be done with it. Except ignore it, eh? . . . No good beginning except with the individual, you know, or with three or four reasonable people gathered in a room. I'm convinced of that, and it's why I've never been other than what they call a college man. See that the college does the right thing by its own people, and the university will look after itself.'
>
> (J.I.M. Stewart 1976: 142)

Lempriere's structure of feeling, combining a long historical perspective with fear of the mob and a trust in individual education, is no accident. Stewart had shown in *Lament for a Maker* (M. Innes 1938) that he knew his nineteenth-century Scottish novelists. He uses a device typical of Galt and William Alexander, in telling us what we are to think of a character through that character's name. John Lempriere's (c 1765–1824) *Classical Dictionary* used to be familiar to any public school child learning Latin or Greek. We are to expect this college fellow to exemplify Hellenism, 'the urge to see things as they are, to take delight in clearness, beauty, intellect, and "spontaneity"' (Honan 1981:349). His surname is significant then, but it is rendered doubly so by his Christian name. Ruminating student agitation in a later novel, Duncan Pattullo evokes the times when the major Victorian enthusiast for Hellenism, 'Matthew Arnold, that prince among dons, had gone round crying woe' (J.I.M. Stewart 1977: 132). Arnold Lempriere exemplifies Stewart's interpretation of what Matthew Arnold thought worth defending: humane values, disinterestedness, aristocratic privilege.

As is usual, Stewart hits the spot. Matthew Arnold, 'the Victorian who matters the most' (Honan 1981: 424), is the man who set the discourse which controls all British university fiction. But that discourse is embedded in much wider and deeper issues about English culture and society. For this, once more, one turns first to Arnold. Perry Anderson says somewhere that England is unique among modern European nations in having generated neither a classic sociology nor a classic Marxism. What fills the space is 'concealed sociology' (Lepenies 1988: 155–95), social criticism masquerading as literary criticism. Arnold's *Culture and Anarchy* (1869) is the source of the masquerade.

Arnold's most significant contribution is his analysis and celebration of culture, a term which – in this sense – he introduced to the English-speaking world (R. Williams 1958: 114) and which, in Lionel Trilling's words (1962: 38), he made his 'personal insigne'. Culture is defined as

> a pursuit of our total perfection by means of getting to know, on all matters which most concern us, the best that has been thought and said in the world; and through this knowledge, turning a stream of fresh and free thought upon our stock notions and habits.
>
> (Arnold 1869: 233)

Culture has to do not with institutions but with personal attitudes and development: it is, he tells us, 'above all an inward operation' (Arnold 1869: 234). To be cultured is to be mentally unsettled, always to know how little one knows. Arnold is no friend of intellectual complacency.

Wolf Lepenies (1988: 158–9, 172) makes Arnold a typically woolly English thinker, strong on example and weak on analysis; a radical subjectivist who placed 'lace covers on a steam-engine'. There are ambiguities enough, to be sure. What, for example, is the relationship between culture and science? His classical education led Arnold to put Greek and Latin at the heart of culture throughout his life, but he claimed not to disparage science. Dudley (1942) shows that this claim was weakened by three factors. First, Arnold knew almost no science, and made little effort to remedy the deficiency. Second, his enthusiasm for science waxed and waned over the years. Third, he used – and did not always discriminate between – two radically different notions of science. The first was the narrow fact-collecting that he thought typical of natural science, the second that organization of systematic knowledge in any field that the Germans call *Wissenschaft*. Clearly in favour of the latter, he gave less unambiguous praise to the former. There was some point in Henshaw Ward turning a weapon against its forger: 'science', he said, 'regards Matthew Arnold as an arch-philistine' (quoted in Dudley 1942: 279). We find the same tension in Arnold's politics: a nineteenth-century Liberal who was so passionate in support of state intervention in education that some commentators have made him (less than convincingly) to be proto-fascist.

Lepenies seems to have a point, but his critique is not wholly fair. In the first place, much of Arnold's social criticism was comparative: look to other countries, he said, and you will see that there is no divine warrant for specific English arrangements. He is no Pecksniff. Second, the more generous (and more English) Peter Keating (1975: 212–13, 226) urges that Arnold's characteristically slippery method of argument was central to his conception of what a cultivated man should do. To be disinterested – the central requirement – meant that one should avoid being trapped in any particular position. To nail one's colours to any mast was a mistake, since defence of an idea could slip into defence of a class.

On 7 June 1867 Matthew Arnold lectured at Oxford on 'Culture and its enemies', coining one of his enduring tags: that culture embodies and engenders 'sweetness and light'. This lecture later was combined with an essay called 'Anarchy and authority', and published as *Culture and Anarchy*. The choice of venue was significant. Arnold wrote to a publisher that 'I wanted to make my last lecture as pleasing to my audience and as *Oxfordesque* as I could' (Super 1965: 409). His most recent biographer expands the point:

> The university was then in trouble. In the exciting political air with talk of 'reform' everywhere, Oxford seemed to many observers a place of the past, losing its prestige and effect.... Arnold certainly aimed to tell a badly divided audience of old Newman Ritualists, Broad Church dons, young university men and students that *their* Oxford still had a crucial role to play.
>
> (Honan 1981: 344–5)

Culture and Anarchy is the base document for a concealed English sociology. Where its most important arguments were first heard, what those arguments meant in that place, matter. The future of culture in England; the future of culture in Oxford. We have Chinese boxes, the smaller mimicking the larger. We now can understand why Emily Bryant rejects 'everything I detest in Oxford and in this society' (Lejeune 1987: 245). To hate one is to hate the other; to cherish one is to cherish the other. As the dying Brereton says,

> 'Our civilisation is at stake and we don't realise it. Surely you can see that we have to defend all this?' He waved an arm in a gesture embracing all the spires and towers of Oxford.
>
> (Shaw 1981: 183)

A central European visitor to Cambridge makes the same point, as he admires a college close in the July twilight: '"Perfect!" said Vorloff. "This is civilisation. And so little left..."' (Clinton-Baddeley 1967: 29; original punctuation).

Civilization, culture, is under threat. It must be protected behind defensible walls. Universities provide those walls. '"The universities are havens for pure research,"' Duncan Pattullo tells Giles Watershute. '"Havens for pretty well everything now,"' Giles replies. '"Every sort of culture contracting within the walls of these institutions"' (J.I.M. Stewart 1978: 19). A minor redbrick university has 'red-brick spires and towers', 'gothic slit windows and . . . battlements', leading an inmate to declare that '"At least it's easily defended, if it should come to *that*"' (Bradbury 1959: 24). The once-new Lowlands University campus 'looks like a modern version of a medieval fortified town, with its subtly interlocked towers and flat roofs and buttresses casting patterns of light and shadow, its elegantly brutal concrete walkways and bridges crisscrossing the facades' (A. Davies 1986: 5). A stronghold.

Another new university seems yet more formidable. This unnamed place is 'set into the moorland, at some distance from Long Royston House', the mansion captured by the university's administration.

> The three buildings were hexagonal heavy towers in a darkish concrete slab: they stood around the one courtyard which was paved in a blueish engineering brick. Two of them shared one wall: the other stood alone. They were and were meant to be reminiscent of northern keeps and millstone grit, older than the pleasant long, low front of Long Royston, as well as rawer and newer. At first sight their lighting was odd, at least from outside. Huge expanses of glazed window, revealing staircases winding, or even large spaces the width of the tower, alternated with deep eye slits, closed and secret.
>
> (Byatt 1985: 273)

With its thick walls, circular staircases, and arrow-slits this place appears admirably designed for the defence of culture. But one would not be wise to rely on its strength: great plate glass windows offer easy entrance to a determined attacker. We are to take it that some universities offer culture a stronger fortress than do others. Lowlands' professor of English, stout defender of the third best English department in the country – the best two are in Oxford and Cambridge – is forced by the powers of darkness to resign his post. He retreats from the bailey of culture's castle to its keep: he returns to his old Oxford college, there to maintain his struggle for humane culture (A. Davies 1988: 229). His action makes sense to readers because other literary representations of Oxbridge have prepared us to see colleges as places built to withstand siege.

The notion of Oxford and Cambridge colleges as defensible spaces is firmly rooted in literary genre. They make ideal settings for detective fiction because the fellows' habitat – 'the material structure in which they talk, eat, and sleep – offers such a capital frame for the quiddities and wilie-beguilies of the craft' (M. Innes 1936: 5). 'A porter closed the great gate of the college', Frank Deasy tells us.

> I stood for a moment, feeling curiously shut in. If I wanted to go and roam the streets of Oxford . . . I should have to ask this man to let me out. And only he could let me in again. It was true that I had been given a key to an unobtrusive entrance elsewhere. But the massive iron-bound gates swinging to were symbolical, I reflected, of how cloistered these places were.
>
> (J.I.M. Stewart 1966: 64)

Until the relaxation of discipline over undergraduates that gathered pace in the 1960s, all that a porter had to do was close the great gate at the customary time and his college was isolated from outside influences. This was invaluable for criminally inclined literary folk. A murder done, it was simple for a detective to limit the suspects to those locked in the college, together with those dons possessing keys with which they could let themselves in through posterns, and those undergraduates who could be shown to have climbed in along well-recognized routes. As John Appleby learns, 'St Anthony's, or any other college' is as tightly contained as a submarine (M. Innes 1936: 10–11). Tantallum, Warlock College, Oxford's porter, expanded the point in Robert Robinson's unconvincing demotic prose.

> 'The only College in the University as no one can climb into, and they've tried 'ard enough, I'll lay. Ladders and scalin' irons, and that kind, but it's no go. Even the windows 'as got bars to 'em. And only one door. This one 'ere. What you'd need . . . is a 'elicopter.'
>
> (R. Robinson 1956: 33)

Using firm boundaries to limit the cast of suspects explains why fictional death has stalked Oxbridge quadrangles and courts so frequently, but almost always at night.

Books talk to books. Assumptions are carried from one kind of book to another. Frank Deasy lives in a novel with only the slightest hint of crime, and that fraud rather than murder. Here, as in many other books, the whodunit's emphasis on the college as defensible space is absorbed and extended to make Oxbridge colleges the ultimate bastion of a threatened culture. In another book, 'Oxford seemed a desperate place, a chaos amid which the colleges barely maintained their ground, like forlorn last-ditch fortresses' (J.I.M. Stewart 1978: 86). But all is not lost. Through joint action in the university which the colleges comprise, further defences against barbarism can be constructed. As is customary, buildings stand for threats and possibilities. In *The Guardians* – significant title – 'the pervasive flaking and crumbling of Oxford grew ominous, as if throwing out a hint of secular and Roman decay' (J.I.M. Stewart 1955: 26). Against this, 'Looking beyond the [hockey] players Quail could see only the bleakly rectangular outlines of large new laboratories. They might have been a massive fortification thrown up by the ancient university with some notion of protecting its northern flank' (J.I.M. Stewart 1955: 44). To the north lies the proletarian threat. Many books about Oxford undergraduate experience open with the protagonists arriving by train. Most breeze in from London, through Didcot. Only working-class students like John Kemp (Larkin 1946) arrive via Banbury, from the north.

The defence of Oxford and Cambridge is critical, we are told, because these are not like other universities. Other places are provincial: important forts against barbarism in their own districts, but less significant in the national picture. Oxford and Cambridge are metropolitan. They are national bastions, national universities refining the cream of British youth. Modern novelists merely block in what J.H. Newman had sketched:

> Never has learned institution been more directly political and national than the University of Oxford. Some of its Colleges represent the talent of the nation, others its rank and fashion, others its wealth; others have been the organ of the Government of the day; while others, and the majority, represent one or other division, chiefly local, of the country party. . . . Oxford became a sort of selected arena for the conflicts of the various interests of the nation, and a serious

University strife was received far and wide as the presage of civil war.

(Newman 1856: 215–16)

Novels show us every district sending its best sons to Oxford and Cambridge, there to be inducted to a national elite. Distinctions are submerged in the university, but maintained in the colleges to give each its characteristic imprint: that variety in unity celebrated as the ancient English universities' greatest gift. The fellows of St Thomas' College, Oxford

> think of the regal splendour of Christ Church, of the catholicity of type in Balliol and its scholarship strengthened and fortified by its Scottish infiltration; we think of the tough North Country basis of Queen's, of the solid virtue of New College, or the athletic vigour of Brasenose.
>
> (Masterman 1952: 241)

The senior members of these colleges may think that their business is concerned principally with the creation and conservation of knowledge, but they are wrong. 'Oxford's greatest contribution to mankind in the past', we are told soon after the Second World War's end,

> has not been scholarship or education. Its greatest contribution has been leadership. Even Oxford with its roots of tradition stretching deep and wide down into the centuries can hardly lead back to life a world that has passed away. Oxford will change, too, but in one respect it will not change. Oxford will still lead, will still continue to breed leadership.
>
> (Morgan 1948: 63)

Clearly here, less openly in many other places, we are told that Oxford and Cambridge are finishing schools for men born to rule.

Morgan implies that this is neither to be celebrated nor disparaged: it is simply to be seen as natural, as inevitable as the progress of the sun across the sky. But things are not quite that simple. Provost Pococke suggests that Duncan Pattullo might contemplate a nineteenth-century controversy, might consider

> how applicable today is an anatomy of Oxford in terms of Benjamin Jowett and Mark Pattison. Balliol and Lincoln.

Rival camps! Pattison saw the function of the university
through what have been aspersed as Germanophil eyes. As a
place of learning and scholarship, at some remove from the
world of affairs. Jowett, although himself so considerable a
scholar, viewed it as an indispensable nursery of rulers and
administrators. . . . The young men of superior privilege
were to be groomed and civilised as legislators. The others, if
they didn't simply enter the church, were to be the backbone
of the higher civil service.

(J.I.M. Stewart 1978: 29)

Stewart sets up a tension between a meritocratic and an aristocratic
conception of Oxford. This tension runs through much of his
fiction, and that of other writers. We usually find it transmuted
into class terms: meritocratic working-class and middle-class folk
on one side, aristocrats on the other. In describing this fuzzily
defined cleavage, most novelists lean to the aristocratic notion of
Oxford's purpose. Like W.G. Morgan, they tell us that the culture
to be protected in Oxbridge is metropolitan. It represents Society
within society (Davidoff 1973).

Covertly class-based, this notion of culture denies other bases
for distinction. Duncan Pattullo's uncle Rory, who thinks of the
two universities as naturally as he thinks of the two sexes, is
Scottish.

I found it unnatural that my uncle, who didn't hale from
England, should talk like my masters at school, who did. At
the same time, I found the fact fascinating, since it revealed
to me the existence of a caste or class unconfined by what I
had accustomed myself to think of as unbreachable national
boundaries.

(J.I.M. Stewart 1974: 187)

This class inclusion requires, and then in its turn asserts, a
conflation between England and Britain. Glowrey, that unre-
mitting scourge of culture's enemies, is a Scot (Lejeune 1987). So,
distantly, is Arnold Lempriere, the standard-bearer for collegiate
disinterestedness. Mungo Lockhart, an undergraduate Scottish
nationalist, settles comfortably in an Oxford college (J.I.M. Stewart
1973). All Britons are invited, are required to join in celebrating
an unproblematic Englishness.

That Englishness is constructed, an artefact; but, like Oxford's role in nurturing leadership, we are required to treat it as natural. Nature is dissolved in culture. We see it happening most clearly in C.S. Lewis's *That Hideous Strength* (1945). Bracton College, one of the three constituent colleges in Edgestow University, owns the adjacent Bragdon Wood.

> If you came in from the street and went through the College to reach [the Wood], the sense of gradual penetration into a holy of holies was very strong. First you went through the Newton quadrangle which is dry and gravelly; florid but beautiful. Georgian buildings look down upon it. Next you must enter a cool tunnel-like passage, nearly dark at midday unless either the door into the Hall should be open on your right or the buttery hatch on your left, giving you a glimpse of indoor daylight falling on panels, and a whiff of the smell of fresh bread. When you emerged from this tunnel you would find yourself in the medieval college: in the cloister of the much smaller quadrangle called Republic. The grass here looks very green after the aridity of Newton and the very stone of the buttresses that rise from it gives the impression of being soft and alive. Chapel is not far off: the hoarse, heavy noise of the works of a great and old clock comes to you from somewhere overhead. You walk along this cloister, past slabs and urns and busts that commemorate dead Bractonians, and then down shallow steps into the full daylight of the quadrangle called Lady Alice. The buildings to your left and right were seventeenth-century work: humble, almost domestic in character, with dormer windows, mossy and grey-tiled. You were in a sweet, Protestant world. You found yourself, perhaps, thinking of Bunyan or of Walton's *Lives*. There were no buildings straight ahead on the fourth side of Lady Alice: only a row of elms and a wall; and here first one became aware of the sound of running water, and the cooing of wood pigeons. The street was so far off by now that there were no other noises. In the wall there was a door. It led you into a covered gallery pierced with narrow windows on each side. Looking out from these you discovered that you were crossing a bridge and the dark dimpled Wynd was flowing under you. Now you were very near your goal. A wicket at the

end of the bridge brought you out on the Fellows' bowling-green, and across that you saw the high wall of the Wood, and through the Inigo Jones gate you caught a glimpse of sunlit green and deep shadows . . .

Half a mile is a short walk. Yet it seemed a long time before I came to the centre of the Wood. I knew it was the centre, for there was the thing I had chiefly come to see. It was a well: a well with steps going down to it and the remains of an ancient pavement about it. I did not step on it, but I lay down in the grass and touched it with my fingers. For this was the heart of Bracton or Bragdon wood: out of this all the legends had come and on this, I suspected, the very existence of the College had originally depended. The archaeologists were agreed that the masonry was very late British-Roman work, done on the very eve of the Anglo-Saxon invasion. . . . [In the fourteenth century] the well with the British-Roman pavement was already 'Merlin's Well'.

(Lewis 1945: 18–20)

Here, indeed, is a subject fit for deconstruction. On one level Lewis gives us no more than the usual approving account of an Oxbridge college's humanely various architecture. But, of course, he gives us more than this. He gives us allegory, controlled by the phrase about gradual penetration to a holy of holies. From the street, the present, we move straight (without having to avert our eyes from the horrors of Victorian Gothic, note) to seventeenth-century rationalism; Newton quadrangle, beautiful but arid. We pass through medieval piety, green, soft and dimly lit, to come – anachronistically – to sweet, brilliant, humble Puritanism. We then pass from history to prehistory and myth, crossing the Wynd (the Lethe?) to reach the Wood's margin. That follower of Palladio, Inigo Jones, concerned to merge ancient models and aristocratic English realities, built the gate. Within, at the wild wood's centre, lies the well. Culture is embedded in English nature. The culture is syncretic: the well, the source, is Romano-British (an earlier, authentic version of Jones's pastiche) but venerated as Merlin's place. Merged with a Protestant mysticism and strong whiffs from *The Golden Bough*, we have been given a high-Tory allegory of English history. Bracton College's varied architecture encodes, mythologizes, this history: richly diverse, we are told, but massively continuous. But these buildings, that recorded history, are nourished and justified by numinous springs. At the heart of the college, at the heart of England, lies the well; authentic British culture (Merlin) legitimized by classical builders.

> And always, through all changes, every warden of Bracton, on the day of his election, had drunk a ceremonial draught of water from Merlin's Well in the great cup which both for its antiquity and for its beauty, was the greatest of the Bracton treasures.
>
> (Lewis 1945:21)

The divine right of kings, God's thumbs-up to England and the English, is asserted, sustained. The holy water passes to monarch, to warden, in the Grail.

The conflation of England with Oxbridge is illuminated brilliantly by Lewis's allegory. But he merely tells us in an open, if displaced, fashion what the routine discourse of British university fiction takes for granted. Englishness is the highest value. If Englishness is to survive then places like Edgestow – Oxford and Cambridge – must be preserved from corruption. We have seen that most modern British university fiction is set in Oxford, and an overwhelmingly large proportion is set in Oxford or Cambridge. When we find ourselves in other places, Oxbridge always provides the measure of not-Oxbridge inadequacy. We now can see the point of this fiction. It is about culture: what it is, how to promote it, how to defend it, who threatens it. Given that, it is no surprise that versions of Matthew Arnold's ideas set the discourse.

This is not new. Mortimer Proctor (1957) showed that nineteenth- and early-twentieth-century English university fiction was narrowly focused on Oxford. This fiction holds little literary interest. Major novelists had no direct university experience. George Eliot spent much time in Cambridge gardens, but her sex kept her out of the colleges. Apart from the famous chapters in *Jude the Obscure*, chapters written by an architect trained in a drawing office rather than a university, major novelists ignored Oxford and Cambridge. But the Victorian university novels – written by minor novelists deploying direct university experience mediated by genre – collectively generated 'a profound exploration of the function and purpose of the university itself' (Proctor 1957: 10). Novelists came to terms

with the old and ever-new question, What are the ends of a
university education? Or even more broadly, What is a
university? [They echoed] the great debate that had
occupied Victorian educational theorists throughout one of
the most lively discussions in all the history of English
education. The central issue was, of course, the value of a
liberal education as against a practical, or useful one.

(Proctor 1957: 190, 192)

What follows this? Exegesis of the social theory covert within the
fiction: that liberal account of the university exemplified, Proctor
thinks, by J.H. Newman and Matthew Arnold. In the latter's view,
the principal task of education was to make people disinterested,
to remove them from the strictures of class and make them aware
– whatever their social origins – of the need to exemplify and
defend culture. Such people, liberated from stock habits, he called
aliens. In them he saw hope for the future.

Thus post-war British university fiction is set firmly in its frame
of Victorian references. A surface reading makes these references
purely literary: books talk to books. '"Half the world"', grumbles a
fellow of St Thomas' College, Oxford, '"still thinks that *Verdant
Green* and *Tom Brown at Oxford* represent the truth, the whole truth,
and nothing but the truth (though some might add *Zuleika
Dobson*)"' (Masterman 1952: 153). These books, and others of their
kind, shared a perspective. In 1875 Mark Pattison noted that

The novelist sets up his *camera obscura* in the middle of the
High Street and lets the passing figures mirror themselves as
they flit to and fro. He gives us what he sees. And he sees all
from the student's side.

(quoted in Proctor 1957: 183)

The Victorian novels made Oxford a shell factory in the war for
culture. Raw young men arrived from town or country, public
school or private tutor. After three years in the university – years of
sport, modest rowdyism, the odd political excursion in the Union,
last-minute study for examinations, but above all years of vigorous
social life in the college – they were despatched into the world,
pointy-headed aliens ready to be fired at culture's enemies.

Many modern novels follow this lead, showing us the induction
of proto-aliens into collegiate culture. Most are undergraduates,

but some are not: Frank Deasy, for example (J.I.M. Stewart 1966), is a college's first visiting Schoolmaster Fellow, and Duncan Pattullo (J.I.M. Stewart 1974) is re-inducted to the same college after many years outside Oxford. Drawing outsiders to Oxford's heart, showing them slowly coming to understand what the university and colleges are for – and thus why they must be protected – is the narrative structure behind most Oxbridge novels. But there is a deeper sense in which all Oxbridge novels are about induction. Here it is not the characters who are led inwards to more private regions, but the reader.

Some not-Oxbridge novels are asserted to contain lightly disguised portraits of real people. Who was Neddy Welch? Who is Howard Kirk? Rumours abound; but they represent little more than routine academic gossip. No more can be expected from the diffuse not-Oxbridge interpretative community. Things are rather different with Oxbridge novels. 'One quickly becomes conscious in Oxford of the contention that all senior persons are known to one another' (J.I.M. Stewart 1978: 92). Gavin Tandom and Marianne Fontenay 'shared a common social world. Here it was in the stalls and pews: a highly integrated society, an eminently endogenous tribe, its territories stretching from Headington to Cumnor, from North Oxford to Boars Hill' (J.I.M. Stewart 1955: 223). Within this little academic world, and its Cambridge equivalent, some novels can be read as slightly disguised accounts of real events and persons. Jago in C.P. Snow's *The Masters* is modelled on Canon Raven (Amos 1985: 269), though Raven won the election in Christ's College, Cambridge and ruled as master until 1950; Skullion (Sharpe 1974) becomes a portrait of Albert Jaggers, erstwhile head porter of Corpus Christi, Cambridge. The book can be read one way by an outsider, differently by an insider. The astute author can play on this possibility. Consider Everard Raven's distress at the arrival of an unwelcome visitor:

'Oh dear, oh dear!' Everard's voice rose to something like a wail of despair. 'We were up at Corpus together. And Corpus men always continue to acknowledge each other, I suppose you know. An excellent custom, I am sure. Have you ever remarked the cold glare that marks the meeting of Balliol men wherever they may be?'

(M. Innes 1945: 187–8)

Is this reportage, or cultivated fun? Only real insiders can tell.

But there are different degrees of inclusion and exclusion. A wider group of people familiar with different colleges' reputations – academic Oxbridge and graduates, let us say – would appreciate John Appleby's gulling a fake private school's principal. Arthur Appleby, a fictive son, is to be crammed for Oxford. Which college should he grace?

> 'We have Christ Church in mind – or perhaps New College. The present Warden of New College, as it happens, is Arthur's uncle. And the Senior Tutor is his first cousin, and the Tutor for Admissions is his godfather. I also know the Chaplain and give him a square meal from time to time.'
>
> 'Quite so.' Captain Bulkington recorded all these striking particulars on the form before him. 'I think I can recommend New College strongly. Just at the moment, the moral tone is particularly good there. Better than at Christ Church, I should say – although that is very good too.'
>
> (M. Innes 1973:109)

The ironical possibilities of this passage are revealed if we know that J.I.M. Stewart wrote it while still a member of Christ Church, that New College had a reputation for manufacturing bishops, and that personal contacts once provided an inside track for undergraduate entry to Oxford and Cambridge colleges.

More of us are able to solve the vexed question of where Wooster garnered his meagre education. Marmaduke, Lord Chuffnell recalls the illuminated Bertie having once 'insisted that he was a mermaid and wanted to dive into the college fountain and play the harp there' (Wodehouse 1934: 76). The Revd H.P. ('Stinker') Pinker, on the other hand, recalls that Bertie's merry smile was '"one of the sights of . . . Magdalen College, Oxford, when we were up there together"' (Wodehouse 1963: 25). Richard Usborne (1976: 190) adjudicates: 'There is some doubt about which college Bertie was in at Oxford. He says Magdalen, but he also says that he bicycled (in the nude, after a Bump Supper) round his college fountain, and that could only mean Christ Church.' It could only mean Christ Church to academic Oxford, to graduates, and to many tourists. We have a less exclusive group of insiders; one which would be able to understand the point of the working-class John Kemp contracting his nearly fatal bout of pneumonia by being thrown into Wooster's fountain (Larkin 1946).

We can play this game through successively less restricted circles. We reach the limit in Doncaster's perception that in deepest New South Wales 'saying "St Catherine's" meant no more than if he had said "St John's" or "St Edmund's Hall." All equally conjured up a picture of lawned quadrangles, jovial porters and ivy-cluttered walls' (R. Barnard 1974: 108). Bereft of any tacit knowledge, this kind of reader must take the words on the page at face value.

Except that authors often are determined that readers should not be left so uninformed. Again and again early pages of a novel are given over to a more or less subtle guided tour round the college and its environs. Some of this is necessary to what follows – the reader should be able to find his way around before the bloodied knife is found in the gowned back – but much of it is redundant to plot needs. It is a means of drawing the reader inwards from one level of inclusion to the next. When first we meet J.B. Timbermill he is merely a rather cranky Anglo-Saxon specialist living in an attic cave, who introduces Duncan Pattullo to 'the pursuit of mere-dragons, marsh-steppers, eldrich wives, whales, loathly worms, and argumentative nightingales and owls' (J.I.M. Stewart 1974: 67). Three years later we see him again. He still is 'the outstanding Anglo-Saxon scholar of his time', but now he is further identified as the author of *The Magic Quest*, a prehistoric fantasy which has enjoyed runaway success among the young (J.I.M. Stewart 1977: 76–7). We leave him, soon to die, sitting forlorn among his admirers; we leave him knowing that J.B. Timbermill is J.R.R. Tolkien. Stewart has drawn us inwards, taken us from full-outsider status to being semi-insiders. Simon Raven does this for an institution rather than a person. When we see Lancaster College, Cambridge first, in a very strange novel about vampirism (Raven 1960), it appears to the uninitiated reader merely to be a large, fashionable, and rich college. The early pages of *Places Where They Sing* (Raven 1970) maintain this anonymity. Then new information begins to be supplied. This is a college with a reputation for leftist politics, and for male homosexuality. One group of readers pins it down. More clues are supplied. The college chaplain dies saving the chapel's celebrated Rubens from a Jacobin mob. A rather wider group of readers pins the place down. Finally, for those who still have not identified Lancaster as King's – the college that Raven left for the Army, believing that it was 'rotted to pieces of tertiary socialism' (Raven 1980: 6) – we are presented with choices about how to spend a large sum of money raised from the sale of land. One suggestion is that it should go to sustain the fabric of the college's famous chapel, and to sustain the equally famous choir that sings in the chapel. Anybody who still has not identified King's College is beyond redemption. But the rest have been moved inwards on the track that leads to full insider status. Although he occasionally slips in details from other colleges, J.I.M. Stewart also plays this college striptease. In *Vanderlyn's Kingdom* (1967) he gives us an unnamed Oxford college that is as large, rich, and prestigious as Raven's Lancaster, Cambridge. There are architectural clues for the initiated reader; a nobly crumbling library, a fountain in one quadrangle. We arrive back there in the *Staircase in Surrey* sequence, initially just as informed or ignorant about the college's identity. Then, in the third novel, *The Madonna of the Astrolabe* (1977), the college's chief architectural glory is revealed to be in danger of collapse. That glory is its great tower, famous throughout Oxford. For those who still do not recognize the college as Christ Church, the hardback novel's cover has a helpful etching of Tom Tower. One can do no more in trying to induct the reader.

But why is the reader to be inducted? Partly, no doubt, in the interest of general education; but also, as with fictional undergraduates and academic visitors, so that in penetrating closer to the heart of the college he or she can come more clearly to see, and value, what it is and what it is for. Having been invited to follow the author within the college's buildings, we are expected – as considerate guests – to accept a text's assumptions about Oxbridge hegemony. A friend explains to Stephen Henderson why he is throwing up his Oxford fellowship for Harvard: 'One wants to get away from a place that is so incontrovertibly the best in many ways – for a while at least' (Trickett 1954: 163). Apparent challenges to hegemony are inverted. A provincial young woman is abashed by an acquaintance being an Oxford don, 'which she associated, wrongly, not with intellectual but with social superiority' (W. Cooper 1950: 70).

In modern Oxbridge fiction, as in its Victorian counterpart, it is the college that matters, not the university. 'Everybody alive might go to heaven on Judgment Day,' Arnold Lempriere believes. 'But these young men were members of the college now' (J.I.M. Stewart 1976: 136). Attachment to the college sets the frame for education; but alien-making, like building Volvo cars, is carried on in smaller groups. College teaching is individual, with the tutor listening to his pupil's weekly essay. Mass teaching is deprecated. University lectures are not important. Arnold Lempriere warns Duncan Pattullo of the arduous obligations devolving on a Reader: "You will also have to give a great many lectures. I believe it's thirty-six in a year. As you will deliver them triennially for the rest of your days, it's advisable to have them typed out on durable paper"' (J.I.M. Stewart 1974: 208). Jane Appleby, John's sister, does not bother to take notes from the Stockton and Darlington Professor's lectures because 'the substance of what the Professor had to say had, in point of fact, been bequeathed to her by an aunt who attended the lectures in 1925' (M. Innes 1951: 157).

Peers are important catalysts in the process of alien-making. Arthur Aylwin, coming to Oxford from a northern grammar school, 'moved fairly easily in a small group of congenial undergraduates, mostly within his own college. From these young men, almost all of whom had been at major public schools, he picked up changed manners and attitudes' (J.I.M. Stewart 1966: 16–17). And, we are to assume, changed their attitudes in return: the process of dis-interest in motion. But the heart of college life is not the undergraduate peer group. It is the staircase. 'In Lempriere's Oxford . . . there was what politicians would call a special relationship between a senior member and the half-dozen or so youths who happened to run up and down the same flight of stairs as himself' (J.I.M. Stewart 1976: 124). Stewart's five-novel settling of accounts with Oxford is called *A Staircase in Surrey*. The name refers not to the English county, but to a college quadrangle. We see three generations' representative inhabitants live, and remember living, in rooms off this staircase. They combine, conflict, and recombine over thirty years, creating unexpected patterns. An undergraduate lecher ends up a high cleric, a bad amateur cellist becomes a master spy. A diffident freshman turns into the college's senior tutor. When Ivo Mumford is accused of being party to gang-raping a village girl, three generations of this staircase's inhabitants combine to spirit him beyond the reach of justice. Obligations forged on the staircase take precedence over niceties like the rule of law. When finally ejected from the college for yet more reprehensible behaviour, Ivo's contacts find a niche for him in that well-established system of out-relief for the well-connected: he becomes Something in the City. Compare his fate with that of two not-Oxbridge derelicts. Thrown out of his lecturing job in a minor redbrick, Jim Dixon is saved from a fate worse than death – real work – by being hired to keep unwelcome visitors from a fabulously wealthy Scottish Nationalist (Amis 1954). Adam Appleby escapes the treadmill of his London University doctoral work when he is recruited on the Embankment to buy books for a limitlessly wealthy American collector (Lodge 1965). Neither of these *dei ex machina* exactly convinces; but what are Dixon and Appleby to do, since they are excluded from the asserted webs of common experience that tie Oxbridge folk to the worlds of power and commerce, to the fountains of cultural capital?

J.I.M. Stewart shows us three generations on his staircase, but also three classes. Nick Junkin, a proletarian product of Coketown Grammar School, has suffered hard times. The three generations of the Mumford family are aristocrats. Duncan Pattullo, son of an Edinburgh painter, carries the flag for the middle classes. The staircase, a microcosm of the college, civilizes those who live off it, regardless of social origins. 'If [the proletarian] Peter Lusby had probably never before met a [well-born] George Tarpark it was equally probable that George Tarpark hadn't before met a Peter Lusby. So here, I told myself, was Oxford education going on' (J.I.M. Stewart 1978: 127). But one of the five novels, *A Memorial Service*, shows that the civilizing process does not always work. Ivo Mumford never should have come to Oxford. Dimly realizing the fact, he sets to forcing the college to throw him out. The fellows try to avoid this end, but their hand is forced when Ivo publishes a criminal libel against a fellow. The victim is Arnold Lempriere, that exemplification of collegiality. He stands for everything that Ivo Mumford rejected. In an earlier book Ivo had caused the death of a working-class undergraduate, Peter Lusby's elder brother (J.I.M. Stewart 1974). Now Lempriere pays secretly for Peter to be coached for the college's scholarship examination. Through him the college does service to Paul Lusby's memory. Collegiate guilt, collected through Ivo, is expiated through Lempriere.

Stewart treats Oxford alien-making in other books. The

'common-or-garden public school boy' Bruno Landreth educates,
and is educated by, the 'common-or-garden grammar school boy'
Luke Tresilian (J.I.M. Stewart 1963: 28). Mungo Lockhart – a
name from *Lament for the Makaris* – and Ian Cardower are
undergraduates united by their Scottishness but radically divided
by class. Lodged on the same staircase, they become close friends.
For a time it seems that they may turn out to be close kin.
Eventually this proves not to be true, but the staircase has made
them all but brothers across a social chasm. Stewart is careful not
to give us an unrelieved celebration of the staircase as a social
institution, however: an elderly homophilic don, a pre-echo of
Lempriere, is befriended and exploited by a group of undergraduates seeking access to his remote rooms for some quiet
pot-smoking (J.I.M. Stewart 1973: 58).

Stewart celebrated the centenary of 'Culture and its Enemies'
with *Vanderlyn's Kingdom* (1967). At the heart of this novel, as of
Arnold's lecture, is the matter of how to defend culture. A Labour
government allegedly bent on modernizing Britain is in office.
Social turmoil is in the streets once more, in demonstrations
against American warfare in Vietnam. The larger world is mirrored
in Oxford: anti-American graffiti scrawled on walls, the Franks
Committee sitting to consider constitutional reform in the
university. To Oxford comes Bernard Vanderlyn, a fabulously
wealthy American, a scientific and military adviser to presidents. At
a college high table the talk turns to culture's imperilled
condition, and the idea of a reservation is floated: an island in
which culture can be kept inviolate while the bad times rage
outside. Encouraged by his sternly liberal first wife, Vanderlyn tries
the idea. He buys a Greek island, and seeks to construct an artistic
colony with all modern amenities; a place in which liberal values
and culture can be preserved from an illiberal world. The
experiment fails. When Vanderlyn's daughter and his second wife
are seduced by Greek servants he abandons the island. Ideas may
be perfectible, but people – or women – are not. Human
imperfection means that culture cannot be defended through
withdrawal from the world. For Stewart, as for Arnold, engagement
is the only strategy. If Tyros has proved to be indefensible then
England's cultural citadel will have to be garrisoned once more.
Back to Oxford.

Adam Morris, freshly arrived in Cambridge, 'had come to the

greatest university in the world (that he had once dreamed of going to Oxford was soon forgotten)' (Raphael 1976: 16). 'Oxford to Joanna', a doctor who has stayed in the city after taking a BA degree, 'was a *little* world. It ended at Park Town where she lived on the north, and at Folly Bridge on the south. Three or four square miles and in it all the learning or scholarship that counted' (G. Butler 1962: 21). Being there, being invited to see oneself as culture's Horatio, does not encourage modesty in undergraduate or graduate. It has the same effect on senior members:

> Oxford dons aren't on the whole deficient in a due sense of their own distinction. They're quite pleased with themselves, if the thing may be vulgarly put. . . . And no Fellow of an Oxford college is obliged to think that anywhere in the wide world outside Oxford itself does anything that may be termed academic advancement beckon to him.
>
> (J.I.M. Stewart 1966: 17, 44)

Gervase Fen muses on the downside of privileged academic life: '"The trouble is, we're all so damnably intelligent at Oxford"' (Crispin 1944: 157) After a limpid description of a college, two fellows discuss the delights of being in Oxford:

> 'It is seducing, isn't it?' Naylor asked . . . 'The place requires our presence for only half a year, and yet we come to behave as if we were Frenchmen, judging the rest of the world wholly barbarous, or Americans, convinced that it's insanitary.'
>
> 'It certainly sells us its own idea of what's important and absorbing.'
>
> (J.I.M. Stewart 1967: 178)

The Greeks had a word for that: hubris. J.C. Masterman's books treat the matter. The narrator of *An Oxford Tragedy* (1933) is Winn, the 60-year-old vice president and senior tutor of St Thomas' College, Oxford. We meet him secure in his position, his scholarship, and his warm appreciation of collegiality. In short, he is smug. But the murder of a fellow, and the subsequent investigation, reveals a dark side to college life that he had not suspected. The certainties dissolve: we leave him contemplating resigning his fellowship. Collapsing convictions are mirrored in the degradation of his previously immaculate prose style:

My friends are all gone, and I'm lonely ... I wonder if, with all their callousness, Doyne and Trower and Shephardson aren't really right? How little the life of a great college like this concerns itself with any individual, how easily it goes on without him! How much would any of them care if I went to-morrow? How long should I be remembered? The individual passes, but the college goes on. ... But I can't bring myself into tune with new ideas. I can't help thinking only of the disastrous past.

(Masterman 1933: 186–7; original punctuation)

We return to St Thomas' College in two later books. In *The Case of the Four Friends* (Masterman 1957) Ernst Brauer, the amateur detective from *An Oxford Tragedy*, prevents a college murder: this is that rare bird, a who-nearly-dunit. Five years earlier, Masterman had published *To Teach the Senators Wisdom*. Some of the characters from *An Oxford Tragedy* are still around: Winn, now 75 and on the edge of retirement; Trower, the ex-Indian Army bursar; Mitton, the ineffectual chaplain; Prendergast. Hubris once more shapes the plot. Those eight fellows left in college at the height of summer are saddled with the chore of entertaining three American visitors that an honorary fellow – a rich bachelor from whom the college expects to do well in time – has wished on them. Since he is so well connected they decide that the Americans must be senators. They will write a collective guide-book, to show their visitors what Oxford is like and how it works.

Masterman uses this slight plot as a peg for two things. The first is a long series of Oxford stories. The second, and more important, is statement and debate about specific features of Oxford life. The St Thomas fellows cover a wide canvas: change in the university since the nineteenth century; local sights and felicities; the relationship between the university and the colleges; academic administration and politics; the tutorial system; the tension between aristocratic and meritocratic entry provisions; the relationship between science and the humanities, between work and sport, between town and university. Their guide-book written, the fellows sit back with a sense of work well done.

Nemesis arrives with the visitors. They prove to be not senators, but female students. This knocks the fellows off their collective balance: nothing has prepared them for such fantastic difficulty.

In approved fairy-tale fashion, the visitors ask the fellows three questions. What influence do the ideas of a particular Harvard education professor have in Oxford? How do students participate in decision-making? What are the women's colleges like? For all their lengthy preparation, these questions stump the fellows. They seem not to have heard of any scholar outside Oxford, let alone an American educationalist. The notion that students should have any say in running university or college affairs is utterly novel. They do not even know where the women's colleges are, let alone what goes on in them. They have to be rescued by their own undergraduates, who answer the visitors' questions and carry them off to punts.

This wise, humane, and measured book warns against complacency. The senators are to be taught wisdom. But who are the senators? Winn and his colleagues think that it is the visitors. Masterman, a Head of House soon to take a turn as vice-chancellor, tells us that it is senior members of Oxford University, men who would be found in the councils of college and university, who lack wisdom. Stepping from behind his authorial persona, he tells the reader openly that 'If I sometimes shudder at the suggestions of reform, I am more often appalled at the obstinate and complacent conservatism of the majority of them' (Masterman 1952: 9). Dons must remedy this deficiency, for another set of senators looms. When university and colleges rely on state funding to a degree never seen before, novel questions about accountability will be asked.

Post-war British university fiction takes Matthew Arnold's assertion of the overwhelming need to defend culture, but transforms it. For Arnold culture was rooted in classical languages and literature. For the modern literary discourse culture is rooted in English literature, the well at the heart of English culture. For Arnold culture was an 'inward operation', rooted in each cultured individual. For the modern literary discourse culture is incorporated in hierarchically ranked institutions. All universities embody culture, but some embody it better than others. To defend culture one must defend the key institutions: one must defend Oxford and Cambridge. An adequate defence presupposes a proper identification of enemies. Smith, blissfully ignorant of *Culture and Anarchy* and much else, tells us that Oxford aristocratic culture before 1914 was untroubled, serene:

But all that is changed now. Today's Top People are insecure but just as arrogant. They can't ignore the fact that changes have taken place – that Oxford has been invaded by the grammar schools, the workers, the scientists, the personality-cult, William Hickey. The world may be blown up any day.

(Smith 1962: 89)

Who needs thermo-nuclear devices when civilisation has already been destroyed? Smith constructs an unlikely alliance of barbarian tribes. It makes more sense to see British university fiction constructing four sets of enemies: proletarians, scientists, women, and foreigners. The next four chapters examine how these hordes are conjured in post-war novels.

Part three

Chapter Five

BARBAROUS PROLETARIANS

'"What have I got left to love?"' asks a character in a routine Oxford novel.

'An ugly, vulgar, illiterate mob who make ten times as much money as I do with less than a tenth of my brain, who call anyone who speaks the King's English privileged, when the only privileged people are the so-called workers, who let the "privileged" pay for their doctors, education, unemployment and every other damned thing and spend their time fighting for more pay for less work, whose highest idea of happiness is dog-racing and the flicks, a land that's daily becoming uglier and more overcrowded, a land where men no longer walk freely, glaring posters on all the hoardings advertising three things only, death on the roads, diphtheria is dangerous, and venereal disease is rampant.'

(Mais 1949: 169)

This character reflects his author's general stance. The world is going to hell in a handcart, and England with it. Who can doubt this when he sees the lower orders growing so uppity?

Oxbridge reflects England. 'In the days before 1914, when Oxford was a home for gentlemen', before 'the social rot set in' (Balsdon 1961: 203), the ancient English universities were safe for aristocratic culture. Now, a host of grumpy conservatives tells us, the places are going to pot. In 1946 Max Beerbohm assured sceptical readers that 'my fantasy [*Zuleika Dobson*] was far more like to the old Oxford than was the old Oxford like to the place now besieged and invaded by Lord Nuffield's armies' (Beerbohm 1911: *Note*). '"But that's just what it's all about,"' one fellow of Lancaster, Cambridge tells another.

'Increased numbers equals democracy in action equals absolute good. Fine views equals privilege equals absolute bad. We have a large area called Scholar's Meadow, which looks nice but serves no purpose. Its beauty provokes as much resentment as its uselessness, and certain people will not rest until it is covered from the Queen's Road to the river with square, grey blocks of cheap and nasty bed-sitting rooms——'

'——Full of cheap and nasty students, all reading socio-logy. Don't tell me. Well, it's got to be stopped.' Ivor Win-stanley breathed heavily through his nose, while little flecks of foam appeared at the corners of his mouth.... 'To build on Scholar's Meadow – an act of vandalism on that scale means the end of everything.'

(Raven 1970: 24)

Once again, this exchange captures its author's foam-flecked attitude. The motto to Raven's *Places Where They Sing* is taken from the Anglican *Book of Common Prayer*: 'There never was anything by the wit of man so well devised, or so well established, which in continuance of time hath not been corrupted.'

In the ancient universities as in the outside world, the root of culture's difficulty is class. Daniel Mond, a humbly born Jewish Fellow of Lancaster, explains the motivation of modern Cambridge students (a significantly not-Oxbridge designation) to Balbo Blakeney:

'They are here to better themselves. To get more of what is going. . . by which I do not mean knowledge, but social status and worldly goods. They have decided that they are not getting more enough quick [sic] enough, and so they are turning nasty with us and all we stand for.'

(Raven 1970: 84)

A corrosive meritocracy threatens all that is rare and beautiful. We also find merit taking over from birth as the basis for prestige in a twenty-first-century Oxford comic dystopia: 'It was a sign of the University's decline from the end of the twentieth century that it could no longer take its peerage neat, but liked it watered down with a strong admixture of practical achievement' (Balsdon 1961: 123). Here, however, the rot has gone much deeper. Latin and

Greek, emblematic of aristocratic virtue, are no longer acceptable university entrance subjects. The compulsory subjects are Chinese, Chemistry, General Civics and Basic Psychology. The university has a permanent vice-chancellor, like not-Oxbridge places: this reform 'was one which for decades progressive dons in the Honour School of Politics, Philosophy and Economics had been advocating in their ill-attended seminars' (Balsdon 1961: 23–4). The tutorial teaching system has been abandoned. University finances depend wholly on the state, college funds on students' state scholarships. High tables and senior common rooms have been replaced by Teachers' Canteens and Teachers' Canteen Rest Rooms. The Oxford Union has been replaced by the Oxford branch of the National Union of Pupils, a body with a very different ethos. The leaders of Oxford's NUP branch are Mr Tanner and Mr Tit. They represent two of the viruses that have destroyed Oxford: money-grubbing attitudes and women.

Raven and Balsdon both rail at the destruction of Oxbridge culture, but they appear to have different targets. This is misleading. Together with other authors of deep-dyed old Right political persuasion (Lejeune 1987; Shaw 1981) they identify two fundamental corrosive doctrines: socialism and utilitarianism. Each has a class location, the first in the proletariat and the second in middling classes. From whence do university novelists derive these class enemies?

Surprise, surprise, from a conservative reading of Matthew Arnold. In writing the essays in *Culture and Anarchy* he intended 'to recommend culture as the great help out of our present difficulties' (Arnold 1869: 233). Those difficulties were social. The book was written in a time of considerable social tension: particularly significant for the argument was that struggle for franchise reform which produced the 1867 Reform Act. Arnold was a liberal, occasionally exasperated by contemporary progressive nostra but maintaining a broad faith in improvement. He was, he said, a liberal of the future if not always of the present. His meliorism made him welcome a widened franchise; but he feared for culture under democracy. The poignancy and urgency in *Culture and Anarchy* come from the clash between contradictory imperatives.

Culture has to be defended at all costs. Against whom? Well, roughly, everybody. Arnold shows us the three great classes of classical political economy – Barbarians (aristocracy), Philistines (bourgeoisie), and Populace (proletariat) – then declares each unworthy of the grail. The barbarians are too corrupt to hold and defend culture, the philistines too money-grubbing. The best that can be hoped of 'the Playful Giant', the working class, is that it can be cajoled not to kick over the social sand-pit. At the collective level policy must aim at civilizing the philistine: hence Arnold's unwavering support for state educational provision. He spent many years as a school inspector among working people, but he thought that the cultural imperative was to educate the English middle classes. And it was education that was needed, not training. Schools can build philistines. Mr Bottles, a genial Bounderby, recalls his youthful years at Silverpump's academy:

> 'Original man, Silverpump! fine mind! fine system! none of your antiquated rubbish – all practical work – latest discoveries of science – lights of all colours – fizz! fizz! bang! bang! That's what I call forming a man!'
>
> (Arnold 1867: 71)

Proletarian riot, the Playful Giant's boisterousness, 'tends to anarchy' (Arnold 1869: 119); but so does 'our strong individualism, our hatred of all limits to the unrestrained swing of the individual's personality, our maxim of "every man for himself"' (Arnold 1869: 95). If culture is to be defended against the mob, then it also needs to be defended against possessive individuals. Jacobinism may be one enemy, but utilitarianism is just as dangerous. In the absence of suitable social forces to manage a defence against these threats, Arnold puts his trust in 'aliens'; declassed individuals from each of his three groups who will recognize their common mission and unite to exemplify and defend culture. Thus he gives us a class theory, but one that looks to the dissolution, the dis-interest, of class. We do not have to play with conceits in order to make Arnold Lempriere an alien. J.I.M. Stewart intends that we should identify him as one.

Arnold's ambiguities made his work a rich quarry for later covert social theorists (Rothblatt 1988). English social criticism as literary criticism divided after his death. One stream flowed through Pater to T.S. Eliot, the other through the Newbolt Report, I.A. Richards, and the Leavises to Raymond Williams. Baldick (1983: 231) makes the distinction theological: high church against low church. For our purposes there is a more useful distinction. Arnold was concerned to think through how civilized values could be maintained under conditions of inevitably widened democracy. *Culture and Anarchy* is a contribution to the central nineteenth- and twentieth-century debate about mass society.

Mass society models construct an image of society as a pyramid (Kornhauser 1959; Giner 1976). At the top sits a small elite. At the bottom lies a huge mass, the overwhelming bulk of the population. The membrane between the two groups contains mediating institutions. These comprise organizations of many forms – employers' associations and trades unions; professional bodies; a multitude of voluntary organizations and interest groups; everything, in fact, from ICI to the Auchenblae Bowls Club. When the membrane works properly, mediating institutions filter and articulate demands from below, soften orders from above. We have that pluralism celebrated by liberal political scientists, in which the state acts merely as the neutral arbiter of policy competition among warring interest groups. But the membrane can be ruptured, and a plural society become a mass society. At this point judgements divide. Mass society is always taken to be bad, but the nature of the evil depends on what one thinks is at risk. The many aristocratic mass society theorists (Tocqueville, le Bon, Ortega y Gasset) take the need to maintain the elite's freedom of action to be paramount. For these people unfiltered demands from the mass – 'the mob' in nineteenth-century language – render government impossible. For the fewer democratic mass society theorists (Hannah Arendt, C. Wright Mills), by contrast, the evil in mass society lies in the excessive ease with which the elite can control and manipulate the broad population.

We can map these distinctions on English concealed sociology. T.S. Eliot exemplifies the aristocratic line, obsessed – in *Notes Towards the Definition of Culture* (1949), for instance – with maintaining unpolluted the pure, thin stream of high culture. Raymond Williams is the most distinguished modern standard bearer for the democratic camp, concerned in *Culture and Society* (1958) to define the grounds for a common culture rooted in the lived experience of most British people. Characteristically F.R. Leavis looked both ways, covering profound intellectual confusion with high-octane prose. And where does Arnold sit in all this? It is possible to read him in both aristocratic and democratic ways; but

107

for all his liberalism of the future and his work as a school inspector, at bottom Arnold was a thoroughgoing aristocrat trying to define circumstances in which an intellectual elite could float free from social determination.

Modern university novels construct an initial image of Oxford congruent with this intention: an Oxford that floats free from, is sharply differentiated from, proletarian towns and cities. Once again, J.I.M Stewart is our surest guide. In *Stop Press* a railway journey permits him a curiously post-structuralist description of the city.

> Oxford – adorable dreamer, cuckoo-echoing, bell-swarmed, lark-charmed, rook-racked, river-rounded – Oxford shivered, lurched, disintegrated into the fluidity of parallax. A few seconds of mere confusion and rhythm asserted itself: at various speeds the grey pinnacles revolved about their axis in the gas-works.
>
> (M. Innes 1939: 40)

Winter twilight raises old spectres:

> The sky, a sheet of lead rapidly oxidising, was fading through glaucous tones to cinerous; lights were furred about their edges; in the gathering twilight Gothic and Tudor, Palladian and Venetian melted into an architecture of dreams. And the hovering vapours, as if taking heart of darkness, glided in increasing concentration by walls and buttresses – like the first inheritors of the place, robed and cowled, returning to take possession with the night.
>
> (M. Innes 1939: 19)

Noble architecture dissolves into medieval monasticism: a physical description conjures an assertion of Oxford's massive continuity.

In the following year *There Came Both Mist and Snow* took us to a West Riding mill town. John Appleby looks out from Belrive Priory, a doomed mansion built – significantly – around monastic ruins:

> Unbroken snow was below us; beyond, the city sullenly resisted the pressure of a leaden sky. To the left, and closer than I had ever realised them to be, back-to-back houses spilt themselves down the valley-side in parallel rows, like grimy tentacles abruptly lopped. Everywhere, above black roofs

snow-powdered, slow smoke rose grey and black to heaven,
so that the city showed like a vast and cinerous altar whose
useless offerings smouldered in a void. A lurid sun hung low
as a furnace door in a foundry, or like a burning football
tumbled between the goal-posts of the brewery chimneys.
And far away down the valley, as if to suggest that here was
but an outer circle in the inferno of industrialism, lay a
blacker smudge that told of iron and steel in a neighbouring
town.

(M. Innes 1940a: 201)

The weather in Oxford and Belrive is much the same. Much the
same language is used in the two passages. But the effect is utterly
different. Oxford is an 'adorable dreamer', heavenly. The mill
town is 'a vast and cinerous altar', an outer circle of hell. This is
Stewart's invariable attitude to the industrial north, derived from
nineteenth-century 'condition of England' novels. Like his
creator, Frank Deasy had little interest in what went on in northern
factories: from his study's window 'Over two thirds of the horizon,
certainly, man-made flames will faintly yet luridly flicker – serving
night-long manufacturing processes which have remained,
through all these years, obstinately beyond my comprehension'
(J.I.M. Stewart 1966: 14). Deasy looks at this view, after many years
as head of English in the city's grammar school, as he prepares to
be Schoolmaster Fellow in a glittering Oxford college.

The lopped tentacles of back to back terraced houses fumbled
blindly yet inexorably towards Belrive Priory. This is strikingly
similar to Stewart's much later description of another mansion's
being swallowed by an industrial town in *The Bloody Wood* (M. Innes
1966: 14, 51), a novel which employs Eliot's *Sweeny Among the
Nightingales* to allegorize (as Greek tragedy) the collapse of
aristocratic English culture. Both join, with *Dombey and Son* and
Hard Times, in the description of yet another industrial city
creeping out to envelop the park of Old Hall, a disgraced mansion
housing a minor redbrick university:

In front of them the straight avenue crossed the park at its
narrowest extent, and just beyond were the outermost
suburbs of the city that stretched, all smudge and smoke and
watery glitter, to a horizon of chimney-stacks and miscellaneous industrial contrivances. But elsewhere the park

109

faded imperceptibly into a sort of no-man's land between country and town: fields creeping round abandoned manufactures, fresh manufactures devouring abandoned fields, hills in places immemoriably wooded and in places scraped and scarred by mines and quarries.

(M. Innes 1956b: 20)

The threat to Old Hall is the threat to the university as cultural citadel. That mansion's minor redbrick is no more than an insignificant fort, but the proletarian and utilitarian pressures threatening this place, if not resisted, eventually will mass against the Oxbridge keep and the aristocratic culture that it defends. Olivia Jory, scion of the family that used to own Old Hall, 'couldn't really regard the University as other than a thoroughly provincial little place, swarming with up and coming young vulgarians, intent upon grabbing places and privileges that her sort was progressively letting slip' (M. Innes 1956b: 67).

Stewart offers two forms of defence. The first is apartheid. Colin Clout and George Lumb, two of Olivia Jory's up-and-coming young vulgarians, struggle for her favours. They are less than gruntled to discover that she has bestowed those favours on her cousin Jerry, thus reuniting the Jory family's two branches. Clout and Lumb are forced to fall back on pursuing Sadie Sackett, a graduate, like them, of Old Hall's 'absurd university'. Aristocracy is to be preserved through endogamy, through exclusion. There are to be universities for proletarians and middling folk; universities that, in principle, are separate from but equal with aristocratic Oxbridge. Stewart had developed this line rather further in the heady days of post-war reconstruction, in *The Weight of the Evidence*. The Duke of Nesfield's hobby is to govern the local major redbrick university. Taking his hobby seriously, he seems to have been reading 'Bruce Truscott's' *Redbrick University* (1943). He explains to John Appleby why Nesfield – '"this sort of university"' - will prove important.

'All these little Toms and Dicks and Harrys – and Susans and Josephines and Gladyses too – come from the workers and the lower middle class; from the people who, a couple of generations from now, will be absorbed in an amorphous and classless material prosperity. Not, mark you, a prosperity running here and there to wealth. Just a nice whack all round and perhaps half as much again for the bureaucracy policing it. Now, where is a little breadth of mind going to come from all this? From Susan and Harry, if you ask me. Lord knows what they're taught: Anglo-Saxon, Fitting and Turning, Political Economy – it doesn't matter very much. The point is that for several years, and when almost grown-up, they rub along in coteries and crowds, and sit chattering on benches which never see furniture-polish from one year's end to another. Moreover, they are in contact with scientists and scholars – a sort of people who often don't very clearly know whether they possess homes and gardens at all. In fact, these universities may temper the coming, attractive materialism rather as chapels and institutes and so forth a little tempered the disgusting materialism of the last century.'

(M. Innes 1944: 21–2)

Thoroughly Arnoldian, Stewart looks to education to humanize the philistines, make them basic-grade aliens. But that education is to take place in a reformed version of Silverpump's academy, in the philistines' own institutions. '" These universities, you know, require for the most part technical men,"' the Oxford-trained Professor Crunkhorn tells John Appleby. '"Applied scientists – that sort of thing." Silly old snob, thought Appleby. "These universities" won't have a soul of their own until they put the Duke's Dicks and Harrys into their teaching jobs' (M. Innes 1944: 26).

Stewart's second solution is to induct a narrow stream of proletarian and middle-class barbarians into culture's citadel. There they are to be transformed into a higher class of alien. His most significant book about Oxbridge alien-making is *The Man Who Won the Pools*; a novel about 'class and that' (J.I.M. Stewart 1961: 216), his response to that social realist Angry Young Men school constructed by the Sunday reviewers. Phil Tombs is an electrician rooted in working-class Oxford's organic community, randomly informed through his trade training and adventitious literary gleanings. A big pools win takes him through a cycle of characters who represent class types measured against Tombs's 'wholesome working-class realism'. Prendick runs the pools company. He stands for new, flashy money: living in a Cotswold mock manor house called Loose Chippings, driving a Jaguar. Prendick's niece and secretary, Jean Canaway, hails from 'The insulated and unchanging English upper middle class. . . .

Something that wouldn't make sense in any other country in the world. But it's there' (J.I.M. Stewart 1961: 217). Hannay, a fake English gentleman, and McLeod, a Lebanese purporting to be a Highland laird, are London crooks attempting to separate Tombs from his money. Lord Mark Thickthorne, an eccentric undergraduate, stands for aristocracy, for old landed money. Peter Sharples and Aubrey Moore are two more undergraduates, the first working class and the second aristocratic. For this novel, like so many by Stewart, is about Britain seen through Oxford's prism. Tombs looks from his home patch towards the colleges.

> And straight ahead down New Street, down this vista – that was the word – of Victorian or whatever it was meanness, shining in that evening light that could do something even with the gasometers, was Christ Church College's tower – only it wasn't a tower but a sort of pepper-pot such as giants might own if they had a fancy for everything superior around them. Phil Tombs looked at this tower, Tom Tower, closing the vista of New Street, and told himself that you don't get things as ruddy beautiful as that by accident. And not just by paying up neither, he told himself. The bleeding thing means something. So, for that matter, does the Primitive Methodist 1843. Buildings do mean things. Funny how everything solid expresses something that isn't solid at all.
>
> (J.I.M. Stewart 1961: 29)

The buildings encode class meanings. The Primitive Methodist chapel stands for working-class rootedness, Tom Tower for an impossibly remote aristocratic high culture. That he can recognize, however dimly, the insubstantial messages locked in red brick and honey-coloured stone marks Tombs out as an unusually perceptive proletarian. Later events tune and develop his antennae, as he makes contact with undergraduate Oxford. He strikes up a friendship with Peter Sharples, who proves to be a much more impressive student than Aubrey Moore. He strikes up another with Mark Thickthorne, and combines with him to design a revolutionary coal-to-gas process. The pilot plant to test the process is constructed at Thickthorne Court. It is arranged to supply both the Court and the village within its walled park. Aristocrat and proletarian work together for the common good. Tombs has moved from an organic urban working-class community to an organic rural classless community. Interest has been stripped from him. We leave him about to get his cultural warrant: '"I seen a man in Oxford. A professor. He says I got to go to Cambridge. . . . he said he'd fix a college, all right"' (J.I.M. Stewart 1961: 239). A new-coined alien, he looks once more towards the colleges:

> Here was the Primitive Methodist 1843 and there in the distance was Tom Tower, Christ Church. It came into his head queerly that they didn't seem so far apart as they'd used to. They pretty well nodded to each other the minute you thought of Prendick's office or of Loose Chippings.
>
> (J.I.M. Stewart 1961: 221)

Galvanized Methodism and gilded privilege close ranks against culture's enemy – philistine utilitarianism. The debt to *Culture and Anarchy* becomes manifest, but in a form that Arnold would scarcely recognize. He thought that 'the Playful Giant' had to be kept sedated. Stewart proposes an alliance between aristocracy and proletariat against the crass bourgeoisie.

The sense of aristocratic Oxbridge assailed by proletarians and utilitarian middling folk structures many accounts of life among students and teaching staff. In *Oxford Blood* Antonia Fraser gives us a novel of undergraduate experience that is riddled with contradiction. The narrative stance lurches around because Fraser cannot decide whether the undergraduate Lord Saffron and his bloody friends are atavistic:

> In an age of grants, declining, and unemployment, rising, it was easy to see how some undergraduates might actively envy Saffron for his advantages. . . . what price the classless society based on merit which many might hope to find at a university if nowhere else in Britain? The cars, parties, dinners of the young and rich ensured them. . . a sour spotlight within the university.
>
> (Fraser 1985: 95)

'The lifestyle of the Golden Kids', she tells us,

> contrasted with that of the vast majority of the under-graduates eating in Hall, living off grants or, rather,

113

struggling with inadequate grants, finding even coffee an expensive luxury and never touching a drop of champagne from one end of term to the next.

(Fraser 1985: 125)

We are told that undergraduate society has been transformed, understandings of what Oxford is about unsettled, by state funding. Many other novels confirm this truth; a couple deny it.

Raymond Postgate presents a picture of Oxbridge undergraduate culture before state grants became widely available after the Second World War. Henry Proctor is a working-class lad who wins a scholarship to St James' College, Oxford, in the First World War. His scholarship will not cover teaching and living expenses: it is augmented by the elders of the strict Gospel Fellowship in which he was brought up. Oxford disturbs assumptions derived from this background.

> 'And all discover, late or soon
> Their golden Oxford afternoon.'

How very untrue (he thought). All do not discover their Oxford afternoon: it is for a privileged few. And how very odd that I should be one of those few, and thinking rather indulgently of the outsiders who will never have it. When I go back home, I become again one of the people who never have a golden Oxford afternoon – in fact, I become so a little even when I think of home – but here I don't even think or like them, and I forget the way they live.

(Postgate 1953: 74)

Proctor's stock notions are challenged in Oxford. Fair enough, one might say: that is what Arnold thought education should do. His tutor clearly thought so, taking 'less interest in his pupil's scientific studies. . . and more in making him "less of a barbarian"' (Postgate 1953: 79). But it does not work. Proctor is removed from the working-class culture into which he was born, but Oxford provides no new bearings. The rest of his life is spent in an unhappy cultural limbo. Death by murder comes almost as a relief.

To Wilfred Sheed's (1967: 42–3) anti-hero, John Chote, 'class was a faint impediment, like a limp, keeping him out of a few clubs, and perhaps later a few jobs, and away from a few other goodies that perhaps he didn't even know about'. Even in a seedy college, Oxford still rubs Chote's raw class nerve.

> At Sturdley there was only a handful of men who had gone to the top public schools, and acquired the fine, luminous unconsciousness; and about the same number had gone to nameless grammar schools and still spoke defiantly, reluctantly, with the meatier accents of their provinces; in between, there was a great pink featureless mass, Britannia's flesh. Chote had gone to an obscure public school, Brinkley College in the Chilterns, reputation so-so, where he had acquired a passable variant of the BBC voice: that was more than enough for Oxford to know.
>
> (Sheed 1967: 42)

State scholarships, we are told, have had little impact on Oxford's old Adam. A public school ethos rules Sturdley, and to have gone to a minor rather than a major school is shameful.

This account is challenged by other descriptions of Oxbridge transformed through state funding. Andrew Sinclair (1959: 50–1) contrasts 'the rich sport-and-no-work world at Cambridge' with 'the work-and-no-sport kids on the government grants'. J.I.M. Stewart asserts change through time:

> During what I could now think of as three [aristocratic] Mumford generations, the colleges of Oxford, as of Cambridge, must have been receiving a steadily increasing proportion of young men who had never been away from home before. There had been more [proletarian] Nicholas Junkins in Tony's time than in his father's, and there were now more in Ivo's time than there had been in Tony's.
>
> (J.I.M. Stewart 1974: 183)

A history lesson interpolated in Stewart's next novel explains the mechanism of change. 'The deeper causes. . . lay in social history and the drift of social legislation' - the factors threatening aristocratic culture in *The Bloody Wood* and so many other Michael Innes country-house whodunits – 'but the immediate cause was simply a change in academic standards'. Before 1945 a ground-level entrance hurdle faced prospective Oxford students. This permitted colleges to choose whom they wished:

most of them took for granted the validity of the proposition
that a body of undergraduates ought to be a mixed lot; that
some should read and some should row; and moreover that
Uncle Rory's 'two universities' owned a particular responsibility to educate, if remotely educable, those boys whom
inherited wealth or tradition was particularly likely to
promote to positions of public responsibility later on. In a
college like my own, these persuasions and contentions produced, class-wise, a very marked effect.

(J.I.M. Stewart 1975: 85–6)

But a cautious change of policy introduced a matriculation
standard 'falling not inordinately short of that required by the
provincial universities'. Colleges could still choose to admit rather
lightly qualified eccentrics, but 'the pitifully thick, the incorrigibly
idle', and the 'pronouncedly inane' were excluded.

I believe that – particularly during the nineteen sixties –
undergraduate feeling as a whole evolved a good deal under
the influence of this growing number of young men who
possessed, among other things, a more adult grip than their
fellows on the economic facts of life.

(J.I.M. Stewart 1975: 85-6)

Stewart gives us a string of these purportedly case-hardened
working and lower middle-class undergraduates. Phil Tombs and
Peter Sharples are set against Aubrey Moore and Mark
Thickthorne (J.I.M. Stewart 1961). Luke Tresilian, a 'common-or-
garden grammar school boy' whose father just happens to have
been a major painter, is set against Bruno Landreth, a cell in
Sheed's Britannia's flesh, a 'common-or-garden public school boy'
(J.I.M. Stewart 1963: 27). The aesthetic Mark Varley is a working-
class son who came to Oxford from a grammar school in Nesfield,
his creator's stock northern industrial city. He is counterposed to
the Master of Ballater, leader of his college's bloodies, aristocratic
dining and hunting yahoos. Dragged before the Dean for having
attacked Varley's person and his room, Ballater asks '"Why create,
man? It's only another upstart little snot-school shite"' (J.I.M.
Stewart 1967: 71). These comparisons culminate in the contrast
between two undergraduates with rooms on the same college
staircase (J.I.M. Stewart 1974; 1976). Both are modestly endowed

intellectually, facing expulsion if they fail a resit examination. They come from sharply different social backgrounds. Ivo Mumford is the son of an ennobled Tory cabinet minister. Nick Junkin is a proletarian son from Coketown, Dickens's disguise for Preston in *Hard Times*. Junkin gets much from Oxford, and gives some back through his talent for student theatricals. Mumford gets nothing and gives back nothing, expressing his baffled resentment through yahoo vandalism. '"Do you know why I'm going to pass their silly exam?"' Junkin asks Pattullo. '"It's because I'm not going to be in the same bleeding galley as that ignorant gnome"' (J.I.M. Stewart 1976: 274). We feel no surprise when Mumford, like Ballater, is slung out of Oxford. He represents a view of the university as aristocratic play-pen which Stewart, unlike Antonia Fraser, consistently reviles.

An assertedly more mixed population generates different accounts of undergraduate subcultures. The routine nineteenth-century distinctions between aesthetes, bloodies, hearties and reading men are displaced. Louis McIntosh provides a much more refined set of categories:

> Oxford's class distinctions are quite different from the upper, middle and lower distinction that is more or less serviceable for the rest of the society. In Oxford there are dozens of different sets, each with one thing in common. There is a set which went to school at Ampleforth; a set which speaks Russian at home; a set which shared an Army barrack-room; a set which sketches Nonconformist chapels; a set which spends the summer in Alexandria; and a set which has dishonourable intentions on the deer in Magdalen Park. Often one person belongs to more than one set, of course.
>
> (McIntosh 1956: 85)

This account of Oxford as a densely networked island of classless distinction wilted under the widespread discovery of class by mid-century English novelists. Five years after McIntosh's book was published, Phil Tombs quizzes Peter Sharples:

> 'Do you mean Two Nations – that sort of thing? Even inside your bleeding college?'
> 'Four, I'd say.' The young man had flushed slightly, almost like he was a teacher beginning to give the kids a talk on sex.

'Etonians, for a start. And perhaps Wykehamists. Then all the people from all the other public schools.'

'That's two? Wouldn't it be a bit a matter of dads and so on, as well as schools?'

'Yes, of course. There are cross-currents one would never get to understand, even if one wanted to. But roughly, that's two. And then there are two quite distinct lots from grammar schools. And it's nothing but dads, this time. White-collar dads – the lower middle class, in fact. And then plain proletarian dads, like mine who's a coalminer.'

(J.I.M. Stewart 1961: 21-2)

Sheed (1967) echoes this, we saw, merely collapsing Stewart's two grammar school categories. But fourteen years later, Leo Bellingham (1981) shows us an Oxford in which students' social backgrounds, and even their genders, are submerged in a common undergraduate culture. And not merely a common Oxford undergraduate culture: these are students working, drinking and fornicating much like not-Oxbridge students. Difference has collapsed. Bellingham seems content that it should be so. Others, we shall see, are not.

Novels show us a few Oxbridge college fellows risen from the lower middle class through (usually midland or northern) grammar schools: Mottram (Masterman 1933); Fothergill (Rees 1945); Albert Woods (W. Cooper 1952); Lewis and Martin Eliot (Snow 1960); Mallory (T. Robinson 1961); Arthur Aylwin (J.I.M. Stewart 1966); Jeremy Shefford (J.I.M. Stewart 1967); Ashe (Shaw 1981). More than half of this company are scientists: a massive over-representation which will interest us in a later chapter when we explore the implications of Bowles-Ottery's assertion that '"the new sort of scientific men [are] rarely gentlemen"' (Vulliamy 1952: 47). Like the physicist Luke – son of a dockyard hand (Snow 1951: 101) – G.S. Clark, a Cambridge modern linguist, is a much rarer bird than these. Lewis Eliot introduces him to us.

His accent became broader and flatter as he warmed up to the nineteenth century romantic-realists: he came from Lancashire, his origins were true working-class. It was very rare, I had thought before, for anyone genuinely working-class to struggle through to the high table, though a sprinkling had come, as I did myself, from the class just

118

above. In the whole history of the college, there could not have been more than three or four who started where he did.

(Snow 1960: 41)

Spawn of the Playful Giant, we might expect Clark to represent a distinct threat to Oxbridge culture. We would be disappointed. He is ultra-conservative, the leader of reaction in Lewis Eliot's college. Less reactionary than Clark, but still a stern defender of the arrangements to which he has succeeded through merit rather than birth, is the literary critic Mallory.

> 'But there's just one thing I'm afraid of – it's that one day someone's going to decide that Oxford's got to be reformed. Let's clear out all the abuses and muddle and dirt, he'll say, and make the place nice and new and cromium-plated, with every square inch serving some useful purpose. And in two shakes he'll have Oxford looking like every other damn' polytechnic you've ever seen and there'll be no more fun left for anyone. . . . I've always thought Oxford a very special place and I don't want it made ordinary.'

(T. Robinson 1961: 163)

Utilitarianism looms, and with it a common greyness to replace Oxford's colours. Both must be resisted. Luke, Clark, and Mallory show that a major defence is the successful socialization of redeemable besiegers. By origin two proletarians and a *petit bourgeois*, they have been permitted to enter Oxbridge through a tightly controlled postern, and then educated to treasure the values of the place. Induction has worked.

Less than ten years after Timothy Robinson's book was published, it seemed that all the citadel's gates had been forced. 'In the sixties and seventies it was the turn of the new universities, Sussex and Essex, for student agitation', Jocelyn Davey (1982: 16) tells us. 'In the late seventies Oxford had its turn.' His chronology is awry. In the mid-1960s Jeremy Shefford, driving a distinguished American around Oxford, is embarrassed to see graffiti attacking American involvement in Vietnam (J.I.M. Stewart 1967). Five years later, the only thing that distinguished Oxford from any other provincial city to Colonel Butler's eye

> was the number of chalked slogans, which ranged from somewhat banal appeals to action against Greece or South

119

Africa, and support for the NLF, Women's Lib and Black
Power, to the rather more intriguing contentions that *Proctors
are Paper Tigers* and *Hitler is Alive and Living in* ——.

(Price 1972: 75)

A year later, Mungo Lockhart and Ian Cardower wandered around
the same city.

A great many of the buildings – colleges, Mungo supposed –
had recently had their walls cleaned or refaced; and on the
inviting surfaces thus obligingly provided were scrawled all
sorts of *graffiti*: plainly the work of rising young scholars in
the university.

(J.I.M. Stewart 1973: 37)

We see from novels as well as newspapers that student agitation was
alive and well in Oxford and Cambridge in the late 1960s and early
1970s. Jocelyn Davey was wrong to limit it to the late seventies.

What Davey did not miss, however, was the widespread
novelistic sense that agitation was a virus introduced from less
cultivated quarters. 'A lot of them. . . had come by coach for the
day from places like Essex and Sussex. I thought they looked too
awful to be ours, even in the distance' (Raven 1970: 220). That was
Cambridge; but Oxford is no different. Duncan Pattullo examines
a demonstration's banners:

A few of these claimed, whether veraciously or not, the status
of a kind of personal standard of one individual college or
another; others announced various Marxist-Leninist, Maoist,
and Trotskyist affiliations; and a surprising number spoke of
regions remote from Oxford's dreaming spires.

(J.I.M. Stewart 1976: 157)

Since this is Innes/Stewart, the one banner which we are
permitted to read declares its bearers' affiliation to 'Dotheboys
Hall Anarchosyndicalist Group'. Of which not-Oxbridge university, or hardly Oxbridge dim college, is Wackford Squeers now
Vice-Chancellor or Master?

Student agitation presents many challenges to Oxbridge. A
college's doctor explains what lies behind the demand for a
students' union at Oxford,

'the providing, at the university's or the government's expense, of a kind of Kubla Khan pleasure dome with everything laid on. A common meeting-place for all students – and the running of it probably more or less left to them. Fairly rational, I suppose. But it's prompted by the imitative instinct and a rather dreay reversed snobbery – being as like a polytechnic or whatever as possible. It's also prompted – much more it's prompted – by straight anti-college feeling. They don't want any longer to live in groups of two to four hundred chaps, presided over by fatherly dons and big-brotherly donlets. They want to be out on their own – ten thousand of them, or thereabouts.'

(J.I.M. Stewart 1977: 154)

Collegiality – the very essence of Oxbridge, the thing that most sets it apart from not-Oxbridge – is under threat. Nor does the threat come only from students. Some clerks prove treasonable. Lancaster College, Cambridge has a devious, unprincipled Master. A group of his college's undergraduates have been jailed for smashing a tomb in the chapel. He trades agreement to allow the released students back to the college for left-wing fellows' agreement not to make trouble over his ennoblement (Raven 1976: 269, 284). One of these fellows had been the foolish Chaplain, Oliver Clowes – '"one of these new progressive clerics who hardly seem to believe in God at all and apparently picture Christ as some kind of revolutionary guerilla from South America"' (Raven 1970: 41) – but he was redeemed by surrendering his life to protect the college chapel's altar against student stormtroopers. A second is Lord Beyfus (note the anti-Semitic play on Dreyfus), a writer of 'scabby sociological tracts' (Raven 1970: 78) manipulated by his remorselessly levelling lover, Mona Carrington. Mona explains to Beyfus why money from the sale of Lancaster farms must be devoted to building new hostels: because '"more people – many more people – have to be educated, despite the obstructionism of a tradition-oriented elite". "Meaning?" "Higher numbers and fuck standards"' (Raven 1970: 77). Tony Beck is an English literature tutor at Lancaster:

'he, if any man living, must realise the importance of standards; and yet, although nothing on earth would make him drop his own, he seems to think that the 'new culture'

121

requires their general replacement by something which he calls 'co-operative evaluations'. These, as far as I understand it, are arrived at in committee or even, ideally, in public assembly.'

(Raven 1970: 39)

Raven has open contempt for what he sees as infantile New Left academics. Other authors are more discreet, but none dissents. In 1986, when leftist agitation was no more than a dimming rosy recollection in ageing hippies' minds, the mock-Oxbridge not-Oxbridge Ashfield University still suffers from subversive polit-icking. Dane combines his occupation of the university's chair of English with a privy life as Britain's secret service supremo. There is a move to remove him from the Deanship of Arts '"and replace him with a little pseud fellow-traveller named Jason who is currently a Senior Lecturer [in history]. Jason is part of the trendy Marx comedy there at the moment"' (Gethin 1986: 23).

Oxbridge students' attempts to copy not-Oxbridge is construed as the threat of a covert not-Oxbridge utilitarianism. This, we have seen, is taken to have a middling class location. But student action is also an emulation of proletarian manners. Youth culture has led Oxford undergraduates to copy working-class dress styles. 'In these tight Levi jeans, and in that anomalous upper garment of American suggestion', Bruno Landreth is 'indistinguishable in the streets of Oxford from a lad out of the motor works' (J.I.M. Stewart 1963: 27). Mungo Lockhart and Ian Cardower, newly arrived in Oxford, are unable to distinguish undergraduates from car workers: '"Why shouldn't they be students? They just happen to have disguised themselves as young heroes of labour from the motor-works at Cowley. Or they may be young heroes of labour disguised as students. Nobody can tell"' (J.I.M. Stewart 1973: 37). Three attacks are mounted on Lancaster College, Cambridge. One is Carrington and Beyfus's attempt to cover Scholar's Meadow with self-serviced bedsits. This seeks to destroy Oxbridge residential patterns. The other two challenge college discipline and organ-ized religion. In the first, an undergraduate is suborned to spend a highly publicized night in college with his doxy. The second is a full-blooded assault on the college chapel on Madrigal Sunday. Both are masterminded from outside Lancaster by a sinister travelling Jewish agitator named Mayerston: '"A prophet," says

Beck, '"to bring the people out of Egypt"' (Raven 1970: 87). His squad of travelling henchmen is 'all of them dressed much alike in elegant yet somehow proletarian garments of leather' (1970: 134). In their elegantly fetishistic uniform disguise, the enemies of culture swim like fish in the proletarian sea.

For these are culture's enemies. Agitation by students and treasonable dons threatens established hierarchies between teachers and taught. That is bad enough. Worse is the threat to established hierarchy among British universities. Such threats had been faced before. A radical Oxford fellow, Herriott had sought to make Oxford more like not-Oxbridge: '"Fundamentally the idea of universal mediocrity had a great appeal for him"' (T. Robinson 1961: 163). Fortunately Herriott was murdered before his plan could mature. Now, a decade later, Oxford and Cambridge risk real marginality: they risk being decentred. The Master of King's College, Oxford fancies that his university '"is a little out of fashion for the moment"' (Price 1972: 80). That marks the deepest threat: the collapse of privilege. Crawford, a Cambridge Whig, had thought this inevitable:

> The one thing on which all serious people were agreed, all over the world, was that privilege must be done away with; the amount of it had been whittled down steadily ever since he was a young man. All the attempts to stop this process had failed, just as reaction in its full sense had always failed. All over the world people were no longer prepared to see others enjoying privilege.
>
> (Snow 1960: 65)

Most university novelists deny Crawford's judgement. If good men prove true then an invaluable privilege can be saved.

> It was not simply fear of failure that was the horror grinning on Audley's pillow [in Ryland's College, Cambridge], but also that he too was a product of that privileged world which took its proved quality for granted. It was a world that had taken some hard knocks as the pressure for quantity rather than quality had built up against it, but it was not beaten yet – and Butler rather suspected now that when its last barricade went up he would be on the same side of it as Audley.
>
> (Price 1972: 139)

Privilege must be defended in Oxford and Cambridge, for proletarian and utilitarian attacks on those places are merely the prelude to a much wider attack on central symbols of English culture. Having levelled Lancaster College, Cambridge, Mona Carrington intends to bring down the monarchy and the House of Lords (Raven 1970: 90–1).

Threads of treachery lead beyond Britain's shores to the KGB, perennially watching for opportunities to sap the English cultural citadel. Was it mere coincidence, Jocelyn Davey invites the reader to speculate, that saw Special Branch brass visiting Nuffield College rather often during Oxford's student disturbances?

> There was a thin line in looking at students. It was absurd to take them seriously, yet one needed to know who was pulling the strings and whom they were recruiting. MI5, with Scotland Yard closely in tow, never forget the message of Cambridge in the thirties – Burgess, Maclean, Philby, and all the rest of them awaiting posthumous identification. The wild student of yesterday could become the highly respectable mole of today. There was no law that kept it all to Cambridge.
>
> (Davey 1982: 16).

How true. Emily Bryant is a mole dug deeply into Oxford's soft underbelly (Lejeune 1987). It appears that Dane's troubles at Ashfield stem from KGB destabilization, until we are shown that Dane, dying, was organizing a masterful piece of black propaganda against the enemy (Gethin 1986). Back in Oxford, Dzerzhinsky Square seeks to set up a high-flying civil service mole by establishing a ringer for a brilliant King's College, Oxford, undergraduate. They cover this attempt with a feigned subversion against students at the new Cumbria University whose boss, Gracey, '"is one of the few provincial vice-chancellors who are determined on quality rather than quantity in his student body"'. This assertedly Oxbridge attitude in a not-Oxbridge university sends David Audley scuttling north for a stint as the first Nasser Memorial Fellow: '"It happens to be an interesting experiment, what Gracey's trying to do here at Cumbria. We [the cloud of British security agencies, that is] thought it made him a prime KGB target"' (Price 1972: 84–5, 112).

Subversion against Oxbridge merges with and mirrors subversion against England. Oxbridge novelists run scared: like many senior members of the two English ancient universities, J.I.M. Stewart tells us.

> For those were days in which all such people subscribed to gloom and doom. The Establishment had not been so frightened, I told myself, since the railings went down in Hyde Park and Matthew Arnold, that prince among dons, had gone round crying woe.
>
> (J.I.M. Stewart 1977: 132)

But this was not the only possible donnish attitude displayed to us in novels. We see some monsters: a few teachers – Beck, Beyfus, and Carrington (Raven 1970), Kirk (Bradbury 1975), Ashe (Shaw 1981) – sought to catch the revolutionary wave. Other teachers declared armed neutrality, distancing themselves through ironic detachment.

> For the second time within a few days I was listening to the voice of young Oxford in insurgence. . .
> 'They don't usually come out again after tea,' Professor Babcock said. 'And they always break up in time for it – just as with their rowing and rugger and so on.'
> In this remark I recognised one resource of senior Oxford in coping with the phenomenon unleashed upon it. Demos were rags and no more.
>
> (J.I.M. Stewart 1976: 153)

For a novelist like Simon Raven this would look like immoral complacency. Stewart would disagree, seeing in it a different kind of defence. Amused tolerance is his habitual stance towards agitation. He applies it to Oxford students in the mass. An administrative building is sat-in, with the intention of bringing the university to its knees by blocking salary payments.

> Then it was discovered they had occupied the wrong offices. This one didn't send the dons their cheques; it administered university estates – and in so devious a manner that the total surcease of its operations would probably pass unremarked by anyone for several years.
>
> (J.I.M. Stewart 1973: 52)

More generally,

> A term would begin in calm, while the young men and
> women rapidly hatched their plots in privacy. Then there
> would be eruptions. 'Demos' would be held, buildings sat in
> by sitters-in, strikes and boycotts decreed, walls scrawled over
> with cheerfully inflammatory graffiti – all in the interest of
> programmes beyond the power of men to achieve. . . . Then
> suddenly it would be all over, since the proponents of various
> forms of revolution had switched to fixing up their charter
> flights for vacations in Istfahan or Cathay.'
>
> (J.I.M. Stewart 1976: 92)

Stewart applies the same technique to individuals. Dave – we
never learn his surname – is an Oxford undergraduate. He holds
inflammatory views, being 'quite capable of asserting roundly that
all property was theft' (M. Innes 1980: 117). Fear not, however.
Dave is the son of the richest man in England, and denigrates the
'bourgeois habit' of photography. Like the young John Appleby,
he drives an elderly Bentley. 'He seemed to be the sort of young
man whose notion of professional activity includes becoming an
officer in the Brigade of Guards' (M. Innes 1980: 104). Dave, not
the proctors, is a paper tiger. Treated gently, age will bring him to
sober sense. The same is true of his mate, the novel's central
character.

> Timothy Barcroft was twenty two, and at twenty had
> experienced brief fame or notoriety. As a student he had
> come to hold strong views on the evils of capitalist society,
> nuclear weapons, sub-human housing, racialism, the CIA,
> and numerous other conditions and institutions that ought
> simply not to be. His condemnations and indignations
> tended to be on the sweeping side, and he was at various
> times a nuisance to sundry authorities with whom he came in
> conflict. Much of this happened because he was a very nice
> young man; and it was one of his chronic troubles, even
> grievances, that many, although by no means all, of his
> elected Aunt Sallys persisted in so regarding him even after
> he had taken a good hard swipe at them. He felt he wasn't

being treated seriously – which is an unforgivable offence against the sensibilities of the generous young. . . . Tim was no more than a confused Oxford undergraduate, who had hung on to his studies because he contrived to see some of them as in some way 'relevant' to the social phenomenon which clamoured to be sorted out.

(M. Innes 1980: 23–4)

Repressive toleration will sort out Tim as it will sort out Dave. If senior Oxford keeps its head, then the essential reasonableness of the place will disarm all juvenile subversion.

One marches and gestures and shouts in 'confrontations' of the most authentic sort. But there are no riot police at the other end of the street, and from below the level eyebrows of their straight-headed Tudor windows the dim and ancient buildings, discouragingly domestic and forebearing and benevolent, survey the shindy with an air of inexpugnable repose. It must be excessively frustrating.

(J.I.M. Stewart 1977: 105)

Sit tight and trouble will go away: that is the message. It derives some support from Oxbridge's asserted marginality in the protest movement. Insurrection's cutting edge – and the journalists gathering like vultures – is to be found elsewhere. Oxford sit-ins are 'adequately serviced with hamburgers, cokes, top pop groups, and instructive allocutions by visiting persons understood to be in the forefront of insurgence in distant places' (J.I.M. Stewart 1977: 104). We have had two of these distant places identified: the new universities of Essex and Sussex. Tribulation at an ex-CAT shows us a third: 'This term had brought new and more assertive students and two lecturers, fresh from the London School of Economics with revolutionary ideas about the way things should be organised' (Pym 1986: 138).

Characteristically Pym's dim ex-CAT cannot even get disruption right (1986: 5): 'This summer the students had rioted, though mildly compared with others who appeared to have more worthy grievances. Ours concerned themselves with trivia, ranging from the provision of slot machines for contraceptives to complaints about the food.' Elsewhere, things are managed better.

> Ashfield University dated back to the 1860s and was not so
> much redbrick as mock-Gothic – the Vice-Chancellor's little
> joke. The establishment tutored in a variety of disciplines. At
> various times these had included riotous assembly and the
> occupation of offices – his second little joke.
>
> (Gethin 1986: 25)

Cumbria University sees a confrontation between the forces of
order and student insurgents on Hadrian's Wall, that earlier
boundary between civilization and barbarism (Price 1972).
Rummidge University is brought to a standstill by student sit-ins,
causing the maddened professor of English to be retired
prematurely after he is detected stalking the campus, defending
culture with his elephant gun (Lodge 1975: 161–2). In central
London an escaped elephant sparks a riot which is quickly
exploited by students carrying banners reading *'We Demand
Participation'* (Hoyle and Hoyle 1971a: 81–2). In Watermouth
University radicalism is so deeply rooted that the machiavellian
Howard Kirk needs to do no more than hint – untruthfully – that
a geneticist unfairly suspected of racist predilections has been
invited to the campus, to bring the university's work grinding to a
halt (Bradbury 1975). Staunton University is to have a fine new
Media Complex, funded jointly by the state and local private
subscriptions. The plan is threatened, and the university's work
disrupted, when students discover that the man running the local
subscription campaign is boss of a company that operates a colour
bar. A protest is mounted against 'tainted money': it collapses only
when it is shown that the demand for discriminatory employment
policies came not from management, but from that unionized
work-force idolized by the revolting students (Raphael 1976:
203–50).

Revolting students melted away as rapidly as they had gathered,
leaving the discourse of British university novels shaken but
unbroken. Curiously unproletarian in origin despite their
protestations – remember Pasolini's description of Paris students
attacking the CRS in May 1968 as the bourgeoisie attacking the
proletariat – they provided an image of what real proletarian
insurrection might look like if the sleeping Playful Giant ever
woke. The working class is always with us, a perennial internal

threat to cultural order. Centuries of practice have shown culture's
defenders how to resist this threat. Science's inexorable rise
represents a more difficult challenge. The next chapter examines
this challenge.

Chapter Six

BARBAROUS SCIENTISTS

In wartime St Christopher's College, Oxford 'there were more people reading science and fewer reading arts, and this Nigel, with the instinctive snobbery of the arts man, deplored' (Crispin 1944: 34). Fifteen years later, C.P. Snow countered that

> No young scientist of any talent would feel that he isn't wanted or that his work is ridiculous, as did the hero of *Lucky Jim*, and, in fact, some of the disgruntlement of Amis and his associates is the disgruntlement of the under-employed arts graduate.
>
> (Snow 1959: 24)

There is a distinct aroma of the primary school playground on the surface of this exchange, but there are deeper currents at work.

Stark stereotypes govern novelists' accounts of science and anti-science. Fred Hoyle's *Ossian's Ride* is a scientific romance marked by the rosiest Utopianism. Aliens have escaped the death of their own planet, and have settled in south-west Ireland. There, in ersatz-human bodies, they strut their scientific stuff. The Industrial Corporation of Eire – their front organization –

> is *science*, science in control of itself, an organisation run by scientists. In the world at large, science is forced to serve many masters. Here scientists are asked to serve only science itself. That is the real reason why we are forging far ahead, of why in a few short years we shall have none to rival us.
>
> (Hoyle 1959: 184)

The hero, a Cambridge-educated mathematician, needs little convincing. Earlier, he had given us a lesson in crude technological determinism:

How wrong it is to imagine that economics represent the prime moving factor in historical change. Give every man fifty pounds and let him spend it on beer, cigarettes, and horse-racing, and there will be no historical change. But give every man a television set costing fifty pounds and there will be a change of significance, a change that may even turn out to be profound. It is not money that is important in itself, but the things that one can buy with money. So much is a mere truism. But it is not a truism to say that what one can buy depends on technology, not on economics. Technology is the key to social change.

(Hoyle 1959: 64)

One wonders what he makes of a Britain where almost every person does have a television set, and the *Sun* sells more copies than any other newspaper. It may be change, but is it development towards ICE's rational science-based Utopia?

Not content with defending science after his lights, in a later joint book Hoyle took the attack to the humanists. Every problem has a simple solution, he assures us. The difficulty is to isolate the relevant evidence.

Physicists would describe most of what happens in everyday life as 'noise.' This is best explained by saying that 'noise' consists of activity without information content. 'Signal' consists of genuine information. A signal-to-noise problem in physics consists in digging out genuine information from activity without content.

With this understood, it is possible to assess what goes on in the press and in our universities. The protagonists of studies in the humanities fail to appreciate the extent to which their problems are of the signal-to-noise kind, difficult problems too, often with little signal. Instead of separating the noise – throwing it away as the physicists do – they spend their energies chasing through every detail of the darned stuff. Students of history do this with ferocious concentration, spending year after year studying their 'period' as they call it. Students of sociology might indeed be described as the ultimate students of noise, literally and figuratively. Instead of putting a smart stop to this nonsense, universities are

131

proceeding energetically to expand it. The predictable consequence is bedlam.

(Hoyle and Hoyle 1971a: 120)

It is no surprise that an uncomplicated scientism like this should generate its opposite. C.E. Vulliamy (1961) might have been thinking of Hoyle when he wrote that

Men of science are curiously naive, and even childish, in their approach to life as a whole. In this respect they are not excelled by the most completely self-satisfied of retired generals or the most authoritative of the clergy. Like so many other people, admirable indeed within the sphere of their own abilities, these cloistered and abstracted men profess, and are dangerously severe in professing, to have a soundness of judgement as valid and as valuable in all the affairs of the world as it is in the laboratory or the study.

(Vulliamy 1961: 92)

Note how Vulliamy attacks scientists by employing a conventionally hostile stereotype of university humanists as 'cloistered' and 'abstracted'; instead of challenging the dominant discourse he turns it against a pariah group, and thus reinforces it. Raymond Postgate (1953: 117–18) avoids this trap while making much the same criticism of scientists' trained incapacity for public affairs. No matter how skilled he may be in his own bailliewick, Postgate tells us, a scientist is likely to make two kinds of disastrous error when crashing into the political and administrative domain. The first is to place excessive trust in theories derived inductively from apparently uncomplicated facts. The scientist fails to recognize that political, economic and social theories are essentially metaphorical, needing the exercise of careful interpretative judgement. The second danger, splendidly illustrated by Hoyle, is a disproportionate self-confidence. Both need the quietus.

Others are willing to share in wielding the bare bodkin. '"Among the benefits of the growth of science, you know,"' Robert Raven asserts, '"is this: that it gives the Theodores – talented, second-rate men – something more or less useful to do. His sort of fair-to-medium intellectual energy is drained off elsewhere"' (M. Innes 1945: 80). Paul Wainwright, professor of English in a minor redbrick, constantly trumpets 'the selfish stupidity of scientists'

(Middleton 1987: 31). He might have been thinking of Edwin Melkarth, an astute self-made chemist and businessman with a string of external London degrees. Offered a doctorate for 200 dollars by a postal university in Nebraska, 'Professor Melkarth, who combined remarkable professional skill with an almost incredible naivety, jumped at the offer' (M. Harrison 1951: 11). In Oxford, within the bleak angularities of Anthea Lambert's laboratory 'forces of incredible violence were controlled by men of unassuming manners and restricted conversation' (J.I.M. Stewart 1954: 8). The Master of King's College speaks of chemistry as though it was 'some kind of physical handicap' (Price 1972: 98). '"Fancy pretending you're educated just because you know how an engine works,"' Hickes snorts. '"These Bachelors of Science are no more educated than my old boot"' (T. Robinson 1961: 99). In the same book we learn that another character, Reece, '"didn't realise the implications of what he was suggesting. He was a typical scientist in that respect, I'm afraid"' (T. Robinson 1961: 163).

British scientists tend, Snow (1959: 18–19) tells us, to be irreligious, to be politically radical, and to be moving up the social scale. Many post-war university novelists reflect these perceptions. Albert Woods is born into the lower middle class in a Midland city, and takes a first degree and a Masters degree in organic chemistry at the local university. He arrives in Oxford on a scholarship, and moves via an Oxford fellowship to a chair at London and a fellowship of the Royal Society. He is prevented from crowning a successful career with a knighthood only when political conviction impels him to bawl out a Cabinet minister's anti-Semitic wife at a party (W. Cooper 1952). William Watershute is a top-flight nuclear physicist with leftist views. He simulates defection to Moscow, and the consequent loss of his Oxford fellowship, in order to bring two dissident Russian physicists under the wire (J.I.M. Stewart 1978). Professor Sharkey, who steps from a moving train as a consequence of disorientation following unwise self-administered sensory deprivation experiments, is an 'Oxford Biologist, aged sixty-seven, Nobel Prize Winner, gentleman of good family, leftist views' (Kennaway 1963: 7). Donald Howard is yet another leftist, a physicist detected apparently faking evidence critical for his Cambridge research fellowship election. This presents Francis Getliffe with a difficult choice: he is torn between ambition for his college's Mastership and a sense that Howard has suffered injustice. That he chooses the moral course and defends Howard follows, we are to understand, from the fact that 'Francis himself, like many of his fellow-scientists, had been far to the left. Now he was respectable, honoured, he had moved a little nearer to the centre, but not all that much' (Snow 1960: 14). The Master whom Getliffe seeks to succeed is a physiologist, 'One of the best biologists alive' (Snow 1951: 78). His privileged position in a privileged university notwithstanding, Crawford asserts that '"The disappearance of privilege – if you want something that gives you the direction of time's arrow . . . that's as good as anything I know"' (Snow 1960: 65). An Oxford physics professor is 'responsible for all the atom-bashing and so forth that goes on' (J.I.M. Stewart 1967: 37).

> Most of Charles Blaine's colleagues suspected him of being a haunted man. He lived, the President [of his college] liked to say, deep in unfathomable mines of never failing skill – a skill which he then had to place in the hands of a society to which only an optimist would issue so much as bows and arrows. Blaine's regular recourse to the idiom of classical communism was thought to be a reflex of this unease.
>
> (J.I.M. Stewart 1967: 59)

Sir Ronald Callender, a microbiologist, 'was the establishment scientist, carefully uncommitted politically, who personified to everyone's reassurance the poor boy who had made good and stayed good' (James 1972: 30). A student is murdered in a Gothic hall of residence at North London College in order to prevent her exposing a young chemistry lecturer's communist activities – which, it is asserted (Nash 1962: 207), would have been '"enough to jeopardise your career as a scientist"'. Finally, Ashe rolls into a single bundle all these elements. He is an outstanding mathematician, but 'he behaves like a sociologist' (Shaw 1981: 4). 'An indefinable accent appeared as his anger rose. . . . "You made the mistake," he said [to his aristocratic mistress], "of thinking I was a gentleman underneath"' (1981: 9–10). Ashe is 'an uncompromising radical, not a socialist or yet a Marxist, but a committed revolutionary devoted to the annihilation of the existing social structure' (1981: 8). He occupies college rooms that 'would have been gracious in other hands. As it was, they exhuded a bleakly utilitarian atmosphere' (1981: 80). Invited to cast his fellow's vote on which part of Beaufort College's fabric should be refurbished, he replies contemptuously:

> It's the Establishment preserving itself whatever you do. This College – Oxford – it's part of the whole bloody corrupt system. Its elitism sickens me and as far as I'm concerned it can fall down, the quicker the better. . . . You can put my vote towards the chapel. It's the most fossilized part of the whole medieval farce. I'll support anything that makes it look more ridiculous, if that's possible.
>
> (Shaw 1981: 17)

When Ashe is found strangled, we are to see that justice has been done through crime. Similarly the chemist Bowles-Ottery poisons himself when sentenced to hang for a murder he did not commit, after having escaped conviction for a string of murders which he did: 'for Justice (like her sister, Truth) may wear the mask of irony' (Vulliamy 1952: 255). The world – Oxford's little world – is well rid of both men. Branchfield, 'this miserable town with its third-rate university' (Devine 1969: 7), is similarly well rid of Rhys-Jones, a potty senior lecturer in zoology who had been employing the chaos engineered by student protest to rid the world of students who he took to be parasites. It is no surprise, given British university fiction's running subtext, that Ashe is murdered by a historian, Rhys-Jones exposed by a classicist.

The cast for Oxbridge senior common room novels typically comprises humane scholars: cohorts of philosophers, classicists and historians, regiments of litterateurs. Scientists are scattered thinly, seldom more than one to each book. They may be rare but, like yeast, their effect is marked. They provide a leaven, usually of malice. This is particularly true of whodunits. Oxbridge scientists have an extraordinary propensity to die violently, or to make others die violently. We have a fine crop of murderers. The undergraduate Geoffrey Ourglass, 'a first-rate scientist – as brilliant as we now realise him to have been unscrupulous' (M. Innes 1951: 301), kills for profit. Among his seniors, Mottram kills the wrong man in attempting to save the woman he dumbly loves from a cad's embrace (Masterman 1933). Bowles-Ottery applies what he thinks of as Social Service Through Selective Elimination – the police prefer to call it murder – to dominant university figures blocking his promotion to an Ockham [Oxford] chair

135

(Vulliamy 1952). Baby Link is abducted, and feared murdered, by a mad Oxford savant intent on using the child as a surrogate baby orang-utang in a psychological experiment (Farrer 1955). Sir Ronald Callender, the eminent microbiologist, kills his son for family and financial reasons, then covers his tracks by hiring a private investigator to look for the son (James 1972). Christopher Roope, a long-haired scientist and a fellow of Christ Church, murders to protect a profitable fraud in the Foreign Examinations Syndicate at Oxford (Dexter 1977). Proffy, identified no more exactly than as 'some kind of scientist', kills two people while unsuccessfully seeking to kill his mistress' son; like Mottram, he is a scientist who cannot even kill competently. His motivation, we are told, is '"The hatred of the old for the young. Must be all too easily encouraged by life at Oxford"' (Fraser 1985: 44, 220). Motives are scattered, individual; much like the motives that taxi-drivers or accountants might have for murder.

Some scientists are victims of murderous violence. Brauer, a Polish fellow of St Nicholas', Cambridge, is executed by men who discover that he had worked, under coercion, as a medical experimenter in Nazi concentration camps (Clinton-Baddeley 1967). Professor Reece is executed 'because he was attempting to spread the gospel of the Natural Sciences (which Dr Browning and Dr Hickes believed to be alien to the Oxford tradition) and, even worse, spread it at the expense of the Parks, one of Oxford's chief ornaments' (T. Robinson 1961: 214). Ashe's murderer is unrepentant about deed or implement. '"I killed him with a Beaufort tie,"' Brereton tells the police, '"as a pathetic gesture of defiance, to show that the heritage of which Beaufort is part has the guts to defend itself"' (Shaw 1981: 182).

Motives here are consistent, focused. It is wrong to kill, no doubt, but in each of these cases a higher moral imperative is wheeled forward: the defence of culture. '"I would kill Ashe again,"' Brereton tells us. '"He and his kind want to destroy a whole culture"' (Shaw 1981: 182). The threat is to Oxford-as-England, of course: the death of Oxford culture would mean the end of English culture. And the threat is widespread. A late J.I.M. Stewart short story (1986: 109–35) has Martin Brand, Galen Professor of Physike and Chirurgerie in Oxford University, suspected of initiating a devastating outbreak of contagious dyslexia in the university. Whether he did it or not, only a scientist could be suspected of spreading word-blindness: the ultimate crime in logocentric humane Oxford. Many scientists, not all of whom end up with a shiv between the ribs, are in the business of changing Oxbridge's nature. Pacey, for example, wants to make Oxford more like not-Oxbridge. He urges that the university should be strengthened at the colleges' expense; that it should take over all teaching from the colleges, which would become mere residential hostels with shared kitchens. He attacks university sport as a waste of time (Masterman 1952: 48, 51, 176). Ashe is – or was – more radical: for him attacking Oxford was merely part of a general assault on privileged British institutions. He was also unusually forthright about his intentions. Most scientists threaten culture not through policy, but inadvertently. Merely being there, living as barbarians in the citadel, they pollute culture's thin, sacred stream.

Scientists erode collegiality. This is for two reasons. First, they lack the tacit knowledge necessary to live easily in a cultured senior common room. Winn notes that Mottram was elected a research fellow of St Thomas' College, Oxford in the expectation that he would ripen into a medical scientist of European fame.

> Socially, however, he was hardly a success. He was shy and silent, sometimes even *farouche*. In manner he seemed almost always to be on the defensive, and he had little or none of the easy companionability of the other men of his generation .... He cared little for sport or literature or society, and after a time he sank as it were into the background of our Common Room life.
>
> (Masterman 1933: 20)

Mottram's suicide note gives his side of the story.

> I can never forget my first night in Common Room. Half the table was discussing a political novel which had just been published, and I had never heard the author's name, much less those of the people about whom he wrote; Hargreaves was discussing cricket, and I had never seen or even wished to see a first-class match; Shepardson was speaking of wine, and I could not tell a claret from a burgundy. All your interests and your conversation and even your jokes were strange and alien and incomprehensible to me. One by one

137

you tried to draw me into conversation, and one by one you gave me up. I was a member of Common Room, but I might just as well not have been there, for all the difference my presence made. I blame no one; you had your language and it wasn't mine.

(Masterman 1933: 148-9)

The second reason why scientists erode collegiality is the way in which they have to go about being scientists. Nineteenth-century colleges had science laboratories, but these proved increasingly inadequate. The university took over the task of providing adequate laboratories (Masterman 1952: 72, 232). A scientist's life, whether as don or undergraduate, came to be centred in university facilities rather than in the college. '"Scientists are a closed book to me"', the Provost of an Oxford college confides. '"They come into college to do some old-fashioned teaching – listening to essays, I suppose, although heavens knows what an essay on molecular physics can be like – and then they go back to some lab or other and get on with their job"' (J.I.M. Stewart 1978: 32). 'It was Mottram's habit to work in the laboratory, which was in South Parks Road, four or five evenings a week. Sometimes he went early, sometimes late, often he stayed for the greater part of the night' (Masterman 1933: 35). Independently of his feelings of incongruity, this would have prevented Mottram from dining much in hall, from being clubbable in the senior common room. He is not alone in this. Fothergill, the only scientist in Fisher College, Cambridge, had rooms which 'were typical of a young, hard-working Fellow with few interests but his work' (Rees 1945: 123). Venables, an Exeter College, Oxford chemist described as Britain's leading bacteriologist, 'spent the greater part of every day and often part of the night in the laboratory . . . "The laboratory was his mistress. No wine, women and song for him"' (Mais 1949: 67). Beaufort, Oxford contained 'one or two scientists whose obscure researches in the Clarendon Laboratory made their appearances in College so rare as to make them unknown to all but the Bursar, who paid their salaries' (Shaw 1981: 61). Seeking to defend collegiate Oxford against 'uniformity and a monotonous mediocrity', Prendergast brings Pacey to boiling point by asserting that undergraduates reading for inhumane disciplines threaten the institution's essence:

138

'Of course the scientists present a difficulty. They are, almost of necessity, cut off from the rest in their laboratories, living in a world of their own – but even they must gain something from the fact that we have a residential system. However much they try, they cannot altogether escape from contacts with humane persons, and they must gain some tincture of culture even if they only see their contemporaries in Hall or on the playing fields.'

(Masterman 1952: 227)

The university laboratories represent an erosion of collegiate Oxbridge, a penetration by not-Oxbridge. Further erosion is to be discovered within this salient. Oxford science readers seek promotion to professorial chairs 'not, as they will invariably hasten to say, because they want status for themselves, but because they want status for their subject' (W. Cooper 1952: 29). The not-Oxbridge university looms, structured by disciplines rather than by colleges. Within a department social relationships are as hierarchical as in not-Oxbridge, and justified in similarly mythic terms: in Oxford, 'Above Dibdin there was the professor of one of the main departments of chemistry. He was always referred to as the Professor or the Prof. His name, like that of certain tribal deities, was never uttered' (W. Cooper 1952: 30). The late Professor Sharkey's Oxford biology department is similarly hierarchical, similarly not-Oxbridge (Kennaway 1963: 18).

The stoutest defence against these threats is to spike the enemy's guns. A good tactic is to acculturate scientific barbarians. Mottram might have been a hopeless case: others are not. The safest policy is to recruit sound chaps, to ensure that a scientist has a suitable educational background. As a result of 'his liberal training in the Humanities and especially in Greek literature', Kerris Bowles-Ottery had a respectable cultural competence: 'He combined, in the rarest way, classical scholarship with immense ability in his profession – that of a chemist' (Vulliamy 1952: 14). The only odd thing about this passage, apart from the unfortunate light shed on it by Bowles-Ottery's subsequent career as a mass-murderer, is the assertion that this general cultural competence is rare. Other novels show us other examples. '"Ah, the right kind of scientist," Ambrose said approvingly. "Classical education. Newton and Darwin, not to mention Leibnitz, of

139

course"' (Davey 1982: 42). Martin is 'an old-fashioned scientist of some kind, who prided himself on numerous extraneous interests. ("I can give you the date of the battle of Salamis," he liked to say. "But can you give me the atomic weight of helium?")' (J.I.M. Stewart 1967: 52). 'Jenkins, a physicist and one of the few science dons in St Old's [Oxford], had just returned from a visit to Harwell. "Reminded me of the common room in a girls' school," he said. "There's a stifling atmosphere of specialisation"' (Spencer 1961: 65). The implied contrast, of course, is the urbane generalism of St Old's Senior Common Room. An Oxford physics professor 'had once christened a laboratory after his favourite character in fiction, and consequently been suspected of communist leanings by some august scientific body whose members imagined that Oblomov was a physicist belonging to the Soviet Union' (Ross 1960: 130). One notes the illiteracy of massed scientists, contrasted with the cultivation of the Oxford man. The apogee of scientific cultivation is an immensely fat man, one of J.I.M. Stewart's finest comic burlesques.

> Freshmen would nudge each other in the street and intimate with awe that there was Mark Bultitude. If they were scientists they cherished hopes that their own tutors (who had proved to be insufferably dull) might be persuaded to arrange for their transfer to the care of this scintillating intelligence. If on the other hand they pursued more humane studies, but were sufficiently well-born, wealthy, good-looking or clever to have some hope of making Mark Bultitude's dinner-table, they importuned sundry uncles, god-fathers, former house-masters and others of the great man's generation and familiar acquaintance, to open up some avenue to this grand social advancement. Of all this Mark Bultitude approved. He valued highly his reputation as Oxford's most completely civilised being.
>
> (M. Innes 1951: 78–9)

Science can be permitted to enter culture's keep. '"Gavin and I are progressive,"' Jeremy Shefford tells Charles Blaine. '"We know Greek and Latin; we know all about the minor Caroline poets. But we think that Oxford should have more and more stinks, and more and more bangs"' (J.I.M. Stewart 1967: 180). But there is to be no automatic right of entry. Posterns are guarded by humanists watchful for forged passports. Only scientists like Martin, deferential to humanism's hegemony, are to be admitted. 'A university would be no use to him without whatever kind of old-fashioned laboratory he pottered round, but he knew that a university ought to contain other things as well' (J.I.M. Stewart 1967: 61). Even Pacey is willing to trade a vague requirement that humanities undergraduates should have to show a modest competence in some natural science for the specific commitment that Oxford science undergraduates must have Latin (Masterman 1952: 228). Artefacts of a micro-culture which suspects and despises science though such judgements might be, scientists must respect Oxbridge *ukazes*. When Callender failed to get a Cambridge fellowship after a brilliant undergraduate career,

> He used to say that it was because he hadn't influence, but I think he may not have been quite clever enough. In Harrogate we thought him the cleverest boy in the grammar school. But then, Cambridge is full of clever men.
>
> (James 1972: 125)

A civilized scientist is conceivable; but only when, like Mark Bultitude, his science is subordinated to the dictates of Oxbridge aristocratic culture masquerading as general culture. Individual scientists like Ashe may deny the legitimacy of Oxbridge privilege, but science in British university fiction mounts no general challenge to hierarchy. Oxbridge science departments tend to generate internal hierarchies. Scientists have their own chiefly totems. Nobel laureateships, fellowships of the Royal Society, gongs – 'Sir Walter Luke: Sir Francis Getliffe: Sir Arthur Mounteney: in five years' time those would be the styles' (Snow 1954: 214) – serve to keep the young bucks suitably deferential while waiting for Buggins' Turn. Snow's social co-ordinates for British scientists – leftist politics, irreligion, upward social mobility – are subordinated in a house-trained university science. Oxford scientists might wear red ties on election days, but '"The wildest and most red of all our Socialists are always the supporters of college tradition and Oxford habits. Whatever they are in politics or in the world, they are Conservatives here"' (Masterman 1952: 48). A physiologist who is master of a Cambridge college continues to dress formally, 'for Crawford, an old-fashioned Cambridge radical, had refused in matters of etiquette to make concessions to the young' (Snow 1960: 64).

If novelists are confident that natural scientists can be house-trained – recalcitrant individuals can always be executed – then they are less sanguine about social scientists. The worst of these are sociologists.

> Despite his cultivated mediocrity of mind, the Senior Tutor had seen change coming. He blamed the sciences for re-establishing the mirage of truth, and still more the pseudo-morph subjects like anthropology and economics whose adepts substituted inapplicable statistics for the ineptness of their insights. And finally there was sociology with its absurd maxim, The Proper Study of Mankind is Man, which typically it took from a man the Senior Tutor would have rejected as unfit to cox the rugger boat.
>
> (Sharpe 1974: 202)

This is *Porterhouse Blue*, combining Tom Sharpe's splenetic world-view with hazy notions of what social sciences involve. Sociology gets the boot here, but in good company. It is not always thus. Elsewhere we find admirable anthropologists (Pym 1955; Davin 1972), sympathetic psychologists (Sutherland 1987), even a less than venal economist (Davey 1976). Sociology, by contrast, almost always is attacked. The only moderately complimentary depictions appear in novels about new universities. Some colleagues of Howard Kirk's at Watermouth are not held up to ridicule: Flora Beniform is intellectually astute but sexually voracious, Henry Beamish well-meaning but doomed, Professor Marvin honest but vacillating (Bradbury 1975). Their modest virtues act to throw Kirk's evil in higher relief. Gavin Pope, Staunton University's professor of sociology, insults all the Vice-Chancellor's dinner guests before crashing drunkenly on the table (Raphael 1976: 212–19): but at least he stands up to his own revolting students. One would expect no less from a Cambridge man.

These apart, fictional accounts of sociology are consistently hostile. There is little point in running through the gloomy calendar. Instead, let us consider a writer from whom we might expect a different attitude. Barbara Pym spent many years working on a social anthropology journal. Given social anthropology's long frontier with sociology, and its own difficulty in penetrating Oxford and Cambridge universities as the result of 'the conservatism and social arrogance of those who were effectively in control of these two great institutions during the early part of this century' (Leach 1984: 6), we might expect her to provide a balanced account of sociology's strengths and weaknesses. Wrong again. Her seventh novel, *An Unsuitable Attachment* (1982), is set, as usual, in London churchy/anthropological circles. These are treated with Pym's usual wry affection. The main character, Ianthe Broome, is a librarian. We are introduced to 'the ill-mannered grubby students and cranks of all ages who frequented the library of political and sociological books where Ianthe worked'. A little later she tells somebody that 'the people who read sociological and political books don't eat exquisite and delicious food' (Pym 1982: 26, 97). Not a nice class of person. In Pym's last published novel Caro Grimstone fears that her husband, an ex-CAT ethno-historian, will be snared in Iris Horniblow's honeypot. Horniblow is a glamorous sociologist. Caro's fears abate at her rival's formal lecture. Introduced by 'the most senior of the grey sociologists', she produces a turgid lecture: 'it became apparent that the dead hand of the sociologist had been at work' (Pym 1986: 75).

This boot-work is time-hallowed. John Kramer (1979: 359) claims that Anglo-American university fiction's first sociologist appears in Robert Herrick's *Chimes* (1926), set in a lightly disguised Chicago. We can forgive him for missing an earlier character, for he turns up in the most unlikely place. A Wodehouse short story written for an American pulp magazine in the first decade of this century contains one Prosser who, for reasons much too complicated to consider here, is 'the literary loaf-slinger'.

> Owen regarded him without resentment. Since returning to London he had taken the trouble of looking up his name in *Who's Who?* and had found that he was not so undistinguished as he had supposed. He was, it appeared, a Regius Professor and the author of some half-dozen works on sociology – a record, Owen felt, that almost justified loaf-flinging and ear-hole clipping in moments of irritation.
>
> (Wodehouse 1914a: 170)

This is an interesting passage. A Regius Professor can work only at Oxford or Cambridge for Wodehouse; he recognizes no other university. Prosser holds that chair in 1910. Yet a sociology chair was not established at Cambridge until the 1970s, and Oxford still tries to pretend that the subject does not exist. Until Cambridge took the plunge in 1988 neither university offered a full undergraduate degree course in sociology. Hence a young woman's experience in 1954 of

> two serious meetings in King's [Cambridge], one on the desirability of introducing a Sociology Tripos, the other on Cambridge humanism. She had no real idea what either sociology or humanism was. . . . Most people at the Sociology meeting did not know what sociology was.
>
> (Byatt 1985: 181–2)

Hence this snippet of Oxford party conversation between a student and an African visitor:

> 'I'm a research student.'
> 'In which faculty?'
> 'I'm a sociologist. We don't have a faculty.'
> 'Really? Do you know, I had heard that, but I could not believe it.'
>
> (R. Williams 1964: 314)

Wodehouse's view of Prosser seems ambiguous. Judgement is reserved on his merit. That stops once Prosser is unmasked as the author, under the pen-name Edith Butler, of glutinous romantic fiction: 'They're simply chunks of superfatted sentiment. She's a sort of literary onion. She compels tears' (Wodehouse 1914a: 165). In Plum's frozen adolescent male world-view to write romantic fiction is the most heinous of all moral crimes. Prosser is damned, and his subject with him.

We never see Prosser do anything recognizably sociological. That is usual for British academic novelists. In Angus Wilson's *Anglo-Saxon Attitudes* (1958), for instance, it is important that one character be an Anglo-Catholic prig. It is not important that he should be a sociologist, and it is clear that Wilson knows roughly as much about sociology as did Wodehouse. Even when a novelist does know a bit more, the judgements remain harsh. J.B. Priestley's *Out of Town* (1968a) and *London End* (1968b) – recently republished in the original one-volume form as *The Image Men* (1984) – are built around two university-based sociologists. They are con-men, abandoning failing careers in philosophy and in English literature at the prospect of running a privately funded research institute. The dismal ex-CAT that takes them in already employs a professor of sociology; a grey, boring man unworthily promoted directly from an assistant lecturership at Edinburgh to Brockshire's chair through television exposure. All three flourish, like weeds.

The most interesting novelist of British sociology is Malcolm Bradbury. He was a student at Leicester in the 1950s, when Leicester had perhaps the best of the few British sociology departments (Giddens and Mackenzie 1982). He knocked around with sociology students. One of them, or a composite of several, appears as Jenkins in his Leicester-based first novel. Compared with Professor Treece – the novel's central, confused character – Jenkins has clear views. What matter if those views change according to fashion's dictates? After a conversation with Jenkins, Treece muses:

> Are there then, he asked with a mind that seemed over the last few minutes to have grown quaintly old-fashioned, in the cast of some barbarian confronted with Athens at its heyday, are there then people who do *that* and call it thought?
>
> (Bradbury 1959: 29)

As with Wodehouse, here Bradbury appears to fudge a judgement on sociology. For the next fifteen years he seemed mildly favourable under an ironic carapace. In 1960 and 1962 he co-wrote exceptionally bad pop-sociological pot-boilers of modern British manners. He contributed to a straight sociology text in 1972. Before that, in 1971 he published a book which impinged on the sociology of literature. In the introduction to that book he claimed to be writing a more substantial (and more clearly sociological) book on the same subject with Bryan Wilson, a distinguished sociologist of religion and Bradbury's friend since Leicester days. That book never appeared. Instead, we got *The History Man.*

This remains the major and, Priestley's books apart, the only British academic novel dominated by sociology. It is set in the new university of Watermouth which, 'having aspirations to relevance, has made much of sociology'. The anti-hero is Howard Kirk. Born into the boundary lands between the upper working class and the lower middle class in northern England, he slogged his unimagi-

native way to a first in sociology at Leeds. There followed a
run-of-the-mill doctoral thesis on Christadelphianism in
Wakefield. At this point he caught History's bus. Sociology, which
had been 'weighty, Germanic and dull' became light, radical and
fashionable. Howard followed; a change symbolized by the
physical shift from the hard constrictions of Leeds to the soft
availability of Watermouth. If History's bus has carried Kirk thus
far, then it can take him further. Indeed, he can try his hand at
driving. He manipulates campus politics as he manipulates
personal relationships, using his penis as the bus's gear-stick:
'"That's just what you are, Howard,' Flora Beniform tells him. 'An
historical rapist. Prodding the future into everyone you can lay
your hands on"' (Bradbury 1975: 74).

One of the people into whom Kirk is most concerned to prod
the future is Annie Callander, a lecturer in English. He crosses
Watermouth's campus to visit her:

> On the far side of the Piazza stands the Humanities Building,
> a different affair altogether from Social Sciences, a place not
> of height, mass and dark, but of length, light and air.
>
> (Bradbury 1975: 204)

To make sure that we get the point, in returning to his own room
Kirk 'goes from the light and air of Humanities to the dark and
mass of Social Science' (1975: 205). Bradbury establishes
judgements through metaphor: places and disciplines are light or
dark, white or black. This distinction draws its power from
Arnold's counter-position of the sweetness and light of culture to
the darkness of anarchy. Bradbury exploits other resources from
liberal cultural history. Kirk is a Marxist, 'the radical radical's
radical'. He privileges abstract theory over concrete experience.
That is the only privilege that he will countenance. His new book
bears the title *The Defeat of Privacy*. 'It's about the fact that there are
no more private selves, no more private properties, no more
private acts. . . .You see, sociological and psychological understanding is giving us a total view of man, and democratic society is
giving us total access to everything' (Bradbury 1975: 73). All of this
is anathema to the liberal humanism that Bradbury admires but
which, like Henry Beamish (whose appearance resembles
Bradbury's own), he believes to be doomed. Thus it is pointless to
complain that Kirk is not a believable sociologist (Cohen 1977:

533-47): he is not meant to be. Of course there is a sociology concerned to lift structural constraint off individuals – Bradbury is well aware of the fact, even referring to Goffman. But Kirk is constructed negatively: he is the antithesis of culture's virtues, a nightmare figure. He is a machiavell.

He is matched by his university. Watermouth's campus is 'a massive urban construct, lit with spots and flashes, throwing out beams and rays in the half-light, the image of an intellectual factory of high production and a twenty-four hour schedule' (Bradbury 1975: 165). We are back with Silverpump's academy: 'lights of all colours – fizz! fizz! bang! bang!' But this is factory as much as academy. Its architecture is different, but Watermouth is kin to Nesfield (M. Innes 1944: 44): 'The place was shutting down; sweetness and light were over for the day; the quest for knowledge was off until nine o'clock next morning.' Both are not-Oxbridge universities working ungentlemanly shifts. Nesfield works from nine to five, with the despised and shadowy 'engineers' working on into the evenings. Watermouth takes this to the limit, apparently working shifts round the clock. Both are knowledge factories dedicated to utilitarian gods. That is why Watermouth has made much of sociology, with its concern for 'relevance'. For Bradbury, in common with other novelists, 'relevance' is a code word for utilitarianism. 'Real' universities, remote from 'the world', resist such barbarism. But real universities find it increasingly difficult to resist utilitarian pressure. This provides the key to a puzzling feature in *The History Man*. Unlike attacks from other authors, Bradbury does not make Watermouth sociology fraudulent. Kirk and his colleagues are model academics: teaching hard, publishing books and papers, running their department. Teaching, research, and administration are performed in a thoroughly illiberal manner, but they are done. Indeed, it is Kirk's, Watermouth's, and sociology's very effectiveness that most disturbs Bradbury. Kirk believes in a History trundling along an iron plateway. Bradbury believes that all that he holds dear is about to be run down by the train.

Why is this so? What makes sociology so unpalatable not only to Malcolm Bradbury, but also to almost all British university novelists? Whence the anathema? The answer lies in British sociology's dominant discourse. Novels celebrate an unquestioned Englishness. Sociology's consistent comparative itch relativizes

English experience, roots it in historical choices rather than a timeless, God-given never-never land. Novels insist that we should genuflect to hierarchy. This has never been easy for British sociology. The conservative view that hierarchy is a natural feature of human society, outside the course of history, has been challenged consistently within the discipline. Thus a recent peer review of British sociology departments produced worthless results since 'the heads of departments took a collective decision not to co-operate'. The reason? That the process of ranking departments 'offends the instinctive egalitarianism that is part of the intellectual bedrock of the discipline' (*THES* 24 July 1987). The lack of strong old-Right intellectuals – like those to be found in German sociology, for instance – has consistently damaged British sociology's general cultural reputation.

This is reinforced by institutional factors. Sociology grew late, and stuntedly, in Oxford and Cambridge. To the extent that it ever has enjoyed – if that is the right word – an accepted internal prestige ranking, then the top group came not from Oxford and Cambridge but the London School of Economics (Halsey 1982b): and even that tender elite growth did not survive the 1960s expansion. Thus British sociology does not fetishize Englishness, is temperamentally unimpressed with hierarchy, lacks its own agreed internal hierarchy, and is weak in Oxford and Cambridge. These features are not calculated to endear the discipline to those writing, and trained to read, university novels' common subtext. Attacked by scientists like Fred Hoyle as well as by humanists like Malcolm Bradbury, sociology is a special case of British fictional science, walled in its own dreadful enclosure.

The mutual suspicion between literary folk and scientists is rooted in European cultural experience. Lepenies (1988: 1) locates it in 'the confrontation of cold rationality and the culture of the feelings – one of those antitheses which marked the conflict between the Enlightenment and the counter-Enlightenment'. In England this conflict produced a famous Victorian debate (Haight 1971: 483–94; Lepenies 1988: 163–74). On 1 October 1880 T.H. Huxley lectured on 'Science and Culture' at the new Birmingham Science College, the acorn from which the major redbrick Birmingham University would grow. He urged the denial of an educational theory which privileged classical languages over natural science. The future lay with science: English cultural elites could recognize the fact and catch the wave, or they could continue to ignore it and be swamped. The response came from Matthew Arnold. On 14 June 1882 he gave the Rede Lecture at Cambridge, on 'Literature and Science'. He urged that literature, in both classical and vernacular languages, still was essential to culture. But that did not imply the exclusion of science. Defining literature as everything ever written or printed, he claimed Euclid, Newton, and Darwin for literature. Defining science as *Wissenschaft* – as no more than systematic study – he included literary scholarship, and much else, within its boundary. The antimony between science and culture was dissolved by definition. This legerdemain did not offend his opponent. Arnold noted that there was 'really no question between Professor Huxley and me as to whether knowing the great results of the modern scientific study of nature is not required as a part of our culture' (quoted in Honan 1981: 416). Both men wanted natural science taught in schools and universities, along with literature. No wonder that, somewhat to Fanny Lucy Arnold's surprise, the two men got on well together socially (Honan 1981: 351).

This easy amicability was not repeated when the debate over science and culture was replayed some eighty years later. On 6 October 1956 C.P. Snow gave that year's Rede Lecture. His topic was 'The two cultures and the scientific revolution', a subject for which he was fitted as a physicist and practising novelist. Literary intellectuals and physical scientists formed, he said, two polar groups divided by 'a gulf of mutual incomprehension – sometimes (particularly among the young) hostility and dislike, but most of all lack of understanding' (Snow 1959: 15). The common European division between literary folk and scientists was particularly stark in England, for two reasons. First, the English have a fanatical belief in educational specialization, unmatched elsewhere. Second, the English let their social forms crystallize much more readily (Snow 1959: 15). His solution was Pacey's; a broader, more general education in which the undergraduate scientist is required to show modest competence in the humanities, and the undergraduate historian, philosopher or student of English literature must do some science.

This was an unexceptionable conclusion to an unexceptionable argument, a restatement of the middle ground reached by Arnold and Huxley. But the Sage of Downing College took exception, and vented his spleen in the 1962 Richmond Lecture. For F.R. Leavis (1962: 10) Snow knows no history. There is no evidence even that he knows any science (1962: 14). 'As a novelist he doesn't exist; he doesn't begin to exist' (1962: 13). This looks like mere mud-slinging, but Leavis's outrageous attack is rooted in his sense that Snow represents something yet more outrageous, yet more dangerous. His 'crass Wellsianism' (1962: 23) is 'a portent of our civilisation . . . our imminent tomorrow in today's America: the energy, the triumphant technology, the productivity, the high standard of living and the life-impoverishment – the human emptiness; emptiness and boredom craving alcohol – of one kind or another' (1962: 25, 26). What is stands stark against what ought to be: Snow's 'relation to the age . . . is characterised not by insight and spiritual energy, but by blindness, unconsciousness and automatism' (1962: 10). Leavis makes Snow stand for Anarchy. Guess who, for Leavis, is Culture's champion. In his admirably temperate first response (1971: 49–50), Snow asserted that Leavis consistently misquoted his words and misunderstood his arguments; in his almost equally temperate second response (1971: 83–4) he claimed that Leavis vilified him for holding views which he had never held, but which Leavis himself once propounded. This mildness, which he interpreted as mandarin repressive toleration, infuriated Leavis yet further (1972: passim). The many commentators on the 'Snow–Leavis debate' (see Cornelius and Vincent 1964) shook their heads over Leavis's lack of manners, and declared Snow the winner.

One thing emerges clearly from the ruins of the Snow–Leavis fracas. Both men were arguing from what is to what ought to be. Both were concerned with moral questions (Trilling 1962: 51). Leavis wanted to rebuild culture's citadel, because culture provides the moral ballast necessary for being fully human. It is this naval metaphor, and not any competing *double entendre*, that made 'lacks bottom' such a devastating Oxbridge judgement on a man's character. Turning to the other protagonist, Snow's Rede Lecture had three topics. Commentators and critics focused almost exclusively on the first one, his restatement of the Huxley–Arnold debate over the relation between humane culture and science. But Snow attached equal importance to the other two: a revulsion at the increasing division between the world's poor and the world's rich, and a doom-laden concern over rapid world population growth. He objected to literary intellectuals disparaging a science which they did not understand, but he also objected to the rightist politics, and – he thought – the consequent inhumanity in which that disparagement was expressed by Yeats, Pound, and Wyndham Lewis, with their 'imbecile expressions of anti-social feeling' (Snow 1959: 17). Once again the argument is grounded, and in a politics much less ambiguous than Leavis's.

This moral substrate always underlies accounts of science in British university fiction. Consider *Monkey Shines* (M. Stewart 1983). A brilliant Oxford undergraduate athlete is turned into a quadraplegic by a motorcycle accident. Despite this, he takes a congratulatory First. Modest family wealth pays for a flat constructed to permit some degree of independence while he works for his doctorate, but the money – and family support – runs out. The solution is Ella, a monkey capable of acting as his nurse and amanuensis as a result of a novel brain enhancement process. This process becomes a military secret. The hero kills Ella when he realizes that the monkey cannot develop a moral sense to match her intellectual prowess. This is a mass-murdering simian, more terrible than anything anticipated in Giles Gott's *Murder at the Zoo*. With Ella dead, we are led to believe that the nightmare is over, not knowing that two Oxford scientists have retrieved a viable foetus from her womb. The monkey could not help its amorality. To advance their own careers, the scientists choose to act immorally.

This novel stands four square in British university fiction. It takes its colour from a literary discourse that makes English educational arrangements sacred, that makes change in English educational hierarchies the end of culture as we know it, that disparages science. Masterman (1933, 1952) urged caution in drawing these conclusions for fear of hubris; most novelists do not see the danger. Consider that conservative high Anglican mystic, C.S. Lewis.

In 1944 Lewis went to Durham University, apparently for the first time, to give a series of lectures. He was intrigued by the place, and exploited the literary possibilities of a small disguised-Oxbridge collegiate institution in *That Hideous Strength*, published the following year. The 'Progressive Element' - a junta of leftist fellows – has persuaded Bracton College's governing body to sell Bragdon Wood. This is bad enough; the Wood is the centre of the college's, and England's, culture-in-nature. What makes it much worse is the purchaser: the National Institute for Co-ordinated Experiments (N.I.C.E.), a government scientific research station. The novel operates in a force-field between three places: Bracton College, anciently established in the ancient Edgestow University; the new and nasty N.I.C.E; and a mystic Christian community in a neighbouring village. The particle bounced around in this force-field, the novel's central character, is a sociologist.

Lewis is an allegorist. N.I.C.E., 'the first-fruit of that constructive fusion between the state and the laboratory on which so many thoughtful people base their hopes for a better world' (Lewis 1945: 22) is a sardonic embodiment of the ideas of that group of principally Cambridge-connected pre-war natural scientists – Bernal, Haldane, Hogben, Levy, and Needham – who forged a fictionally fateful nexus between science and leftist politics: 'The central purpose behind all of Bernal's writings', Wersky (1978: 185) tells us, 'is to show that only in socialist society can science take its rightful place as the chief servant of human liberation.' Lewis's account of the internal politics of the college is a displaced account of the contemporary politics of Magdalen, Oxford; his own college. But this can be extended. It makes sense to think of the entire force-field as Oxford: the humane college, the university science laboratories, the college chapel. At a different level the force-field stands for the tension between humanities and science, and between science and religion, in English society. Manichaean imagery specifies judgements on the three sectors. The Christian community is white, the laboratories black. The college is an institutional site for struggle between white and black, as the sociologist – representing a possible third position between science and the humanities (Snow 1971: 57–8; Lepenies 1988: 157) – is a personal site for the same struggle. Since this is a Manichaean fable, the novel's climax is an apocalypse in which white triumphs by the skin of its teeth. A series of huge explosions leaves a vast smoking pit where N.I.C.E. used to be. But not only the research establishment is destroyed. The whole of Edgestow, with its ancient university, is blown to kingdom come. Bracton College reaps the wages of its sin in having sold England's soul to science and the state. The sociologist learns that there is no third position. Having chosen the side of the angels just in time, he comes through physically unscathed and much wiser.

That Hideous Strength is evoked powerfully in what might prove to be J.I.M. Stewart's last major novel, *The Naylors* (1985). He returns here to questions about the relationship between science and culture that had appeared frequently in his earlier books. Forty years earlier, for instance, we had been told about 'one of the radical issues between the old and the young. Is science the disinterested pursuit of knowledge which the world may apply if it will? Or is it an activity always dependent upon economic and political demands?' (M. Innes 1944: 30). Scientists often appear in his thrillers: time and again he had ignored Hubert Minto's demand that 'Atom-spies ought to be put on the index with sliding panels and mysterious Chinamen – I'm raising the motion at the next meeting of the Detection Club' (Ross 1960: 55). Stewart's natural scientists habitually walked the boundary between science and espionage. 'Orchard is a great mathematician. For some reason – I don't understand such things – that makes him the best chemist in the country. We've been trying to rope him in [to wartime government science] for years. No good – a very abstract scientist indeed. But he walked into the Ministry the morning after Prague' (M. Innes 1940b: 126). Two sets of villains seek to kidnap Humphrey Paxton in order to make his father, 'beyond question the greatest of living physicists' (M. Innes 1949: 5), betray his country. John Day is a British nuclear scientist who defected to Russia. Discovered washed up on a highland beach, he declares that he was trying to undefect. At the book's end we learn the truth: having failed to rise to the top of Soviet nuclear science, he was seeking to sell his skills in south America (M. Innes 1955). Owain Allington set out his wares in a different market. He

> 'was involved with atomic energy at a pretty high level. And a feeling got around that he was doing a little horse-trading in that line.'
> 'Good God! You don't mean with the Bolsheviks?'
> 'No, not that. But with some inquiring gentlemen from the Near East.'
>
> (M. Innes 1968: 160)

In other books Stewart moves to less-trampled ground; the biological and psychological sciences. In *Operation Pax* (M. Innes 1951) John Appleby thwarts Geoffrey Ourglass's scheme to develop thought-control drugs; in *Hare Sitting Up* (M. Innes 1959), a mad biologist's threat to release a deadly virus.

All these books show a conventional respect for state authority. Consider a curious art theft. Vermeer's *Aquarium,* the jewel of Scamnum Court's collection, is stolen and overpainted with a pattern which John Appleby recognizes as the plan of Waterbath Research Station. "'The mere detailed lay-out of the Research Station could be so informative that it is among the country's top secrets at this very moment'" (M. Innes 1952: 216). Such faith: if the government says that Waterbath's layout would be useful to an enemy, then every sinew must be strained to keep it secret. In *Operation Pax* John Appleby and Mark Bultitude are worried by Ourglass's research line, but doubly worried by the fact that his enterprise is private, not warranted by the state.

All these threads are drawn together in *The Naylors.* This is yet another Oxford novel, but one that cuts into the discourse from many different directions. George Naylor is a cleric – a clerk in holy orders, reminding us yet again of Oxford's monastic origins – who has lost his faith. He is an honorary fellow of his (and Duncan Pattullo's) old college, harried by Father Adrian Hooker, an Oxford physicist turned theologian with a roving commission to round up lost clerical sheep. Note the many puns in this name. An American usage makes 'hooker' a call-girl; not relevant. English usage makes him a shepherd ('crook' becomes 'hook' in some districts): but Stewart is also pointing us to Richard Hooker (1553–1600), author of a famous treatise on the proper relationship between church and state (Coplestone 1963: 322). Father Adrian Hooker recounts (J.I.M. Stewart 1985: 23–4) the Oxford story that gives his task its shape: J.H. Newman's journey to Mark Pattison's deathbed to ease what he thought was Pattison's doctrinal perturbation (V.H.H. Green 1957: 321–3). Pattison refused to cross to Rome. George Naylor refuses to regain his faith. Newman withdrew defeated. Hooker sacrifices his mind in protecting a crowd of children from a pack of radioactive cats.

How Hooker came to get too close to these hot cats is the subject of the book's second Oxford plot. Nursing his unbelief at his family's comfortable country house below the Ridgeway (the house is called Plumley, which a place-name scholar with a taste for modern letters might decipher as 'Wodehouse's field'), George Naylor meets a stock character from the Oxbridge novel: the gilded undergraduate. In Oxford Simon Prowse has been '"hogging all the prizes . . . for writing poems in ancient Greek"' (J.I.M. Stewart 1985: 108). Out of Oxford, he has been arrested at an anti-nuclear demonstration. Would this not discountenance his tutors? Not at all.

> 'The dons don't mind a bit,' he tells George. 'They'd like to have the guts themselves . . . Superficially, nothing looks more utterly conservative than, say, an Oxford senior common room. But in point of training and economic status, the wholly clerkly class is essentially Jacobin.'
>
> (J.I.M. Stewart 1985: 139)

This inversion of the discourse's usual account of donnish political proclivities – 'A small closed society of this self-perpetuating sort might be expected to exhibit a conservative collective mind' Duncan Pattullo had told us (J.I.M. Stewart 1978: 9) – warns us that old resources are being used for new purposes. We have been told this before, in the parallels between Newman and Hooker, Pattison and Naylor. The same message is borne through Naylor's disenchanting walk around that Oxford which he used to love. The last words in the chapter describing this perambulation quote the heading of a leaflet which has been thrust on our attention twice before: 'THE WORLD NOW STANDS ON THE BRINK OF THE FINAL ABYSS' (J.I.M. Stewart 1985: 49).

Oxford stands for England in the usual discourse. Stewart extends the metaphor. Oxford now stands for the world. Culture, civilization, faces the apocalypse. Hence the recourse to C.S. Lewis's *That Hideous Strength.* Simon Prowse is revealed not to be preparing for his final examinations with a local vicar, but organizing an attack on a government research establishment located in a neighbouring village, the Institute of Animal Genetics. Why should an anti-nuclear activist concern himself with a biological station? Because the experimental dogs and cats in this place are being used to test the effectiveness of an anti-radiation pill for humans: 'the government, or whatever body funded the place, was eventually going to use them as instruments of thought-control. *Swallow this* – people would be told – *and you needn't even shelter under the stairs*' (J.I.M. Stewart 1985: 183). Stewart's nasty scientists merge: Ourglass's interest in thought control is placed at the service of nuclear warfare. But this is state, not private, enterprise. With the ground prepared by the oblique reference to Richard Hooker, we see Stewart question state action for the first time: one must challenge legitimate authority, he tells us, because the state is acting evilly.

In properly Manichaean fashion, shades of moral grey are polarized towards the white of good and the black of evil. Punning the method of relaying election news from the College of Cardinals – another oblique reference to J.H. Newman and to Christ Church, Oxford (emblem: a cardinal's hat) – smoke colour establishes moral judgements. Despite the Innes-ironic name of its Director, Dr Scattergood – note the pun on radiation – the Institute of Animal Genetics is black.

> Perhaps because seeming so deliberately pitched in depressing surroundings, it suggested at a first glance a large receptacle for the indigent aged – a high incidence of senile dementia among whom might explain the necessity of its being enclosed within a perimeter-fence some ten feet high. In such establishments it may often be remarked that facilities for mass-incineration have for some reason constituted a high priority in the design, and so it was here. Crowning the Institute there was a chimney-stack of surprising height, and from this arose into the sky a faintly quivering column of oily black smoke.
>
> (J.I.M. Stewart 1985: 171–2)

Aspects of this establishment might suggest a geriatric hospital, but other features – the high wire fence, the obscene experiments on pets rounded up indiscriminately from the neighbouring district, the oily black smoke – recall that central twentieth-century nightmare, the concentration camp. Simon Prowse and his friends challenge this obscenity. The start of their attack is signalled by a smoke signal from Tom's Tump (a neolithic ancestor of Tom Tower?), a long barrow on the Ridgeway. Hooker, Naylor, and Scattergood

> all looked at the Tump – or, rather, at a small column of smoke rising close beside it. And, even as Scattergood spoke, the column broadened, thickened, climbed. It was a great white shaft in air. Momentarily it mushroomed and spread; became as a cloud in the heavens shaped like the hand of

Man. Then it was again a simple column of smoke, white in the sunlight. Almost as an effect of dialogue, of drama, it confronted, across the vale, the black smoke still issuing from the tall chimney-stack of the Institute of Animal Genetics.

(J.I.M. Stewart 1985: 176)

White smoke marks the onset of good's attack on evil. White confronts black. But, unlike C.S. Lewis's untroubled Manichaean-ism, here white is not absolutely good. The pillar of white smoke recalls God's direction finder for the Israelites; but it is also a mushroom cloud, and the shape of a man's – indeed, Hardy-like, Man's – hand. For Stewart as for Lewis, man, not God, got us into this mess. Can man get us out, without recourse to God's grace? Both think not; but while Lewis puts his money on grace, Stewart has no solution. Literary criticism – British university fiction's panacea – no longer gives any purchase on moral issues. He tells us this by having Hilda Naylor, George's niece, quote William Faulkner's words on receiving his Nobel prize. '"There are no longer problems of the human spirit, he had said. There is only the question: When will I be blown up?"' (J.I.M. Stewart 1985: 145). The attack on the Institute is copybook university fiction material. Tom's Tump has the same status as Lewis's Merlin's Well: it is the very root of English historical experience, of Englishness, legitimizing the struggle against evil. Evil has to be confronted, but Prowse's activism brings disaster. His plan combines the carnival aspects of anti-nuclear marches – mothers and children bedecked with placards – with the direct action of animal liberationists. A small group of the latter, using the mums and toddlers as a decoy, penetrates the station's security and frees the experimental animals. The children, seeing their lost pets, make for the irradiated cats. A huge human tragedy is averted only by Hooker putting his faith to use, and suffering the glowing animals to come to him at the expense of his fine mind. A massive radiation dose puts an end to his scholarly career, to his hitherto likely succession (J.I.M. Stewart 1985: 124) to the office of Nolloth Professor of the Philosophy of the Christian Religion at Oxford University.

We are left with no better guide to action than Hilda Naylor's doomed passivity. But if Stewart can give us no solution, he has posed the problems in a rivetingly original fashion. The *Times Literary Supplement*'s reviewer (25 January 1985) identified 'the extreme oddity so liberally revealed in *The Naylors*' only because he did not recognize the frame of references in which it is set. Taken as an Oxford novel about the moral dilemmas presented by militarized science it is impeccable, swirling history against current events, science against culture, assonance against dissonance. This novel shows what the British university novel can do when the discourse is used as a resource rather than a constraint. And this from a man in his eightieth year. Ripeness, as they say, is all.

Chapter Seven

BARBAROUS WOMEN

'Why,' asked G.B. Shaw's Professor Higgins, 'can't a woman be more like a man?' For much British university fiction this question is disastrously mistaken: the real task is to assert how irreducibly different men are from women, and to defend the difference. This colours accounts of women's experience in Oxbridge and not-Oxbridge universities as student, wife, or lover. In British university fiction women are subject to what a critic has called, felicitously, textual harassment (Jacobus 1986: 85). Challenges to this harassment are interestingly modest.

Given their monastic origins, it is little surprise that novels about Oxford and Cambridge should treat women as threatening interlopers. '"I judged [Tandon] to be of the aggressively celibate type – such as still exists, you know, in the colleges,"' says Elinor Fontaney to Quail; '"A negative attitude to women in general, and a positive dislike for women of education"' (J.I.M. Stewart 1955: 134). The prospect of admitting women to Comyns College, Oxford, unmans Jake Richardson. This direct literary – and etymological – descendent of Jim Dixon finds his thing drooping in direct proportion to women's success in forcing open the doors of Oxford men's houses (Amis 1978). The prospect of admitting women to Porterhouse, Cambridge, is particularly abhorrent to the college's Senior Tutor: 'Sickly unisex would replace the healthy cheerful louts who had helped to preserve the inane innocence and the athleticism that were his only safeguard against the terrors of thought' (Sharpe 1974: 202). Here, as elsewhere, opposition is based on more than simple homophilia. '"There has been no greater mistake made in Oxford"', says the Bursar of St Thomas, '"than the abolition of compulsory chapel, except of

159

course the admission of women and the abolition of compulsory Greek"' (Masterman 1952: 140). Secularization, decline of the classical curriculum, letting women in: these are three aspects of a single degradation, the erosion of difference between Oxbridge and not-Oxbridge.

We are shown that fears of this erosion have a long history. '"Nobody thought of women playing any part in University life when I was an undergraduate,"' says Winn of the 1890s; '"I really do not think that there were women in Oxford – certainly it never occurred to us to miss them"' (Masterman 1952: 105). An Oxford don from this generation surfaces gently in the Bodleian Library:

> A long low wheeze, as of air let gently out of a bicycle tyre, made Jane glance to her left. Dr Undertone had opened his eyes and was looking at her in great astonishment – rather as if, on returning to his immediate surroundings, he had discovered himself seated next to a studious walrus or erudite dromedary. This was disconcerting to Jane, but, on reflection, not at all surprising. During a large part of Dr Undertone's reading life, it had to be remembered, women – and particularly young women – must have been an unusual sight in Bodley.
>
> (M. Innes 1951: 172)

Women are constructed by Winn as invisible, by Undertone as not-human. In either form they threaten culture's citadel. Once women have breached the walls of Oxford and Cambridge novelists start to give us distinctly unflattering representations of female education. The women's colleges are very different from the men's. Pursuing enquiries into yet another Oxford murder,

> The policemen walked through the huge, single quadrangle of Walpurgis, by lawns and gravelled walks, populous with litter-bins and tennis-courts. There was nothing here of the quaint, the cramped or the medieval: Walpurgis was large and airy and modern, and had been designed exclusively for big, normal, strenuous, red-legged young women with glasses.
>
> (R. Robinson 1956: 54)

We are required to understand that Walpurgis is in Oxford but not of Oxford. It is a sham, a feeble emulation of a real college.

Where a proper ancient men's college has rooms opening off staircases, these female places have 'small, unsolidly modern' (Crispin 1944: 123) bed-sitters ranged along corridors. It is not just that the corridors 'swam in a strange effluvia composed in equal parts of floor-polish, cosmetics and cosy secrets' (R. Robinson 1956: 56); their very existence asserts women's colleges' kinship with not-Oxbridge universities, with their halls of bed-sitter residence. The architecture of another Oxford women's college evokes a much more specific redbrick comparison. St Mary's

> was a rambling, unco-ordinated sprawl of buildings in harsh red brick set off by occasional excrescences in white stone .... The front entrance ... was silent and spacious, its tiling and panelling suggesting a lavishly equipped mental hospital whose inmates pay enormous sums for the privilege of being shielded from the incomprehension of society.
>
> (McIntosh 1956: 25)

Since this is Oxford we are shown a privileged asylum, but the institution is recognizably of a kind with Bradbury's (1959) minor redbrick university housed in a converted public lunatic asylum. Here, as there, the account of the building contaminates our view of its inmates.

Of necessity being, like lunatics, possessed of less than full citizenship, women cannot understand what it is to be an Oxbridge undergraduate. Where men display a varied aristocratic eccentricity, women demonstrate a depressingly uniform lower middle-class taste: 'in every window the back of a postcard reproduction of Van Gogh's *Sunflowers* was clearly distinguishable' (R. Robinson 1956: 55). The daily routine for men and women reflects this difference between aristocratic and *petit bourgeois* styles. Women get up too early.

> The women undergraduates were the first abroad – cycling along the streets in droves, absurdly gowned and clutching complicated files, or hovering about libraries until the doors should open and admit them once again to study the divine mysteries which hang around the Christian element in *Beowulf*, the date of the *Urtristan* (if any), the complexities of hydrodynamics, the kinetic theory of gases, the law of tort or the purposes of the parathyroid gland. The men rose more

161

circumspectly, putting a pair of trousers, a coat, and a scarf over their pyjamas, shambling across the quadrangles to sign lists, and shambling back again.

(Crispin 1946: 27)

Women lack a proper sense of direction:

Outwards towards the Banbury or the Woodstock Road an unending stream of battered sports cars bore cohorts of male undergraduates, discreetly concealed amid golf clubs, shot-guns, and riding kits. Inwards towards the lecture-rooms and libraries of the University rode an answering army of young women on bicycles bearing large baskets bulging with massive volumes, as if they were the delivery service of a community given literally to devouring books.

(M. Innes 1951: 158)

These bicycling women lack academic discrimination: 'Girl students in wringing-wet gowns were going to odd little afternoon lectures, of the sort that men would never be so foolish as to forsake their strong tea and anchovy toast for' (Liddell 1948: 172). Arrived at their destination, these females – not-Oxbridge 'students,' note, rather than Oxbridge 'undergraduates' – present an unlovely sight: 'The lecture room was full of young women in short gowns, carrying bulky handbags and enormous tattered bundles of notes; they smelt inimitably of facepowder and (vaguely) Irish stew, and they were dressed in woollen clothes' (Larkin 1946: 70). Women's behaviour in lecture rooms is unacceptably different: 'On the wooden benches about twenty undergraduates sat, the women gowned, chattering feverishly, the men ungowned, staring absently about them' (Crispin 1946: 158). No doubt the men were wondering how they came to be in such unaccustomed circumstances, such extraordinary company. We see more Dr Undertones in the making.

Some forms of lunacy can be cured, or at least coaxed into remission. '"Janet was one of our *most* successful girls,"' gushes Miss Puncher, Mistress of St Helena's, Oxford. '"Engaged in her second year, married in her third. She never took Schools. An excellent career"' (Balsdon 1961: 68). Anthea Lambert's marriage means escape from the fellowship of St Cecilia's, Oxford, where tea-drinking and gossip replace the port-drinking and scholarship of

the men's colleges (J.I.M. Stewart 1954). 'After a time,' says
Nicolette Simney,

> I didn't think much of Oxford. I was the wrong sex for what
> goes on there. Young women who could get tense on cocoa
> and whose diet was a muddied amalgam of precocious
> pedantry and belated crushes just didn't turn out to be my
> cup of tea any more than the little Emma Bovarys who were
> hopeful of careers on the London stage.
>
> (M. Innes 1946b: 19)

Having achieved this rational insight Nicolette, like any cured
lunatic, can be returned to normal society: like Janet and Anthea,
she leaves. Oxford is no place for a sensible woman.

Wives confirm this uncharitable diagnosis. 'Dons commonly
marry fools', Vulliamy (1952: 25) tells us. Gavin Limbert is

> A nice Cambridge boy, who had made squiggles in his
> notebooks between lectures on Julius Caesar and more
> lectures on Caesar Augustus. And held an exhibition above a
> tea-shop. And was told by all the wives of all the professors
> that he was a True Artist.
>
> (M. Innes 1952: 38)

We are invited to join in uttering a curse on 'these self-satisfied
dons' wives' (Rees 1945: 218–19). Whence the curse?

We are driven back to the monastic roots of Oxbridge. Until
nineteenth-century reforms, only a college's head could be
married. Other dons had to be celibate, or at least unmarried.
Their modern descendants remain, says Michael Innes (1936:
123), 'obstinately unconvinced of the necessity of the modern
amenities either for themselves, their wives, or their children. Only
recently, indeed, did they *discover* wives and children.' This discovery does not transform attitudes completely. '"When I first came to
live in Oxford,"' says Arthur Aylwin, '"I thought High Table and
common rooms and dining clubs and all the rest of it so many
deplorable relics of a vanished celibate society. Now I'm inclined
to see them as among the blessed alleviations of family life"' (J.I.M.
Stewart 1966: 30). Balsdon's dystopia of twenty-first-century
Oxford under a feminist onslaught imagines one men's college
being sacrificed to the women. The notion that all colleges could
become mixed he regards as too far-fetched to be credible even in

a work of fantasy: 'in a co-educational world, where could men escape to be alone?' (Balsdon 1961: 14). Little wonder, then, that one wife hated Cambridge 'with much the same sort of jealousy as other wives hate their husbands' regiments or clubs' (Raven 1970: 126). Most particularly, wives threaten collegiate mateship. As the Master of Beaufort tells Ashe, his college's house radical,

> It's always better having the Fellows in College. The undergraduates like us to be accessible, and it helps the College spirit if we're seen around. Half the trouble these days is that so many of us are married and submerged by families in North Oxford. There was a lot to be said for the old monastic ideal.
>
> (Shaw 1981: 16)

As a group dons' wives clearly are a Bad Thing. Treated individually the picture is rather more mixed. We are shown some admirable Oxford spouses. Mrs Vereker, wife of the President of St Thomas', is 'a remarkable woman, not very artistic, not very clever, and yet, by virtue of character and a deep instinctive sympathy for others, a kind of natural leader' (Masterman 1933: 52). Mary Aylwin is sensible, capable, and intelligent, a strong buttress for her husband's bid to gain election to his college's provostship (J.I.M. Stewart 1966: 155). Janet McKechnie, wife of an Oxford classics professor and Duncan Pattullo's childhood sweetheart, is endowed with native Scots good sense (J.I.M. Stewart 1974, 1975, 1978). Mabel Bedworth supports her Oxford senior tutor husband by surreptitiously mothering a succession of homesick undergraduates who fall safely in love with her (J.I.M. Stewart 1978). Alice Mannering, aristocratic wife of a humbly born Cambridge fellow, brings him family connections that greatly assist the smooth acceleration of his career (J.I.M. Stewart 1979: 130). To set against these positive accounts we are given less flattering portraits. In Oxford we are shown the foolish and snobbish Mrs Jobling, wife of a college's head (J.I.M. Stewart 1955). Gervase Fen's wife manages an appropriate answer to a question. 'Fen gazed at her with something of the triumphant and sentimental pride of a dog-owner whose pet has succeeded in balancing a biscuit on its nose' (Crispin 1944: 70). Cambridge novels give us cohorts of unappealing wives. Lady Muriel Royce is the aristocratic but graceless and tactless wife of a dying master (Snow 1951). Lady Mary Evans is Sir

Godber's bigotted aristocratic Fabian spouse (Sharpe 1974). Mona Carrington is Lord Beyfus's *de facto* wife, threatening to withdraw her bizarre sexual favours in order to force him to lead the attack on Lancaster College's privilege (Raven 1970). Patricia Llewyllin attacks her husband through calculated sexual promiscuity (Raven 1970). Alice Jago is 'driven to inflict on [her husband] the woes of a hypochondriac, the venom of a shrew, the faithlessness of one who had to find attention' (Snow 1951: 279). Her nature and conduct lose her husband support in a close election:

> It would be awkward if she spoke in that strain to others, I thought. . . . Nothing would give more offence, nothing was more against the rules of that society; I decided that Brown, as manager of Jago's caucus, must know at once. As I was telling him, he flushed. 'That woman's a confounded nuisance,' he said.
>
> (Snow 1951: 119)

Since the novels' gaze is riveted so firmly on the men's colleges, we see little of female Oxbridge academics. Stewart provides us with an unflattering view of the species in Diana Sandys's comment on Noel Gylby's plan for advertising Sappho chocolates as lesbian delights: '"I rather think you'll have female dons – all tense and arm in arm, no doubt, as you want – going to their favourite sweet-shop and asking for *Sap-foh*"' (M. Innes 1937: 157). Invited to watch the grace and culture of dinner in Warlock College's hall, we get an unpleasant close-up view of 'Pearl Corker – the manly Corker of Walpurgis Hall. Beneath the table her knees were spread wide apart, and the elastic end of one woollen knicker-leg obtruded (R. Robinson 1956: 26). A policeman ruminates on a later encounter with this formidable Pearl: '"An educated woman. Thank God my girl's going in to be a stenographer"' (ibid: 56). We get distant views of Dame Helen Gardiner, emeritus Merton Professor of English Literature at Oxford (Dexter 1981); of Professor Babcock – and of her college's Bursar, Cecilia Basket, a general's daughter who pulls a pistol on a drunken college servant when he threatens her with a cleaver (J.I.M. Stewart 1976). We see (after her untimely death) Miss Termag, Mistress of Sapientia College. She wrote the stern Termag Commission report, which recommended that women should take over just one men's college after narrowly rejecting the attractive idea that all men should be thrown out of Oxford. Miss Puncher, her counterpart at St Helena's, is close to being elected vice-chancellor (Balsdon 1961). We see Mona Carrington refusing to speak to Beyfus until the door is closed, for 'a life spent in a women's college had given her a horror of being overheard' (Raven 1970: 68). We see Helen Burns, who can decide whether Sefton Goldberg is elected to the coveted Disraeli Fellowship in a Cambridge college: 'Sefton watched in amazement as she moved her mouth and made real words and sentences . . . Sefton felt as if he were listening to the rabbits talk' (Jacobson 1983: 96). We see Duncan Pattullo's niece (and, it is thought for a time, possibly his illegitimate daughter) Fiona Petrie, living with a female novelist in a hinted lesbian relationship (J.I.M. Stewart 1976, 1978). We are shown two politically treacherous women: Mona Carrington, a left infantilist Girton anthropologist; and Emily Bryant, an able historian who is a fellow of a men's college that has opened its doors to women, and a Russian agent. Bryant is ugly (Lejeune 1987: 32). Petrie may be lesbian. Anthea Lambert is attractive and heterosexual, but her inclination as well as the terms of her fellowship lead her to escape St Cecilia's. A normal, sensible woman should seek to leave Oxbridge. If she stays, then she has to avoid getting ideas above her station:

> Ruth is not what might be called a passionate supporter of women's lib; indeed, she seems to enjoy being feminine. But as Caval Professor of Mathematics at Oxford she is properly conscious of her identity and not at all disposed to think that her role in life is to cook for me. . . . 'You've been very good, Peter, in not trying to stop me being a professor, but what's so difficult about being a woman is that only half of me really wants to be a professor – or rather I *do* want to be a professor, but another me wants to cook and make cushions and even knit socks for you.'
>
> (J.R.L. Anderson 1981: 9, 117)

Given the relatively small number of novels set in such places, women are much more evident in not-Oxbridge universities. Lacking sex-segregated colleges, these places display a promiscuous mixing of men and women. At Nesfield, a major redbrick, 'girls hurried past, bespectacled, notebooked, serious;

girls loitered past, nudging, giggling, powdering; men skylarked, shouted, bit into sandwiches' (M. Innes 1944: 7). But contact is less promiscuous, conduct less unconstrained, in the ghastly gentility of Nesfield's hall of residence for women:

> In the gardens of St Cecilia's Hall young ladies, equipped with secateurs and suitable gloves, gathered flowers. On the terrace other young ladies walked with Miss Godkin's dogs. Under trees young ladies sketched. And through open windows and across the lawn floated the strains of violins and harps, pianos and cellos, discoursed by young ladies for whom, by the doom of Miss Godkin, musical accomplishment had been decreed. One could see at once that throughout the Hall refined cheerfulness and cultivated gaiety reigned. Indeed these qualities, together with unpunctuality, needlework, dips into *Country Life* and *The Queen*, unpainted fingernails, intelligent conversation, politeness to servants, and the use of Received Standard English, were required by Miss Godkin from eight fifteen in the morning to ten o'clock at night. Young ladies who so far wished to become girls again as to read film magazines, make bets on horses, discuss boys, discuss girls, toast bloaters before gas fires, consume grocer's port, fan dance, croon, pinch, weep, become deliciously sick on chocolate peppermint creams, tell each other about their homes and their neighbours, their mothers' troubles with hire-purchase and their fathers' triumphs with dogs: such recalcitrant elements could indulge their backslidings only in the nocturnal seclusion of the spare, but dainty and maiden-like, cubicles with which Miss Godkin provided them. By day life at St Cecilia's was elegant and controlled; it combined, Miss Godkin was accustomed to say, the variousness and verve of a noble household of the Renaissance with the dignity and repose of an English country seat. And some of the girls had to stay three whole years.
>
> (M. Innes 1944: 181)

Teachers' wives continue to be unsympathetic characters. The monied and socially ambitious wife of an ex-CAT's vice-chancellor is 'almost Lady Macbeth' (Priestley 1968a: 18). Hilary Swallow makes trouble for the head of Rummidge's English department by seeking to resurrect her MA studies: '"it puts us in rather an awkward position. I mean, the wife of a colleague . . ." If his colleagues had to have wives, he intimated, the least they could do was to keep them at home in decent obscurity' (Lodge 1975: 198). Elsewhere, the wife of a classics lecturer maintains a ludicrous salon, unable to see that her pretension is pricked by her provincialism (M. Innes 1944: 91–4). She is the literary ancestor of Neddy Welch's appalling wife, who keeps a similarly ludicrous salon. Happily she has not reckoned with Jim Dixon's incompetence at madrigal-singing and his penchant for smoking in bed (Amis 1954). Tom Cochrane is a senior lecturer in geography at Edinburgh. His wife is a professor of sociology.

> It didn't worry him unduly that Flora ranked higher in the university hierarchy than he did. But it did disturb him that Flora enjoyed incessant committee meetings, continual arranging of this or that, and endless entertaining of university personnel in whom Tom hadn't the slightest interest.
>
> (Hoyle and Hoyle 1971b: 143)

Olivia Jory 'was much too young and immeasurably too rare to be conceivably one of the considerable number of learned ladies on the staff' of a minor redbrick (M. Innes 1956b: 11). Elsewhere, too, learned ladies are not an impressive lot. Miss Godkin, Warden of St Cecilia's Hall at Nesfield is 'an assured and thoroughly illogical woman' (M. Innes 1944: 95). Margaret Peel is a lecturer in English, a neurotic leech bent on sucking Jim Dixon dry. Other women on the staff of Dixon's minor redbrick include the sexagenarian Professor of Philosophy and the fifteen-stone Senior Lecturer in Economics (Amis 1954: 107). In an ex-CAT Dr Hazel Honeyfield, nicknamed Honeypot, is a sociologist whose research interests include the status implications of potted plants. Priestley describes her (1968a: 53) as 'a rather small, delicious brunette, about thirty, midnight and cream when in repose, sparkling and dimpling as soon as she talked or listened, no matter how idiotic the subject'. This machine for generating sexual fantasies is balanced by Dr Lois Terry:

> badly dressed, thinnish, with mousy and rather untidy hair, and would be generally considered quite plain, though Tuby, more perceptive than most men, decided it was because she

had no excitement inside, no strong current of feeling, to light her up.

(Priestley 1968a: 104)

Watermouth has the prim Annie Callendar, historically pro-grammed to be Howard Kirk's prey, and Flora Beniform – a specialist on troilism in Walsall – who sexually devours Howard along, it is implied, with many other men (Bradbury 1975).

We need to notice one striking feature in the accounts of women's place in British university life that we have considered thus far: everything was written by men. What sorts of accounts do women provide? Sometimes there are strong continuities with what we have seen.

In a novel with a mid-nineteenth-century setting Mary Lamont waits to join the second cohort of students in Oxford's embryo women's college. She gives us an account of the embattled attitudes to be faced even from liberals like her father, a painter:

> My father says that the coming of women has ruined Oxford. Before we came, he says, what a pleasant world it was, with women kept safely beyond Folly Bridge. He's joking, of course, because in the first place he likes women's company, and there are always plenty of wives and daughters about, but what he means is that none were students of the University. We might attend the lectures on Art by Professor Ruskin (and indeed I did), but until the last year or two we were not found at the lectures on Greek, Latin or Mathematics held in the Colleges for the young men undergraduates.

(G. Butler 1973: 10)

The lively, vivacious and married Thea Sylvester is appointed to be the mock-Oxbridge not-Oxbridge Buriton University's professor of archaeology. '"I was very glad that they gave you the Chair"', says Miss Eliot, a retired medieval historian soon to be murdered.

> It seems extraordinary, fifty years on, that I should still be thinking that it's a boost for women. . . . I've sometimes wondered whether it wasn't the fault of people like myself – my generation of teachers, I mean. Perhaps our pupils were afraid of becoming like us.

(Mann 1973: 85-6)

169

> Students come to Rachel Ambrose [Cambridge], Sharon was thinking, sustained by visions of fountains in medieval courtyards and tendrils of creeper tawny-scarlet over grey stone walls: to get to this place they have to come past the warehouse and the gasworks, past the supermarkets and the Strict Ebenezer chapel [to] . . . the tall Victorian houses, with their porches and flights of balustraded steps, crowned by stone urns pricked over with cacti, the sharp roofs with their barge-boards and dormer windows, the pepperpot baronial tower.
>
> (Myer 1988: 13–14)

Meanings encoded in bricks and mortar tell us that this is a very marginal college indeed. The university does not permit Rachel Ambrose students to sit for its degrees. Ann Livingstone is enchanted by the architecture of Oxford's men's colleges. Then she arrives at her women's college. Her sensibilities are affronted. She is accommodated in a Victorian building, 'that monstrous pile of red brick, with the small, arched, Gothic windows, crudely pointed in yellow brick' (Day 1961: 140). She is horrified by her room in this pile. 'Didn't they, in any case, always have "rooms" at Oxford? They always had in the books she had read. Why should she, then, be consigned, like an underprivileged typist, to a sordid bed-sitting-room?' (Day 1961: 141).

> On that first evening in College, dinner had been another insult to Ann's sensibilities and cherished preconceptions. Where were the cloistered calm, the low-voiced exchanges of wit, the erudite references? After the first meal, she did not think she could live through three years of them.
>
> The dining-hall was large and without character or beauty. Its rough plaster walls were finished off in white swirls, like cheap frosting, and the wooden beams that imitated rafters, shone with yellow varnish. The refectory tables showed the same shoddiness. There was nothing to relieve the eye, nothing moderately pretty to look at.
>
> (Day 1961: 156)

Things do not mend when the other inmates appear. 'The swarming girls coming in singly or in groups did nothing to improve the hall; Ann could not bear to look at them either. Many still wore their hairy sweaters and skirts, and their faces shone like the rafters. The noise they made was intolerable' (Day 1961: 156). Later, Ann reports to a man that

> All the women at my place stand around in hairy, knee-length socks, drinking mugs of cocoa, and looking at the notice-board to see what jolly games they're going to play in the afternoon, or whose class they're in for Anglo-Saxon.
>
> (Day 1961: 187)

Classes imply school, not Oxbridge university. The teachers – fake-dons – confirm this impression. Their nature is summed up in the college's Principal with her grey, cropped hair, beaky nose and reserved manner. These suggest

> the true academic, vowed to the life of the mind, medievally scholastic. Only gradually did it become obvious to Ann that behind this noble exterior cowered a vulgar and trivial mind; one without real learning, culture, or wisdom. As the months went by, the Principal disclosed herself as a woman obsessively concerned with the rituals of good form, the preservation of law, the keeping of rules. Her guardedly formal manner was not a defence for the sensitive intellect, for she had no intellect. It was the defence of the frightened woman, charmless, neurotic, against any sort of human contact.
>
> (Day 1961: 137)

An image of what an Oxford women's college should be like – gracious buildings, erudite dons – crashes against the awful reality. Female undergraduates should be feminine, but they clump around in hairy clothes. This is appropriate for a man: hairy tweeds hint at Augusts spent blasting birds from a Scottish sky. Hair on a woman is mannish, superfluous. Day measures her women's college against a feminine version of British university fiction's dominant discourse, and finds it grievously wanting. 'The hierarchical character of a woman's college, with its petty disciplines, and its strict observance of protocol and rank, came to her as a shock' (Day 1961: 137). Hierarchy and bed-sitters. The dreadful light breaks. Ann is in Oxford but not of it, immured in not-Oxbridge. On her new bicycle she pedals 'the mile of suburban road that separated her from the "real" and central Oxford' (Day 1961: 141–2).

Margaret Forster shares Lois Day's structure of feeling. In *Dames' Delight* Morag, an undergraduate at a top Oxford women's college, tells us about her first dinner in hall: 'I thought I'd never seen such a revolting sight than all those crowded tables full of jabbering, excited females. They were so ugly. . . . The sight of the high table distressed me even more' (Forster 1964: 18, 21). The spectacle might be distressing in its own right, but it is rendered doubly so by the contrast which it provides with life in the men's colleges:

> I'd only been a witness to one college dinner before. It was at Ian's college when I'd sat on the hall stairs in the gallery above and listened to the riot below – glasses breaking, some crazy violin going, spontaneous obscene speeches, complete abandon. I'd felt quite moved by all the deep male roars and envied the tremendous camaraderie which was theirs. But this was a mockery.
>
> (Forster 1964: 108)

This is life in the women's colleges as men understand it: a pale imitation of the real Oxford. Like Day's *The Looker In*, *Dames' Delight* is a feminized novel of apparent Oxbridge undergraduate disillusion – a good male example is Wilfred Sheed's *A Middle-Class Education* (1967) – which reaffirms the discourse at a deeper level.

A.S. Byatt (1985: 110) gives us a very different account of a Cambridge women's college. Returning to Newnham after a quarter of a century, Frederica 'saw it as beautiful – graceful in scale, civilised in space, humane'. At first glance this looks like the celebration of male Oxbridge, but some adjectives – beautiful, graceful – make it teeter on the edge of something else. Consider P.D. James's account of New Hall, Cambridge. She makes plain what Byatt hints at: the college's feminine architecture.

> With its Byzantine air, its sunken court and its shining domed hall like a peeled orange, [it] reminded Cordelia of a harem; admittedly one owned by a sultan with liberal views and an odd predilection for clever girls, but a harem nonetheless. The college was surely too distractingly pretty to be conducive to serious study.
>
> (James 1972: 76)

There are tensions in this passage. New Hall's buildings promote frivolity rather than scholarship; this is not a proper college. But the frivolity follows from its being a harem, an enclosure for women whose life's task is to give men sexual pleasure. The undergraduates and their teachers are to be seen as victims rather than predators.

Variations on this view underlie women novelists' accounts of wives as victims. Helen MacInnes (1948: 196) shows us the Junior Fellow of an Oxford men's college, a Labour voter who determinedly wears a tweed jacket at high table. As he feasts, he thinks guiltily of his wife dining at home on scrambled eggs and a baked apple. Margaret Yorke invites us to

'Think of all those poor lonely dons' wives with their tomato soup on their trays and the Sunday film on the box, while their husbands dine in hall. What a dreary life.'

(Yorke 1973: 138).

These accounts support dons' wives; but they are kin to male authors' more ambiguous sympathy for wives abandoned to poached eggs (C.P. Snow), tinned salmon (Robert Robinson) and tinned spaghetti and sausages (Simon Raven).

Some other women's accounts of academic snares are more interesting. Celia Fremlin (1975) gives us Lena, the mad first wife of Ivor, an Oxbridge classics professor. Lena was a brilliant Minoan scholar, herself a college fellow. Unmarried at 34, she was romanced by the devastatingly handsome 18-year-old Ivor, her pupil, who then used her work to build his own career. Gwendoline Butler (1960) gives us Marion Manning, fellow of St Agatha's, Oxford. She is an anthropologist who turns to English literature after her husband dies, and develops a bizarre second – semi-Australian – personality. In her doomed, posthumously published campus novel Barbara Pym (1986) gives us Caro Grimstone, married to an ethnohistorian in an ex-CAT. Caro is blackmailed by her husband into purloining a manuscript from the bedside of a dying anthropologist. What drives her to this action is fear that her husband is falling into the clutches of Iris Horniblow, a glamorously boring sociology lecturer.

Caro's dilemma is patterned on that in Barbara Pym's Oxford novel, published thirty-five years after it was written. Francis Cleveland is a fellow of Randolph College who falls for a female pupil but is much too timorous to carry through a successful elopement. His wife holds a deliciously wry attitude to the rigours of his academic life:

> Margaret Cleveland, who had at one time helped and encouraged her husband with his work, had now left him to do it alone, because she feared that with her help it might quite easily be finished before one of them died, and then where would they be? Francis was like a restless, difficult child if he had nothing to occupy him. This book meant that he spent long hours in his study, presumably working on it. It would not be at all convenient for Mrs Cleveland to have him hanging about the drawing-room, wanting to be amused.
>
> (Pym 1985: 14–15)

We see that women authors' accounts can give us a wife as minder as well as victim. A secretary is surrogate wife to the Warden of Pentecost, Oxford: 'For the hundredth time, she wondered if the old man was as innocent as he looked. Did he realise how carefully she briefed him? Did he *mind*?' (Farrer 1957: 15). Proper wives type their husbands' manuscripts. This skill is learnt early: some London University anthropology postgraduates

> had been fortunate enough to win the love of devoted women – women who might one day become their wives, but who, if they were thrown aside, would accept their fate cheerfully and without bitterness. They had learned early in life what it is to bear love's burdens, listening patiently to their men's troubles and ever ready at their typewriters, should a manuscript or even a short article get to the stage of being written down.
>
> (Pym 1955: 49)

'Newnham was in those days [1954] outside, but not far outside, Cambridge University proper', A.S. Byatt (1985: 110) tells us. Today it lies within the walls. Other recent novels show us women penetrating the Oxbridge citadel. The context is changing sexual mores. Duncan Pattullo muses on change in Oxford: 'The dimensions of the sexual revolution which had come about in Junkin's time were to be among the more striking impressions of my middle years' (J.I.M. Stewart 1975: 139). Fornication was not new. Of women in former men's colleges: '"They sleep in?" "Some of them do. Still, some of them always did, didn't they?"' (Dexter 1983: 44). Jemima Shore enjoys 'agreeable memories of other sported oaks in her Cambridge days, doors in men's colleges shut not so much in her face as behind her back' (Fraser 1985: 42). What is new is the treatment of fornication as routine (Shaw 1981: 4, 134, 136), and the grudging opening of men's colleges to women (and, of course, the reverse). Grilling a potential witness, PC Walters misses a *double entendre* rooted in historical change:

'Where does Miss Edgeley work?'
'She's an undergraduate at Brasenose.'
'Do they have women there?'
'They've always had women at Brasenose, haven't they?' said the brunette slowly.

(Dexter 1981: 58)

Entirely novel is 'this new intelligent generation of women under-graduates, the post-Brideshead types, living in colleges in equal numbers and on equal terms with the men' (Fraser 1985: 49). Inspector Morse contemplated the change as he

watched the two young lovely ladies as they walked out through the Porter's Lodge. They must be members of the college – two outward and happily visible signs of the fundamental change of heart that had resulted in the admission of women to these erstwhile wholly-masculine precincts.

(Dexter 1983: 43)

This provides delicious new possibilities:

'Do you know Serena of Christ Church?' He swept on: 'Isn't it enjoyable hearing that? I'm old-fashioned enough to adore it. These days I only go out with girls from the best men's colleges, or rather the former men's colleges that were formerly the best. Rachel of Magdalen, Allegra of Trinity, I don't know anyone at Balliol yet unfortunately.'

(Fraser 1985: 83)

We need to be clear about what has happened. Antonia Fraser's *Oxford Blood* celebrates not the fall of the citadel, but women's admission: their shift from being in Oxbridge to being of Oxbridge. Women appear at dinner in the hall of Duncan

Pattullo's college, leading him to reflect that 'this liberty, gained almost without a struggle after centuries in which the mere notion could scarcely have got into anybody's head, wasn't creating much of a revolution in Oxford life' (J.I.M. Stewart 1978: 153). The underlying discourse is not disturbed. As in otherwise valuable feminist anthropological studies of Oxford and Cambridge academic wives' evaporating exclusion (Ardener 1984; Sciama 1984), the triumph celebrated is not the denial of social closure through education but the inclusion of one group – middle-class women – hitherto excluded. This deserves applause, but no more than two cheers. The third cheer must be held back for a time when the dominant discourse is overthrown rather than circumvented. '"There's no lady here. I'm an Oxford professor," Ruth objected. We laughed. "There's no arguing with that," I said' (J.R.L. Anderson 1981: 151). How true. How very true. How sad.

Chapter Eight

BARBAROUS FOREIGNERS

There is an apocryphal story about a headline in *The Times*: 'Fog in Channel', it is reputed to have declared: 'Continent Cut Off'. As *The Times* once claimed to be the epitome of Englishness (before being owned successively by a Canadian and by an Australian who became an American citizen), so that headline summarizes a characteristic national xenophobia. The English do not like foreigners. The main drawback of 'abroad' is that the place is full of them.

The treatment of foreignness in university fiction is a touchstone of this attitude. Two positions are possible. An uninterrogated notion of Englishness makes foreigners at best comic, at worst dangerous. Acting against that we have a feature derived from the historical origin of the university. Medieval Latin permitted clerks from monasteries in many different countries to talk without impediment. The higher knowledge, it is asserted, permits the monks' descendants to do much the same. A university might be in England, in Scotland, elsewhere in Europe, in Australia or New Zealand, in the United States and Canada, in black Africa. None of this matters; the community of scholars is international. One's peers are those folk interested in one's chosen field of study, regardless of national location.

Thus we confidently might expect to find representative cosmopolitans in British university life. It is true that fictional British university teachers appear in exotic locations: Caribbean islands (J.R.L. Anderson 1977; Davey 1982), alpine ski resorts (Yorke 1972), South America (Lejeune 1987), New South Wales (R. Barnard 1974); so it goes on. All these alien sojourners come from Oxford or Cambridge, and their movements appear untrammelled by the mundane obligations of teaching. Not-Oxbridge teachers appear abroad only in vacations, and only at conferences (Lodge 1984; Lejeune 1987).

Cosmopolitanism is to be found abroad, then. But not at home. In only one book are we shown a British university with a significant not-English population: Jocelyn Davey's *A Treasury Alarm* (1976). Here, in early pages before the action moves across the Atlantic, we see an Oxford inhabited by a richly diverse scholarly population. Turks and Hungarians make urbane conversation with Englishmen in college senior common rooms. Against this background moves the novel's central character; Ambrose Usher, a philosophy professor who spends much time working for semi-official arms of government. In another book

> Ambrose was introduced as an Oxford friend. Blue eyes took him in, and seemed satisfied. Ambrose felt slightly relieved. These ultra-Englishmen had a way of reminding him by a look that he himself had been born in a little town in Serbia called Uschze, memorialised in the Usher family name. True, he had lived in England from the age of three, but still . . .
>
> (Davey 1982: 37)

Jocelyn Davey is the pen name of Chaim Raphael whose career, a blurb tells us (Davey 1960), was 'somewhat similar to that of his detective, Ambrose Usher'. Born in Middlesbrough; educated at a grammar school; having held two short-term fellowships; being Jewish: Raphael had a head start in identifying marginality in Oxford. His ethnic background made him value cosmopolitan attitudes. He ruptures the dominant discourse, and thus shows us its routinely resolute little Englandism. The discourse's dark side is revealed when two graduates at St Margaret's, Cambridge, return for a reunion, to find that their old rooms are occupied by an Egyptian and 'a Zionist', presumably an Israeli. '"D'you know what they call this landing nowadays? . . . The Gaza Strip"' (B. Cooper 1963: 223).

Cooper gives us an unusually obnoxious little dig, but his use of two hapless foreigners as markers of not-Englishness is entirely characteristic of British university fiction. Many books have one or two such, their freedom of action strictly limited. Some foreigners are innocents: a Turk, Nuri bey, casts a bemused alien eye on Oxford undergraduate mores (Fleming 1965). Some foreigners are comic. In Oxford's University Parks 'recumbent Ethiopians read the *Economist* or the *Spectator*' (J.I.M. Stewart 1954: 10). A Venetian wore

> a T-shirt upon which the word 'Oxford' was imprinted in large letters beneath a representation of three crowns and an open book. But this appeared to be a tribute to, rather than a claim to residence within, a celebrated place of learning, since its owner was a boy of eleven or twelve.
>
> (J.I.M. Stewart 1972: 126)

In these cases the comedy flows from ludicrous presumption, from not-English people pretending to be English. Foreigners can be dangerous, like the senior wartime French Quisling who masqueraded as a French Canadian scholar in post-war Oxford in order to evade just retribution, and murdered to keep his secret safe (Farrer 1957). Foreigners can think themselves dangerous, but be merely comic. Mr Afraim Olo, a London postgraduate, 'liked to drink Ovaltine while he composed articles of a seditious nature for his African newspaper' (Pym 1955: 77). In St Saviour's, Oxford, M'bola 'and a harmless little West Indian from Balliol . . . were together all evening hatching anti-imperialist plots' (T. Robinson 1961: 90). Mr Eborebelosa

> had been sent over from West Africa to be educated and groomed at the expense, he explained to Treece on the first day, of a terrorist society devoted to driving out the British . . . . [Treece] was quite prepared to help Mr Eborebelosa be a terrorist, if that really was his fulfilment, and people out there seriously felt they had to be terrorists; but surely, in any case, reason would prevail and he'd work in a post office or a government building, creating rather than destroying.
>
> (Bradbury 1959: 26)

Eborebelosa becomes a pitiful figure later, as his inability to handle minor redbrick university life is revealed; but he exists for two reasons. The first is to permit Bradbury to pillory funny foreigners, as when Eborebelosa cannot manage a proper English lavatory. The second reason why he exists is to allow Treece a wallow in liberal confusion and guilt. Like anyone from 'out there', his value lies in throwing a stronger light on what it means

179

to be 'in here'; even when, like Treece, one is tortured by feeling only partly 'in here'.

There are degrees of foreignness. Duncan Pattullo, a Scot, says of Martin Fish, an Australian, that 'he was a kind of half-foreigner, like me' (J.I.M. Stewart 1975: 40). Colonials, Jews (Jacobson 1983; Raphael 1976), and the not-English British occupy a limbo between the heaven of Englishness and the hell of abroad. This can be an unsettling place, breeding structural radicalism. The urbane Snow (1960: 47) notices 'an Antipodean who had come to Cambridge determined not to be bowled over by the place'. We consider white colonial limbo dancers here. In Chapter 9 we examine the fictional fate of semi-colonials from the United States.

British university novelists' typical attitude to the white dominions – Canada, Australia, New Zealand, and South Africa – is uncomplicated. They are worth no more than open contempt. Logan Bester is raised in the splendour of Nova Scotian faded plush, but escapes to Cambridge (S. Gray 1965). This is the only reference to Canada in British university fiction. New Zealand, so small and so distant, also almost avoids notice. Just two references. In the first, the Oxford-educated Desmond Collier is detected in having accepted a post at a university in New Zealand. '"I'm sorry for [Collier and his family], that's all I can say,"' a character declares (Trickett 1966: 49). In the second case a London academic has failed his wife's expectations of professorial status. He was offered one chair, she confides, but 'unfortunately in New Zealand' (Raphael 1980: 90). Clearly out of the question. South Africa gets no more attention. A rugby-playing Rhodes Scholar at St Saviour's, Oxford, gets a patronizing put-down: 'It's the same with all these colonials . . . no imagination' (T. Robinson 1961: 149). Sam Barrett is a South African Rhodes Scholar from an earlier generation. An undergraduate at St Mark's, he is the leader of the college's 'bad men': the idle and rowdy. Thrown out, he marries the sister of his former college's junior clerk. '"But she isn't a lady,"' expostulates the Vice-President of St Mark's. '"Nor am I a gentleman,"' replies Barrett (Cole and Cole 1937: 43). There is no hint of sympathy from this celebrated Fabian husband and wife: Barrett is just a bounder. Settled as the landlord of a country pub-cum-brothel, 'he looked, somehow, a good deal more of the colonial than he had at Oxford' (Cole and Cole 1937: 70). Blood will out, as the Nationalist government was soon to assert in South Africa: until, that is, an embarrassingly large proportion of the Cabinet failed the sanguinary tests for Aryan ancestry.

Among the white dominions the major literary counter-state to England is Australia. Partly this follows from the ten years' Adelaide sojourn of the most important modern British university novelist. We saw in Chapter 2 that until he was on the point of returning to Oxford in 1949 J.I.M. Stewart never wrote about the part of Britain in which he was working at the time. This self-abnegation he broke consistently for Australia. Nor is his opinion of the place flattering. Thirty years' living back in England gave a nostalgic glow to his one positive account as Sir John Appleby, retired Commissioner of the Metropolitan Police, is dined by a group of Anglophile high professionals in a comfortable house high in the Flinders Ranges (M. Innes 1976: 17–38). That apart, Stewart flays the country. In *Lament for a Maker* we learn that Ranald Guthrie attempted suicide on first seeing Fremantle from the deck of his emigrant ship (M. Innes 1938: 121). In the next book, 'reading *Little Grains of Sand*, which was Mrs Birdwire's account of wanderings in Central Australia, [Bussenschutt] was appalled that such places should exist, and yet further appalled that they could be celebrated in so excruciating a prose' (M. Innes 1939: 75). '"I was impressed,"' says the villainous Mr Hoppo in *Appleby on Ararat*, '"by the towns – cities, one should really say. One didn't expect them; one had thought only of the Great Outback. In Melbourne one might almost be in – well, in Glasgow"' (M. Innes 1941: 7). If one of the less-fashionable parts of marginal Britain can be pressed into service to show Australia's awfulness, then other kinds of marginality will also serve. Adrian Waterbird explains to John and Judith Appleby the dreadful fate that awaits both him and Ralph Jenkins, inmates of an Oxbridge crammer:

'I get through this rotten exam, or I'm booked for New South Wales. You see, my family has some property there. But I don't know anything about it. Full of blacks, I expect. . . . As for Ralph, he's going to be put in a bicycle factory.'

(M. Innes 1973: 71)

Examination failure for Waterbird will see him enlisted in the ranks of the remittance men. This, for Stewart (his tongue firmly in his cheek), is where Australia's future lies: 'it has the advantage over Canada. . . of being three or four times as far away' (M. Innes 1938: 121). Exiled before the war, Ranald Guthrie soon has company; '"the ne'er do weel cousin you used to keep in Australia"' (M. Innes 1968: 124) and that pair of beauties, George and Denzell Simney.

> 'George and Denzell, you know, came out to Australia when they were little more than lads, and before George looked like being heir to the title. They weren't altogether reliable boys, I'm afraid. There had been some trouble about banknotes, and they had done some more or less permanent injury to a lad in the village who had offended them, and there had been an affair with a girl in which they had been – um – a little too impetuous in their methods of courtship. So they were sent out with the idea of taking up land and perhaps entering Australian politics later.'
>
> (M. Innes 1946b: 117)

A country in which George and Denzell could look forward to a political career must have a ropey social structure. So, we are told, it has. Given the conventional British colonial wisdom about class emigration – East Africa for officers, Canada for non-commissioned officers, Australia and New Zealand for other ranks – we should not expect Australia to exhibit aristocratic virtues. Stewart shows us sham aristocracy: snobs amid the Ocker corn, people aping English models in ludicrously inappropriate circumstances.

> I had gathered [says Nicolette, Lady Simney] that the Australian Simneys were folk of the severest social sense. They were, in fact, pastoralists – a word which suggests robed and bearded persons living in tents, but which (it seems) is simply synonymous with gentry and applied to exclusively-minded folk living retired lives amid millions and millions of sheep.
>
> (M. Innes 1946b: 18)

Joyleen Simney having married in to this gentry from Bondi – 'I gathered this must be some dressy Sydney suburb,' Nicolette tells us – 'was making the important discovery that to live in the neighbourhood of a Dismal Swamp is socially disadvantageous' (M. Innes 1946b: 24). No doubt she knew Martin Fish, a pastoralist's son at Oxford in the late forties who also admits to being acquainted with Dismal Swamp (J.I.M. Stewart 1975: 285). Names' absurdities reflect that of the whole country. Yet the assertion of that absurdity does not go wholly unchallenged. Arnold's liberalism of the future peeps through Stewart's delicate hint of a possible Australia that is absurd on aristocratic English terms, but not totally to be despised on its own.

'But quite often,' explained Lucy [an English Simney], 'there *is* nobody in particular. The Shropshire Mortimers have cousins in a place called the Flinders Ranges. And they say that there is nobody in particular within hundreds of miles of them. Nobody, that is, except ordinary colonials.'

Gerald put down his knife and fork, and I could see that he was quite quickly learning to be less annoyed than amused by talk of this sort. 'But we are all ordinary colonials,' he said. 'Except of course those of us who are indigenous and black.'

(M. Innes 1946b: 34)

Rather later, Gerald develops these crypto-democratic sentiments:

'The old colonial days were for the most part disgusting, so far as I can make out. But Australia has her chance now. A decent sort of social-democracy can conceivably be set going there. Spiritually and culturally it will be something thoroughly inglorious. But it will be a whole heap better than most other places'.

(M. Innes 1946b: 123)

This is post-war reconstruction Stewart; Gerald Simney's hopes for Australia are cognate with the Duke of Nesfield's hopes for his local redbrick university.

Other British university novelists are no more charitable than Stewart. David Lodge (1984) excoriates snake- and spider-infested north Queensland, with its inhumanly sticky climate. Sefton Goldberg (Jacobson 1983) looks back with relish to Sydney, notably to the cohorts of long-legged, available girls: but Australia looks good only by comparison with the horrors of Wrottesley Polytechnic. Goldberg's apotheosis is to be his unmerited return to Cambridge. A later novel (Jacobson 1986) makes Australia a barbarous bare canvas for the crusading zeal of a rightist, Catholic, Leavisite missionary from Cambridge. The least varnished of all opinions come from the Balliol-educated Robert Barnard. In *Death of an Old Goat* (1974) he bade a less than regretful farewell to Australia, part-way through an academic career that moved from an Accrington technical college to the University of New England at Armidale, then to Bergen before ending in an English chair at Tromso. The book is set in Drummondale, a gauze-thin disguise for Armidale. Drummondale society is dominated by graziers, Stewart's pastoralists. They are stupid men; ostentatious in their flashy cars, philistine utilitarians. They despise Aborigines but combine in a fatuous rain dance when drought threatens farming profits. Their wives are snobs, obsessed with fake culture. The local police, theoretical defenders of liberty and the rule of law, violently repress local Aborigines. The police chief is irrepressibly randy, steadily working his way through the Drummondale wives. All police are corrupt, so completely in the pocket of the local political bosses that they refuse to pursue a murder charge against a respected local headmaster until he has killed a Balliol-educated English lecturer who sought to expose him. Bill Bascomb dies a victim of corruption and Australia, a first-rate victim of the second-rate. But for an Oxford man death comes as a release. "It's so difficult for you young men, just out from England. Torn between two civilisations. . . ." "Two?" said Bill, passing his glass' (R. Barnard 1974: 177).

Academic life in such a country cannot be worth living. The wise recognize this, and stay at home. Ideally one should not even think of the place. An amateur Rorschach test is taken in Oxford:

> What this blot suggested to him was the continent of Australia rotated clockwise through an angle of ninety degrees. The discovery was not enlightening. Australia, he was convinced, was an area of the world's surface with which his subliminal self held no conversation whatever.
>
> (J.I.M. Stewart 1955: 10)

Phil Tombs makes the same point more succinctly: 'Nerts to Australia' (J.I.M. Stewart 1961: 53).

Blissful ignorance is the best defence, but others lie behind. Margaret Woods is untroubled by her husband's proposal that they should quit Oxford for Australia: 'even Albert's restlessness could not make him do anything so silly' (W. Cooper 1952: 209). But people do silly things. Should a British savant fall for the siren song of the south seas then he or she should contact the nearest escape committee immediately. Duncan Pattullo's Oxford college recruits a new fellow. He, 'bald and abraded, was understood to have escaped in middle age from some professorial assignment in the antipodes' (J.I.M. Stewart 1978: 37). Elsewhere we learn that Australian universities are able to equip their students with an inadvertent innocence. Diana Kittery, a sensuous Eve to John Appleby's Adam in their Pacific island Garden of Eden, is tempted to a rash comparison.

> 'There!' she whispered. 'You see? They don't even attend to each other any longer. It's just like people in Capek.'
> He stared at her, perplexed. Here in the green shade her flesh, golden-brown as impossible toast on a hoarding, held half-lights like old bronze. 'Diana, one day you will get right in the target area. Chekhov, perhaps. What makes you so literary? I suppose you enjoyed the Australian higher education?'
> She looked at him suspiciously. 'I took out some classes,' she said briefly.
>
> (M. Innes 1941: 41)

Foreigners bring dangers for English universities, generating a cruel paradox. Different colonial practices meant that while one could think properly of a black – a visibly not-French – Frenchman, a black – a not-English – Englishman was a manifest absurdity (Kiernan 1969: 96–100). Yet state policy required that colonial leaders, of all skin-tints from ebony to pinky-grey, should be educated to accept the enlightened hegemony of the Queen Empress and her descendants. English leaders are manufactured in Oxbridge. Colonial leaders can be rendered safe only by incorporation in Oxbridge culture. Yet the process of incorporating foreigners threatens the sanctity of English culture's citadel. The solution is to restrict the flow of foreigners to a trickle small enough to be acculturated by conventional means. Ethiopians lolling in the University Parks may be incongruous, but at least they are reading *The Economist* (J.I.M. Stewart 1954). At much the same time, Mahmoud and Amin formed a 'black vanguard'. In the late 1960s this would have had them construed as members of a popular liberation army preparing to assault Oxford. That is not what Atiyah (1952) meant: they were the first fruits of a policy concerned to give an Oxbridge polish to a few carefully selected students from a black African colony being prepared for neo—colonial independence. Lo Ping, Lo Ling, and Lo Ting return to China to teach in local universities, their Oxford degrees ensuring that they will carry culture's banner high in Mao Zedong's land (Hsuing 1952). Educating such folk provides assurance that colonial political independence will bring no difficulty to Oxford, to England, to Oxford-as-England. An earlier insurance policy had seen Oxford University develop a quintessential neocolonial device. The Rhodes scholarship took one or a few barbarous chaps (now, rarely, chapesses) each year from each barbarous nation in England's informal cultural empire, and groomed him in aristocratic England's finishing school. The extent of the informal cultural empire thus demonstrated is revealing. Germany was included before 1914: after the unfortunate events of that year recruitment was restricted to the white dominions, selected black colonies, informal dependencies, and the United States of America. Oxford novels show us Rhodes scholars from South Africa, Australia, New Zealand, and the United States. Only Sam Barrett, the South African cad, resists Oxford culture and society: the others are models of successful socialization.

Novels assure us that this fits wider experience. Foreigners are usually successfully socialized in Oxbridge. The mark of success is deference.

> Only a Philistine of the first water could fail to be impressed by the beauty of the dining-hall of St Thomas'. . . . Brendel, seeing it for the first time, and passing a long lingering glance over it all, was visibly impressed. 'Now I think I understand your Oxford traditions,' he said to me.
>
> (Masterman 1933: 17)

Ernst Brendel is a visitor, a Viennese academic lawyer. Mahmoud's father is another visitor, this time from a black African colony. He is entranced.

> It was a sun-flooded June afternoon. The grey buildings and the great beech and chestnut trees stood out nobly, suffused with light, cutting out the edge of their still, superb patterns against an enamel sky. The lawns in the quadrangles stretched their smooth, generous immensities with a sweet abandon, golden-green in the sunshine like carpets in

186

paradise, and though the houris were not in evidence, Sheik Ahmed – making a mental reservation on the point – turned to his son, his eyes dilated with enchantment, and said: 'Mahmoud! If our Prophet's paradise turns out to be anything like this, by God I shall be satisfied!'

(Atiyah 1952: 43)

Now that is the right kind of visitor: rich, well-connected and blinded by aristocratic privilege.

Doing his best to become accustomed to such privilege, to live by the smallest details of its mores, is the Regius Professor of Belles-Lettres, a man for whom Oxford was once as rich and strange as it proves for Sheik Ahmed.

The alarm rings. It is 6.45. Rudyard Parkinson stretches out a hand to silence the clock, blinks and yawns. He opens the door of his bedside cabinet and pulls out a heavy ceramic chamber pot emblazoned with the College arms. Sitting on the edge of the bed with his legs apart, he empties his bladder of the vestiges of last night's sherry, claret and port. There is a bathroom with toilet in his suite of rooms, but Rudyard Parkinson, a South African who came to Oxford at the age of twenty-one and perfected an impersonation of Englishness that is now indistinguishable from authentic specimens, believes in keeping up old traditions. He replaces the chamber pot in its cupboard, and closes the door. Later a college servant, handsomely tipped for the service, will empty it.

(Lodge 1984: 99)

Rudyard Parkinson shows that even the crassest colonial can be inducted to Oxbridge given time on the institution's side and deference on the postulant's.

Making Parkinson Oxonian was not too difficult. Brendel had Viennese culture as a counterweighing impediment to Oxford. Sheik Ahmed had his Islamic faith, which led him to join many male novelists of undergraduate manners in deploring the shortage of houris. Parkinson had no counterweight. Oxford wrote on him as on a clean sheet because, as Bill Bascomb told us in Drummondale, the white dominions have no culture of their own. A 1930s Otago student struggling for New Zealand's Rhodes

187

Scholarship pours out his frustration to his professor: '"That's what I want to get away from, sir. Our metaphors are borrowed, our novels, our plays, our poetry. Schools, universities, politics, nothing's indigenous, it's all second-hand"' (Davin 1970: 177).

This explains the discourse of novels set in the dominions. The most interesting is Robertson Davies's *The Rebel Angels* (1981) which uses Toronto University's vestigial collegiate system to produce a pastiche of many kinds of Oxbridge novel. We are in the College of St John and the Holy Spirit, usually known as Spook. The description of college buildings – Spook's 'Collegiate Gothic' with rooms off staircases and baths in 'another wing of the college, in the great Oxbridge tradition' (R. Davies 1981: 13); Ploughwright's modern buildings ranged around quadrangles, with access through a tower-guarded gate (1981: 59) – tells us where we are in literary space. The novel's typical figure is the bachelor don: not one major character is married. Dramatically lost and found literary texts litter Innes-inspired Oxbridge whodunits. Robert Robinson (1956) gives us Chaucer's *Book of the Lion* in a fake version; Dorsey Fiske (1980) gives us the real lost manuscript of Shakespeare's *Cupid and Psyche*. Davies sets his argument in this stream of novels by giving us two literary frameworks which appear to be unconnected. The first is a Rabelais manuscript, with some attached letters. The second, its significance signalled in the book's title, seems to be Milton's *Paradise Lost*. Half the novel is written through a narrative headed 'The Second Paradise'. We have a colourable Adam, a colourable Eve, a more than colourable Satan. We comfortably assume that *The Rebel Angels* is to be the university as Milton's second Paradise, the Garden of Eden. Then Davies violates our expectations:

> 'Oh, Simon, you must remember the Rebel Angels? They were real angels, Samahazai and Azazel, and they betrayed the secrets of Heaven to King Solomon, and God threw them out of Heaven. And did they mope and plot vengeance? Not they! They weren't sore-headed egotists like Lucifer. Instead they gave mankind another push up the ladder, they came to earth and taught tongues, and healing and laws and hygiene – taught everything – and they were often special successes with the "daughters of men". It's a marvellous piece of apocrypha, and I would have expected you to know it,

because surely it is the explanation of the origin of universities!'

(R. Davies 1981: 263)

Adroitly, Davies moves us from theological poetry to humanist prose. This apocryphal story becomes attached (1981: 283) to the work and legacy of Paracelsus. Rabelais's discovered, then stolen and recovered manuscript letters to Paracelsus conjure a world where humanism is incompletely separated from science, religion from alchemy. Davies connects his two literary frameworks; but he does more. He returns to the early modern world to find a new and more profound justification for the modern university as a cultural citadel resisting populist politicians, for the centrality of humane studies. If in this he out-Oxbridges Oxbridge novels, then in some ways he disturbs those novels' assumptions. Foreigners are not aliens in melting-pot north America. Collegiate women are less likely to be taken to be dromedaries. These apart, 'the fact that Spook was a New World college in a New World university made surprisingly little difference' (R. Davies 1981: 22). This is true in absence as well as presence. Davies tells the reader a great deal about Paracelsus. There is one famous story that he does not recount. In Basel, in 1527, Paracelsus pinned a list of his forth-coming medical lectures to the university's notice-board, with an invitation for any interested person to attend the lectures. This refusal to limit knowledge to properly matriculated persons outraged the university authorities. His silence about this episode suggests that it outrages Robertson Davies just as deeply. More generously we might suggest that it had to be suppressed in order to maintain the integrity of that Oxbridge discourse within which he bedded his novel. *The Rebel Angels* is a remarkable Oxbridge-abroad novel, employing the conventions of the college detective novel and the novel of collegiate manners. With remarkable skill and wit, Davies builds the book around meanings clustered in the chapel: a distanced religious symbolism suffuses narrative and imagery. Once Davies has done it in Canada we realize what an obvious resource lay waiting for Oxbridge novelists. None took it up; British university fiction's secularized discourse closed off the possibility.

The Rebel Angels is unique in giving us Oxbridge abroad. The usual procedure is to use Oxbridge as a covert measure for dominion universities' inadequacy. As the Dismal Swamp Simneys incompetently aped real English gentry, so fake Australian universities ape their real English counterparts. Drummondale's institution

> was situated three or four miles out of the city of Drummondale: the city fathers had insisted on this, for they feared contamination. The first one saw of it was a series of blocks and huts at the bottom of the hill, which Professor Wickham pointed out by name as some of the colleges into which the university was divided. Up the hill were toiling strings of students in jeans and odd green gowns, and at the top of the hill there were more blocks and huts, which were apparently the departments, and a large Edwardian gentleman's residence which sprawled and straggled in all directions, and had caused John Betjeman to chortle appreciatively. This was the nucleus of the university, and now housed the administration who not unnaturally kept the best thing for themselves.
>
> (R. Barnard 1974: 28)

The reference to Betjeman is the key to this passage. We know that we may see some local colour – colleges called Daisy Bates and Menzies rather than Girton and Christ Church; Merv Raines the professional Ocker, an Australian literature specialist – but that everything else will be comfortably familiar. We have hutted colleges, odd green gowns. We have a campus built around what passes for a mansion. We have a university centred in departments rather than colleges. We have animosity towards a dominant administration. We have, in short, a fake-Oxbridge not-Oxbridge British university dumped down on the other side of the world. Oxford controls the discourse, even at this distance. Bill Bascomb, the second corpse, is newly out from Balliol. The first corpse is Belville-Smith, an Oxford English professor on a British Council junket, slain to prevent his exposing a former scout from Jesus College who has bluffed his way to the headship of a private boys' school through a spurious claim to be an Oxford graduate. The action is centred in the university's English department whose head scraped an inglorious second-class Oxford degree through his wife's calculated fornication with key examiners. That achieved, he 'speedily returned to that haven of Oxford seconds, his home land' (R. Barnard 1974: 160). So it goes on. The university's fake-Oxford structure frames a fake-Oxford murder. The setting is exotic, but the action is as provincially British as warm beer. We might be in Watermouth but for the gum trees.

Pohutokawas along the shoreline tell us that we are in New Zealand, but English models rule once more. This is more surprising than in the case of Drummondale. Robert Barnard was no more than a disgruntled sojourner in Armidale; New Zealand university novelists are much more firmly set in their country. Dan Davin, Michael Joseph and Karl Stead took New Zealand first degrees before heading off to be polished in Oxford. Wayne Innes enjoyed all his higher education in New Zealand.

Wayne Innes's *The Department* (1983) claims to be set in Sydney, but this is a legal fiction resting on the happy accident that both Auckland and Sydney have harbour bridges with middle-class suburbs on the North Shore. The description of the university, its strongly behaviourist psychology department, and the building in which that department is housed all mark the setting as Auckland. Innes has an Auckland psychology doctorate. His novel takes its scatologies from Tom Sharpe's *Porterhouse Blue*, its arguments from *The History Man*. With Bradbury, Innes believes that social scientific barbarians have penetrated the citadel. Just as the humanistically inclined Henry Beamish presents no obstacle to the machiavellian Howard Kirk in Watermouth's sociology department, so there is no real chance for the humanists in Auckland's psychology department to resist the dominant behaviourist faction's barbarous utilitarianism. Innes also follows the British model in an unrepentant misogyny. Lesbian feminists infest the Auckland campus. It is not clear whether Innes finds utilitarianism or feminism the greater threat. Certainly his anti-feminist obsessions lead him to blow the chance to write a good British-style university novel attacking behaviourism: an obvious task that has never been attempted in Britain because local university novelists are so dismally ignorant about social science.

Dan Davin's two university novels display a finely flowering cultural cringe towards Oxford as the centre of the cultural universe. In *Not Here, Not Now* (1970) 1930s Otago undergraduates struggle for escape through the Rhodes Scholarship: just as Davin did. This book swallows whole the deferential assumptions underpinning the Rhodes. *Brides of Price* (1972) maintains the genuflection as an expatriate New Zealand social anthropologist shuffles between Oxford and Auckland while trying to decide whether to allow his name to go forward as a candidate for an Oxford chair. In the first book Davin has an academic advise a student that should he get the Rhodes, he should read Greats and hope for a career with Oxford University Press. This was Davin's own career. His advice is wickedly satirized by J.I.M. Stewart (1974: 295) in the absurd figure of Charles Talbert, an OUP proof-reader looking to crown his career with the unlimited opportunities of the Secretaryship to the Delegates.

If these two authors are scarcely worth reading unless one is writing a book on university fiction – with Dan Davin's novels flawed by their craven fawning on Oxford and Wayne Innes's single book by his failure to seize a golden opportunity – then the last two New Zealand university novels are more interesting. The best of the lot is M.K. Joseph's *A Pound of Saffron* (1962). His theme – how can the respect for others' opinions that must mark university life be protected against *Realpolitik?* – looks forward to *The History Man* more than a decade later. But this theme is carried in a narrative that owes a strong debt to Innes/Stewart. *A Pound of Saffron* bears close comparison with Michael Innes's *The Weight of the Evidence* (1944) as a study of attenuated charities among teaching staff in not-Oxbridge universities. It bears close comparison with J.I.M. Stewart's *The Man Who Won the Pools* (1961), but with the emphasis on the possibility of a merger between working-class Oxford and collegiate Oxford transmuted into the possibility of merging Maori Auckland with Pakeha (non-Maori New Zealand) Auckland. As Bill Pearson (1952) noted, the structural position of Maori people in most New Zealand writing corresponds to that of working-class people in British fiction. Joseph's book is profoundly and wittily literary. The plot turns on a student production of *Antony and Cleopatra*, with Cleopatra played by a Maori woman. The director subverts the text in order to celebrate the manipulative Octavius. This director is an Oxford-educated Auckland English professor with an Octavius complex, a man who manipulates others in pursuit of a UNESCO sinecure (shades of Lodge's much later *Small World*). When forced from his Auckland chair he takes a similar job in the Republic of Costaguana, Conrad's mythical South American setting for *Nostromo*.

The most recent New Zealand university novel is Karl Stead's *The Death of the Body* (1986). As befits the work of a major critic, it has a much more ambitious form than its predecessors. We are in Auckland once more, but we glimpse (twice, to make sure that we get the point) the campus through a fountain: flickering, fragmented, broken. This image, together with the novel's recourse to cinematic techniques – the relentless use of flashback, the frequent description of places as if they were being filmed – and the interlarding of first-person and third-person positions, fractures the narrative. The Cartesian subject is displaced, dethroned. The author or his central character no longer warrants the truth of what we see, no longer warrants that there is a single truth to be apprehended. Certainly there is no privileged access to truth. Truth is multiple, located in multiple realities. Stead gives us New Zealand's first post-structural university novel. Surely here the dependence on British university fiction's dominant discourse will be broken?

Not a bit of it. Strong overlapping threads tie New Zealand back to Britain, Auckland to Oxford. Harry Butler, the central character, is a professor of philosophy. The relationship between his professional interest in the mind–body problem and the complications about minds and bodies that breed in his life outside the university set up those ironic parallels that proliferate in the typical British university novel. Butler is a New Zealander, but he took a postgraduate scholarship to Oxford. This is germane to Stead's purpose since Butler practises Oxford philosophy in Auckland; but it also establishes a strong connection back to British university fiction's interpretation of Arnold as the Oxonian standard-bearer for liberal humanism. Stead plays on this connection. There is a death in *The Death of the Body*, signalling a link to the many British college detective novels. The book's climax concerns a thwarted attempt by two lesbian feminists to discredit Butler for sexual harassment. This bounces off rather recent events on the Auckland campus, but it also looks back through Wayne Innes to the characteristic misogyny of the British genre, firmly located in what J.I.M. Stewart once called 'the queer semi-monasticism' of Oxford and Cambridge.

These points are buried rather deeply in the text; but Stead also establishes much more prominent connections between marginal New Zealand and the cultural centre. *The Death of the Body* has two intertwined plots. One concerns Harry Butler's life and times in Auckland. Here Stead writes in the third person. But he interlards a first-person narrative. Here an author figure complains about how difficult it is to write about Butler, and takes us on a Cook's tour of those parts of Europe that a New Zealand academic might visit on leave, as he struggles to make sense of the obdurate material in the first plot. This first person narrator seems to have his feet in Europe and his head in New Zealand; but this is an illusion. He writes about New Zealand from Europe, but constructs a novel whose central character is torn between a Pakeha background and European accoutrements: his Porsche, his mistress's Italian shoes, his Oxford philosophy. Butler is not interested in what it means to be a Pakeha in New Zealand. Unlike *A Pound of Saffron*, Stead's book lacks a single brown face. Butler establishes meaning by looking across the world to Oxford, not across his own city to the heavily Polynesian districts of South Auckland.

The fashionably fractured narrative fails to mask a deeply contradictory text. Karl Stead wants to retain the links to Oxford, to Europe, to the right-Arnoldian notion of a privileged high culture warranting Harry Butler's practice as a philosopher in Auckland. But he also wants to ride the latest critical windsurfer, post-structuralism. So we are given a text that is internally incoherent, a forced marriage of two incompatible partners. Despite its formal pretension to relativism, *The Death of the Body* is an appropriation of New Zealand experience for European purposes: a traveller's tale. That is no surprise when Stead has thrown up his university chair so that he can travel more lightly. But it is a shame that a writer with such a strong feel for the physical presence of Auckland should not take the multiple social realities of the city – and the nation in which it sits – more seriously. He faces a choice. He can write from a narrow, and increasingly anachronistic, conception of what constitutes high culture: the implication of *The Death of the Body*'s content. Or he can take the post-structuralism of that novel's form seriously in future books, and explore much more widely the range of ways in which it is possible to be a New Zealander in our times. We must hope that he chooses this second option. Unlike Dan Davin, he is too good a writer to lose to the siren songs of Oxford's screaming choirs.

We have exhausted the list of post-war New Zealand university novels for reasons which will become clear in a later chapter. For Australia and Canada we have taken only one example. Robertson Davies's *The Rebel Angels* and Robert Barnard's *Death of an Old Goat* display a dependence on British models which matches that in New Zealand novels. But not all Canadian novels are like this. Susan Haley (1984) gives us a straightforward campus staff romance – later transformed into a glutinous television mini-series – that one would assume was set south of the forty-ninth parallel if she did not insist on the Canadian location. Gildas Roberts (1974) gives us a farcical novel set in a lightly disguised Memorial University, Newfoundland, but modelled on contemporary American drug culture novels. Not even all Australian novels defer to Britain. Don Aitkin's *The Second Chair* (1977) takes us to a new university. A sociology professor is killed in a campus road accident. The novel examines his replacement's appointment. This looks like meat and drink for the British genre. An account of the internal politics of a professorial appointment can draw sustenance from Snow, the excoriation of sociology in a new university from Bradbury. None of this happens. The dead sociology professor was widely respected. We never see such an animal in a British novel. Aitkin, a political scientist, shows an acute inside knowledge of sociology: the choices facing the appointments committee make sense. That, too, sets his novel apart from the British literature. It is distanced further by its optimistic tone, so refreshingly different from British counterparts. Whence these differences? Look for clues in the built form, as we saw in Chapter 3. Bradbury's Watermouth campus exemplifies English social history, the transmitted cultural understandings that weigh like a nightmare on the minds of the living novelist. Aitkin's unnamed university is first shown to us in an immensely elevated crane shot. The campus buildings form 'a combination of diamond, circles and arcs' (Aitkin 1977: 2). Architectural whimsy rules, as in Lowlands and so many other dreadful fictional British new universities. But here 'the building worked well and there were few grumbles about it' (Aitkin 1977: 2). The absence of Pommy whingeing tells us that we are in a different literary space. Aitkin's novel breaks the British discourse because it looks to a competing discourse that lacks the pervasive

pessimism of British novels. Aitkin looks to America. We must
follow his example.

Chapter Nine

AMERICAN DIFFERENCE

Americans are difficult people. The notion of 'Commonwealth literature', with Cromwell pressed into validating the dying embers of monarchical Empire, can confine to inferior status those people who insist on writing about white dominion universities. But the United States cut their leading strings in 1776, and 'American literature' quite fails to catch the proper nuance of dependency on English literature. These colonials have gotten uppity, and English university fiction is lost for suggestions about how to bring them back into line.

The usual defensive tactics are employed. Consider Innes/Stewart. His novels show us that the first line of defence is induced admiration for England, for Oxford, for Oxford-as-England. The Rhodes scholarship is invaluable here. Grant Feather arrives from Harvard (M. Innes 1953) some years after Quail had made the same journey (J.I.M. Stewart 1955). Dick Evans from Princeton is supposed to be studying jurisprudence, '"But principally I'm going to write a book on Caravaggio"' (M. Innes 1940b: 72–3). Garth Dauncey is a literary specialist who sweeps Anthea Lambert off her feet and out of her dreadful women's college (J.I.M. Stewart 1954). Leon Kryder, 'a Rhodes Scholar from Princeton' (M. Innes 1956a: 12), sparks a discussion of 'Yanks and English' at an Oxford college reading party in Devon. What do these Rhodesian folk have in common? They share impeccable Ivy League academic backgrounds. Nobody here hails from Bob Jones University. They share rapidly acquired Oxbridge protective colouring. Dick Evans has a gentlemanly interest in art history, though he is a lawyer. Quail, returning to Oxford in *The Guardians* (J.I.M. Stewart 1955), is a fabulously wealthy bachelor who swims easily in senior

197

common room life, just as he had thrown bread rolls many years before on the scholars' table. He is a model of successful socialization; so are they all. They defer.

When not caught so young, Americans are rather more difficult to train. Colin Clout finds a new face in his dreadful minor redbrick's library:

> The middle-aged scholar had grey hair worn rather short; rimless glasses with a glint of gold at their sides; and a face of monotonous pallor, of which the chief feature was a mouth which might have been supplied by a single deft stroke of a knife. His clothes were good and quiet and loose and casual. He had a modest air of high distinction. Clout concluded that he came from either Princeton or Yale.
>
> (M. Innes 1956b: 100)

He came from neither. Milder is a fake professor, but a real villain. It is so difficult to tell one from the other among Americans. Even Louise Vanderlyn (J.I.M. Stewart 1967), an Anglophile trained in English philology, is not as comforting a figure as she might be. First encountered by Jeremy Shefford while she is searching for that Red Barn from which Jude Fawley glimpsed Christminster, Louise proves to be an American liberal of disconcertingly steely purpose. One could imagine her demanding that Oxford should stop making ritual nods to Arnold, and do something about implementing his liberalism of the future.

If socialization fails, then the second line of defence is to patronize American universities. Nudd Manor, one of Innes/Stewart's innumerable crumbling stately homes, is discreetly up for sale. Currently housing a major private art collection, its curator

> 'has in some manner educed expressions of interest from at least two reputable seats of learning in the United States. One of them has even had architects and surveyors down to Nudd, looking into the possibilities of extensions to the house – dormitories and so forth.'
>
> 'Dormitories? Are they thinking of starting a prep school?'
>
> 'No, no. Recollect, my dear Domberg. "Dormitory" is a word used by the Americans, very absurdly, to describe what we should call a court, quad, or even hall of residence.'
>
> (J.I.M. Stewart 1972: 195-6)

That really puts American universities in their place: below Cambridge, Oxford, and not-Oxbridge. Tom Elder is educated in English at Oxford, then can find no better employment than as an assistant lecturer in not-Oxbridge. Discreet plagiarism rapidly takes him to the headship of his department, where

> he proved a ruthless dictator – chasing out the young men and women who were investigating *Sexuality in 'The Waste Land'*, and *Samuel Beckett's New Anatomy of Melancholy*, and *Intentionalism: a Challenge*, and so forth, and appointing in their place serious students of palaeography, typography, critical bibliography, and similar essential tools of a sound literary scholarship.
>
> (J.I.M. Stewart 1983: 52)

But Elder's plagiarism is detected by an American academic who forces Elder on pain of exposure to write his 200,000-word doctoral dissertation on 'Subjective and objective components in the metaphysical substructure of James Joyce's *Finnegan's Wake*'. This appalling task completed, he is set to work ghosting a book on *The Rhetoric of Being and Becoming: Modes of Counterpoint in Prose Fiction*.

> Elder soldiered on. His personality became shifty and eccentric. He would slink into the university library at unfrequented hours, and borrow or steal books on outlandish philosophical terminologies that young Adrian Peppercorn's dim notions of what was modish in literary criticism required. Eventually people simply forgot about Elder; he became just another failed scholar in an obscure provincial situation. Not so Peppercorn. No professor was held in higher regard in the Great Republic.
>
> (J.I.M. Stewart 1983: 59)

Peppercorn's apotheosis flows partly from Elder's hard work; but mostly, we are to believe, it flows from the critical illiteracy of American literary criticism and the feebleness of the universities in which that criticism is perpetrated.

As is usual, Innes/Stewart provides a thread to guide us through the labyrinth of British university fiction's attitude to America and Americans. His view of the Rhodes Scholarship's socializing potential is confirmed in two novels written by American recipients. One, G.J.W. Goodman's *A Time for Paris* (1958), is no

199

more than a picaresque trail around glamorous parts of Europe, with an Oxford episode that confirms the text's prevailing aristolatry. Alan Kennington's *Pastures New* (1948) is more interesting. Two graduates of Knapsack College, Centreville, Kansas, head off for post-war Oxford to do second first degrees – the then-standard polishing process for foreigners, whether from Kansas, New South Wales, or Glasgow. Both are enchanted with Oxford. The woman, Marty, admits that '"In a way, I almost want to get my three years safely over. Before some new Education Bill abolishes Oxford, or else changes her utterly"' (Kennington 1948: 66). Her male companion

> despised those countrymen, Rhodes Scholars especially, who come up with their tails down. There was a certain type that was subdued from the start, pressed down by the weight of someone else's centuries. Sometimes they clung together, holding hollow little collegiate evenings in each other's rooms, made aggressively prickly by the inversion of their inferiority complexes. Sometimes they tried with patient earnestness to do the Right Thing in the English way . . . With the result that all their days at Oxford were spent on a tight-rope. They were afraid of seeming too crudely American, and so amusing the English. They were afraid of aping the English too sedulously and so arousing the contempt of their own compatriots. Their choice seemed to lie between huddling clannishly together or becoming slavish Anglophiles.
>
> (Kennington 1948: 161)

Conflating Oxford with England makes the choice simple for Lane and his creator. Slavish Anglophilia is the thing: since Oxford is ineffably superior, anybody who does not genuflect must have an inferiority complex.

Like all good things, adoration of Oxford can be taken too far. Socialization can be too complete. Browning, a Harvard-based visiting lecturer at St Saviour's, kills two people and attempts to murder a third in a misguided attempt to return Oxford to what he has been persuaded to believe are its proper conservative ways (T. Robinson 1961). His is a rare failure, however; and at least he performs the right action, even if his reason is flawed. His motives would appear plain and admirable to the American author of another college murder mystery. Dorsey Fiske spent a year in Cambridge after Radcliffe. *Academic Murder* (Fiske 1980) describes Cambridge, town and gown, in an awed and reverential tone that strongly recalls the murderous Browning.

Travellers' tales about America reverse the flow of bodies without changing attitudes. John Lyons (1974–5: 123) notes a developing subgenre: 'novels by itinerant Englishmen who write novels about itinerant English novelists who come to the wilds of America to teach their trade'. He lists Pamela Hansford Johnson's *Night and Silence, Who is There?* (1963), Christopher Isherwood's *A Single Man* (1964), Malcolm Bradbury's *Stepping Westward* (1965), Michael Kenyon's *The Whole Hog* (1967), John Peter's *Take Hands at Winter* (1967), and Thomas Hinde's *High* (1968). It is curious that Lyons missed Wilfred Sheed's *A Middle-Class Education* (1967) and David Caute's *The Occupation* (1971), though David Lodge's *Changing Places* (1975) was published too late for his survey.

Lodge is the odd man out in this company. The formal balances between Morris Zapp and Philip Swallow in *Changing Places* mean that Zapp will find a mixture of good and bad in not-Oxbridge Britain, and Swallow will find a similar mixture in state university America. But the balance is not even. Swallow goes to Euphoric State. The name summarizes his attitude, and that of his creator. After the cramped constraint of Rummidge, American university life offers Swallow vast and enticing possibilities. In *Small World* (Lodge 1984: 66–7) he confesses to Zapp that he was so taken with the intensity of experience at Euphoric State that he nearly did not come back, and that his head was in California/Euphoria for months after his feet returned to Birmingham/Rummidge.

This celebration of American university life is extremely rare in British fiction. Much more typical is Malcolm Bradbury's jaundiced account in *Stepping Westward*, rooted in contemplation of the differences between university-based British and American liberalism. The American version is optimistically assertive, its British counterpart pessimistically defensive. Bradbury summarizes the difference in an image. American academic liberalism is an A-frame house with all the lights on and no curtains drawn. Everything should be exposed to public view:

Walker had an image of Party as a vast nudist colony. In it people had no privacy and no defects were concealed. Sex and friendship hung in the cold air like summer pollen, and exposure, of self and of others, was the essential ethic of the place.

(Bradbury 1965: 357)

We are left to draw the contrast. British liberalism, we are to conclude, is about making cosy accommodations in the dark corners of private clubs. Yet Bradbury, an outsider yearning for inclusion, prefers the British form. Parisian madams used to call masochism 'the English vice'.

Stepping Westward is one round in Bradbury's interminable tussle with the question of what it means to be a liberal humanist, and how one can manage the task outside Oxbridge. (Basic answer: with the very greatest difficulty.) Wilfred Sheed's *A Middle-Class Education* is another approach to the same question, with the United States again adduced as a horrible example. John Chote is in Oxford but not of it: a member of seedy Sturdley College rather than a properly glittering place, indolently wasting his undergraduate years. In the first part of his book Sheed gives us an account of profound disillusion with Oxford and the notion of liberal undergraduate experience that novels claim it treasures. Then Chote unworthily wins a travelling scholarship to the United States. He enrols at Madison University. Faced with a bewildering range of courses,

Chote sank back and allowed the departmental head to weave his skilful way through the maze. It was a far cry from the perennial Oxford don shaking the tobacco out of his sweater and asking vaguely what one was doing in his room on a Tuesday, when of course it was really a Wednesday.

(Sheed 1967: 262)

Snider, Chote's head of department, speaks of his university as a factory, as a 'plant'.

'Plant' was a good word for Madison University. Chote filled out some exhaustive forms and stood in line and checked in at a little window; and soon after that, the place was banging away full blast. Determined-looking men in leather jackets and sweaters poured into it every day in relentless shifts; and far into the night, the lights burned bright in every corner of the campus, as education was rapidly manufactured and packaged, and prepared for the June – or February – labels.

(Sheed 1967: 262)

The imagery is industrial; clocking in, shift-work, production, packaging. But the utilitarian resonances of factory production chime antiphonally with the dominant discourse of British university fiction. The description of the university as factory looks back to Nesfield in Michael Innes's *The Weight of the Evidence*, forward to Watermouth in Malcolm Bradbury's *The History Man*. Enrolment recalls the minor redbrick professors and their dependent hierarchies settling in to do business with first-year students in Michael Innes's *Old Hall, New Hall*. Even being under the authority of a departmental head places Chote firmly in not-Oxbridge. Semestral examinations apart, Madison is set not in American literary space, but in not-Oxbridge England. Like Robert Barnard's Drummondale, it is a thoroughly familiar British institution set in unfamiliar circumstances. When Chote throws up his studies and returns abjectly to Sturdley, deferring to the collegiate values that he previously had rejected, he is simply accepting the dominant discourse. Travel narrows the mind.

In all this work British novelists, and their house-trained American emulators, commit precisely the error against which J.C. Masterman warned in *To Teach the Senators Wisdom* (1952): *hubris*. They assume that transatlantic visitors to Oxford must be well connected and well conducted, that British travellers bear culture into the wilds. But what if they should prove to have their own robust ideas about what matters in higher education, like the three female undergraduates who stumped Masterman's fellows?

American university fiction represents a major challenge to its British competitor. There is so much of it. In 1957 Mortimer Proctor counted 131 British university novels published between 1828 and 1925, with another 28 appearing between 1925 and 1956. For the United States in the same periods John Lyons (1962) lists 44 and 171 books. This book's appendix lists 196 British university novels published between 1945 and 1979. The corresponding American figure (Kramer 1981a; Kramer and Kramer 1983) is 439.

More important than numbers is discourse. British university fiction, we have seen, runs in very narrow limits, closely focused on the defence of an authorially constructed Oxbridge liberal humanist culture. Lyons shows that the American literature is much more varied. The first university novel was Nathaniel Hawthorne's *Fanshawe* (1828), but the genre did not begin to develop until a spate of novels – initially about Harvard, then widening to consider other elite universities – began to appear from the 1870s. These were written by former undergraduates 'enchanted with the mid-nineteenth century novels of rowdiness at Oxford' (J. Lyons 1962: 7). Thus American university fiction starts in emulation of *Verdant Green* and *Tom Brown at Oxford*. But it soon develops its own flavour. The major books – Charles Flandrau's *Harvard Episodes* (1897), Owen Wister's *Philosophy Four* (1903), and Owen Johnson's *Stover at Yale* (1912) – take an outsider's view of Ivy League life: and these outsiders are not seduced. All three argue that colleges need to be democratized, their antediluvian curricula modernized. This is not what one finds in contemporary Oxbridge novels of undergraduate experience, with their celebration of what exists as eternally good. Some later American novels extend the argument. Honoré Morrow's *Lydia of the Pines* (1917) and James Linn's *This Was Life* (1936) take Harvard-trained young instructors to western state universities. They go to scorn mass public co-education but stay to worship. Where are the equivalent British novels that have Oxbridge-educated teachers celebrating not-Oxbridge university life? And where are the British novels that rail at the injuries suffered by whole categories of people inside universities? Amanda Cross's *A Death in the Faculty* (1983) – *Death in a Tenured Position* (marvellous title) in the American edition – examines the death of Janet Mandelbaum, Harvard's first tenured professor of English. Kate Fansler, a New York English professor, investigates. She shows that Mandelbaum killed herself in her office, unable any longer to bear the slings and arrows of misogynist Harvard. But when male English staff discovered her death, they shifted her body to the men's washroom in order further to discredit the notion of Harvard women. In common with Alison Lurie's *The War Between the Tates* (1974) – which we will consider later – Susan Kenney's *Graves in Academe* (1985), and Valerie Miner's *Murder in the English Department* (1982), Cross's feminist critique of university life has no counterpart in British university fiction. Antonia Fraser's *Oxford Blood* equivocates; Valerie Grosvenor Myer's *Culture Shock* plays arch little Cambridge literary games. Nor does the British literature have anything to compare with American university novels denouncing racial intolerance. J. Lyons (1962: 153-4) lists Earl Miers's *Big Ben* (1933), Nolan Miller's *The Merry Innocents* (1947), Grace Jamison Breckling's *Walk in Beauty* (1955), and Everett Marston's *Take the High Ground* (1954). M.K. Joseph's *A Pound of Saffron* (1962) is a New Zealand example; but the British discourse's proscription against taking foreigners seriously prevents such arguments developing in the Old Country.

Lyons shows us that some modern American novels appear to run parallel with the British genre. Satires on progressivism in British university education – Bradbury's *The History Man*, Balsdon's *The Day They Burned Miss Termag*, Raven's *Places Where They Sing* – are matched by Mary McCarthy's *The Groves of Academe* (1953), Randall Jarrell's *Pictures from an Institution* (1954), and Alison Lurie's *Love and Friendship* (1962). Recent accounts of the British university raped by businessmen – Andrew Davies's *A Very Peculiar Practice: The New Frontier* (1988) and Frank Parkin's *The Mind and Body Shop* (1987) – are echoes of much earlier American books like Robert Herrick's *Chimes* (1926) and Lawrence Watkin's *Geese in the Forum* (1940). Yet even here the parallels should not be stretched too far. The southern Beauregard College in *Geese in the Forum* has been brought low by an imposed Yankee progressivism. The enemies are utilitarians, but first and foremost they are carpet-baggers. American cultural specificities refract the English argument.

It is this refraction, the collision between the dominant British discourse and a less limited American discourse that is well able to look after itself, that makes the United States such difficult territory for British university fiction. Let us pay a little more attention to satires on progressive education. Dacre Balsdon's *The Day They Burned Miss Termag* (1961) is a dyspeptic farce about a twenty-first-century Oxford brought low by the state, women and proletarians. Simon Raven's *Places Where They Sing* (1970) is one of the first British fictional responses to 1960s student militancy, with a recourse to hostile accounts of the 1789 French Revolution. Malcolm Bradbury's *The History Man* (1975) attacks sociology, new universities, and Marxism as a single dreadful syndrome. The tone of all three is defensive, a spluttering outrage. This contrasts with the tone of comparable American novels. *The Groves of Academe*, *Pictures from an Institution*, and *Love and Friendship* share close kinship. They are all satires on liberal arts colleges. Mary McCarthy uses this setting for mildly comic purposes, but she then turns her book to a topic often considered in the British literature: the defence of academic freedom. Jocelyn College hires Henry Mulcahy, a shifty and unattractive Joycean. When told that he will not be retained when his contract expires, Mulcahy claims that he is being victimised for his former Communist activities. Jocelyn's liberals rally to his defence. Then it is revealed that he never was a Party member. Trapped in webs of liberal guilt, the college president resigns in the hope that his successor will be able to fire Mulcahy. McCarthy gives us a novel that appears to run parallel with Snow's *The Affair* (1960) and J.I.M. Stewart's *The Aylwins* (1966). But *The Groves of Academe* is a very different book. Written against the illiberal crusades of the author's namesake, Senator Joe McCarthy, this novel is more optimistic and less equivocal than its British counterparts. Mulcahy might be a rogue, his case flawed. But that simply makes the principle stand out more clearly. Resistance to tyranny is an absolute obligation that must be maintained even in messy circumstances.

McCarthy writes very well. So does the poet Randall Jarrell. There is a second link. As Gertrude, the academic visitor to Benton College through whose eyes we see the place, Mary McCarthy is reputed to play a leading part in Jarrell's *Pictures from an Institution*. This is a gently pointed satire on a liberal education that rests on Antioch College's democratic work-study programme and the Great Books programme made famous at St John's (J. Lyons 1962: 158). The book is quietly hilarious, understated, and deadly in pinioning its targets. Alison Lurie's *Love and Friendship* is a less gentle but no less impressive book about genteel liberal education.

We find ourselves in the Languages and Literature Division of Convers College, a small New England liberal arts college. Convers is famous for a particular course, Hum (for Humanities) C.

> Hum C was often called the theoretical (or the actual) centre of education at Convers. All incoming freshmen were compelled to take it; more than that, all incoming instructors in the Languages and Literature Division were compelled to teach it. In many ways their individual futures at Convers depended on how well they did so, how quickly they caught on . . .

Hum C was taught by a sort of mean Socratic method: that is, the teachers would ask difficult questions and when a student gave the wrong answers the teacher would just mark a black mark on his paper and write some questions on it. 'The meaning of this word (or line) depends on the words (or lines) which surround it at the time I use it', was the basic answer to the current set of questions, but the students had to find this out for themselves, and nobody was allowed to tell them. For one thing, this statement or any similar one was too full of abstract words to be written on the blackboard. For another, it was believed that the students had to learn the truth themselves in terms of their own experience.

(Lurie 1962: 22–3)

A new instructor, Holman Turner, has to make sense of Hum C. His wife Emmy, the novel's central character, watches him struggle with it. But she soon falls in love – or sex – with Will Thomas, a rat fink from Music. Hum C questions now have to be answered for real. Abstract words like love and friendship have to be brought down to the level of her own experience before she can understand that the meaning of her actions depends on the actions of those who surround her: before, that is, she can make a proper decision about whether to continue her torrid affair with glamorous Will or stick with boring Holman. The philosophical complexities of Hum C form a paradigm for Emmy's [read *Emma's*] moral quandry. As in all Alison Lurie's university novels, personal relationships are set against a disciplinary background that is carefully chosen and expertly explored. That is true of *Imaginary Friends* (1967), with its incisive account of American sociology. It is true of *The War Between the Tates* (1974), which focuses on political science. This last novel is directly comparable with Bradbury's *The History Man*, published the following year. Both concern universities embroiled in change.

The War Between the Tates is a Vietnam novel. Like Karl Stead's New Zealand equivalent, *Smith's Dream* (1971), it is concerned with what the Vietnam War did to nations that fought in that doomed imperial venture. Add one consonant to Lurie's title and we get 'the war between the states', a conventional name for the American Civil War. Thus while at one level the novel treats the break-up and uncertain reconciliation of Brian and Erica Tate's marriage, at a deeper level it is about major fissures in early 1970s American society: the arguments over national policy in Vietnam, women's rising consciousness, intergenerational conflict. Lurie looks for an appropriate setting for these issues, and finds it in the university.

But not just in the university. If the philosophical Hum C provided a palimpset for the dilemmas of extramarital courtship in *Love and Friendship*, then Lurie is careful to choose precisely the right disciplinary background for the Tates' struggle. The Vietnam War was an exercise in international relations carried on through napalm and Agent Orange. Women's struggles concern the gender distribution of power in America. How better to make the geopolitical collide with the personal-political than to set the novel in a department of politics and international relations?

Brian Tate is a professor of political science in upstate New England's Corinth College.

> He is forty-six, and according to local criteria a success. His students think him interesting and well-informed. His colleagues think him competent and fortunate; many of them envy him. He holds an endowed chair in the Department and is the author of two scholarly studies in his field and a widely-used and profitable text; he has a beautiful and intelligent wife, two attractive and intelligent children, and a desirable house in Glenview Heights. They are not aware that internally, secretly, he is a dissatisfied and disappointed man. He bears the signs openly: a sharp W-shaped frown between his neat dark eyebrows, a pinched look around the mouth. But those who see these signs assume Brian is disappointed not by his own condition, but by the condition of the world.
>
> (Lurie 1974: 24-5)

He is disappointed by both. But there is a third, congruent disappointment: the professional. For Brian Tate the world, his kind of political science and his own career are all out of joint in the same way. His marriage has gone stale: it is bogged down. His career is bogged down. The United States are bogged down in a colonial war. These very different levels are mediated by Brian's practice in the university. He approaches personal relationships as he approaches his kind of political science. 'An admirer of George

208

Kennan's early writings, he had long subscribed to the doctrine of separate spheres of influence, both in national and domestic matters; he attributed the success of their marriage to this doctrine' (Lurie 1974: 4–5). But in the 1970s George Kennan's calm, misogynous liberal certainties are breaking down in personal relations, professional life, university politics, and national politics. The United States are embroiled in Vietnam. Brian and Erica's teenage children have turned into a surrogate Vietcong, surly aliens. Brian's kind of political science is on the skids. He has a great future behind him.

Wendy, his student, saves him by seducing him. Her indiscreet letter is discovered by Erica Tate. 'The war', Lurie tells us, 'has begun'. Erica throws him out, straight into Wendy's wholly eager arms. He makes a momentous discovery.

> Brian had known for some time that he and his colleagues were not living in the America they had grown up in; it was only recently though that he had realised they were also not living in present-day America, but in another country or city state with somewhat different characteristics. The important fact about this state, which can for convenience's sake be called 'University', is that the great majority of its population is aged eighteen to twenty-two. Naturally the physical appearances, interests, activities, preferences and prejudices of this majority are the norm in University.
>
> (Lurie 1974: 29)

A radicalizing vision. Brian changes his clothes, his hair-length, and his political convictions. His new radical career briefly suffers when he is identified as an ally of an extreme reactionary in his department. This is a calumny: Brian was trying merely to have his colleague hounded off the campus. Erica Tate is similarly radicalized, but by the women's movement. Her new career plays ironic games with that of her estranged husband. But in life as in war, attrition grinds them down. Slowly they tire. At the book's end Erica seems prepared for a wary truce with the disillusioned Brian. All wars end around a table, whether in Geneva or the kitchen.

The symmetries between Brian and Erica are not complete. Alison Lurie uses her sharply ironic eye and tongue to show that foot-loose professors have an easier row to hoe than do foot-loose professors' wives. This feminist stance is the only thing that disturbs the formal elegance of her argument. The personal, the political, and the professional reflect and refract in a dazzling display of literary craft and control. And central to this display is a deep understanding of American political science. It is not enough that Brian Tate belongs to this coven. He has to cleave to one line within it, interact with others who hold different views, and change his position in ways that would convince an insider. Lurie has to know a great deal about the internal politics of political science, and deploy that knowledge appropriately.

Lurie's skilled depiction of sociology in *Imaginary Friends*, of political science in *The War Between the Tates*, has no counterpart in Britain. Social science is *terra incognita* for British university novelists, something to be ignored or slighted rather than understood. This is true even for authors who know more than most. Frank Parkin, educated as a political sociologist, writes about philosophy in *The Mind and Body Shop*. Malcolm Bradbury puts a considerable knowledge of British sociology to wholly disreputable purposes in *The History Man*. Consider the striking parallels between Brian Tate and Howard Kirk. Both are radicalized conservative liberals. Both have problems – political, intellectual, sexual – with wives and students. They might have been cloned. But there is a significant difference. Brian Tate is inserted into history. It is his seduction by Wendy, and Erica's discovery of his infidelity, that set the novel's machinery in motion. What then happens is the result of Brian's intentions, other people's intentions, and happenchance. Looking backwards Brian might be able to construct a coherent line that he followed through this morass of choices and chances, but things seem less clear-cut as he lives his life forwards. Alison Lurie gives us an account of personal change that coheres with sociological accounts of personal careers. She gives us good humane social science. By contrast, Bradbury gives us execrable social science. At Leeds Howard Kirk decided to insert himself into history. At all subsequent stages of his career he faces no dilemma, no choice. He knows exactly how to get his way, how to do others down. Through his privileged insight into others' desires and intentions, he plays on other people as on an organ. Nothing surprises him. No unanticipated consequences throw his devious plans out of joint. This will not do. No sociologist worth his or her salt would ignore such factors. Lurie worked from inside political science. Bradbury works from outside sociology, constructing a wholly unconvincing picture of the sociologist as social engineer, cynically and expertly manipulating others to his own predetermined ends. That some reviewers and readers took him to be providing a convincing description of the discipline shows how outrageously and complacently ignorant the British scribbling classes are about social science. In the United States, where social scientific ideas are much more widely disseminated and sociology is treated as just another discipline, no author could escape censure for such slackness.

We have spent long enough on American novels for a book concerned with the British discourse. Two conclusions emerge. First, while there are many potboilers in the American literature, at its best that literature writes its English competitor off the page. Partly this has to do with the presence of major novelists in the American list – Nabokov, Wolfe, Malamud, McCarthy, Barth, Lurie. But this is only part of the explanation.

The rest has to do with my second conclusion: unconstrained by the narrow limits of the British discourse, novelists writing about American universities can tackle more issues, and in more interesting ways. We considered some of these issues rather earlier – mass education, the position of women, the position of blacks. What about less tangible matters? Take exile. There are British novels which appear to be about exile. Robert Barnard's *Death of an Old Goat* (1974) maroons Bill Bascomb in Drummondale. Dan Davin's *Brides of Price* (1972) moves uneasily between Oxford and Auckland. In D.J. Enright's *Academic Year* (1955) English literature specialists yearn for England under the Alexandrian date palms. But these books treat sojourners, not exiles. Bascomb stays in Drummondale only because he is dead. Davin's hero will settle in Oxford. Enright's characters return to England on leave and to retire. By contrast, Nabokov's *Pnin* (1957) gives us a white Russian professor bemused in America, stoically ravaged by separation from the country to which he never can return. *Pnin* is a novel in a quite different class from *Academic Year*, and not simply because it is so much better written. Many British novels make Oxford into England. John Barth's *Giles Goat-Boy* (1966) is far more ambitious, allegorizing human life as American university life: commencement, flunking, graduation. Many conventional British university whodunits turn on lost or discovered literary texts. Nabokov's *Pale Fire* (1962) is unprecedented, an extraordinary exercise in intertextuality: the novel is nothing but a poem's text and academic commentaries. Only Lodge's *Small World* (1984) shows anything like that sort of virtuosic formal ambition. Many British novels touch on philosophical debates about free will in the course of their defence of liberal humanism. Only Bernard Malamud tests the idea fully. In *A New Life* (1961) S. Levin, a cosmopolitan New York Jew, takes a job teaching English in a western agricultural university. His experience prefigures most of the English-in-America novels that were soon to follow: Levin's being dumped off the train in the middle of nowhere exactly predicts the arrival of Bradbury's hero in *Stepping Westward* (1965). At one level, then, *A New Life* is the harbinger of conventional British travellers' tales. But it is more. The novel's title asserts potential, possibility. What Malamud chooses to give us is a determinist text. Levin got his job not on his merits, but because his new head of department's wife fancied the look of him. He believes that their affair just happened. She knows better. We leave him as he leaves the college with his new wife and family, victim of a relentless fate. The absence of choice makes *A New Life* sound like *The History Man*, but the effect is very different. Bradbury piled historical inevitability on Kirk's machiavellism. Malamud uses determinism to undercut Levin's dreams of freedom, to work against the text's surface meanings. *A New Life* takes its place in Malamud's long contemplation of the fate of being Jewish, of being sentenced to history.

It is the American university system's significantly different history that generates a significantly different discourse in university novels. Wolfgang Weiss (1988) shows the value of understanding the experience of British and American universities over a very long time period through the interplay of history and literary discourse. Thus far we have concentrated on fiction. We now must turn to fact. In British universities the 1980s have produced fact that few would have accepted as fiction twenty years earlier.

Part four

Chapter Ten

DARK DAYS AND BLACK PAPERS

Let us take stock. In earlier chapters we saw that the discourse of post-war British university fiction has two leading features. First, Oxford and Cambridge, the ancient English universities, form the template against which other kinds of universities are measured and found wanting. Second, the university is treated as culture's citadel, besieged by four barbarian hordes: proletarians, women, scientists, and foreigners. This chapter picks up a thread dropped right at the beginning of the book, by connecting the worlds of novel-writing and politics.

We will begin with a puzzle. Why is the discourse of British university fiction so stable over four decades of radical change – somewhat uncomfortable expansion followed by very painful contraction – in the British university system? One way to tackle this puzzle is to consider the educational background of novelists. Tables 2 and 3 summarize that background.

Table 2 shows us that almost all British university novelists for whom I can find information are graduates. We see that over half of these graduates hold first degrees from Oxford, over three-quarters from Oxford and Cambridge. A significant proportion of not-Oxbridge authors subsequently developed an Oxbridge connection. Thus C.P. Snow and Glyn Daniel ('Dilwyn Rees') moved, from Leicester and Cardiff respectively, to Cambridge fellowships. Frank Parkin's tragically curtailed academic life began at the London School of Economics and ended in an Oxford fellowship. 'Margaret Yorke', not a graduate, worked in two Oxford college libraries. P.D. James, who also has no degree, was born in Oxford and lives in Cambridge. Immediately we see one obvious reason why Oxbridge should bulk largely in British university fiction. But there is a second reason, buried in novelists' disciplinary experience.

Table 2 Location of British university authors' first degree

	N	%
Oxford	48	39.7
Cambridge	20	16.5
Major redbrick	3	2.5
Minor redbrick	3	2.5
London	6	5.0
Scotland	5	4.1
Wales	3	2.5
New English	0	0.0
Abroad:		
Canada	1	0.8
New Zealand	1	0.8
Switzerland	1	0.8
USA	1	0.8
No degree	10	8.3
No information	19	15.7
Total	121	100.0

Table 3 Subject of British university novelists' first degree

	N	%
Archaeology	2	3.5
Classics	12	21.1
English	20	35.0
History	12	21.1
Mathematics	2	3.5
Modern languages	1	1.8
Physical sciences	2	3.5
Social sciences	6	10.5
Total	57	100.0

It is more difficult to find information about what novelists studied than where they studied: Oxford and Cambridge graduates, in particular, think it much more important to tell directory readers about their college than their expertise. There is no obvious reason why reticent novelists should show a pattern different from that in Table 3, which shows what can be discovered about novelists' first degree subjects. English reigns supreme, followed by classics and history. Fourth in the list comes social science. Relative to undergraduate numbers, the first three are massively over-represented. Other disciplines scarcely get a look in. What unifies English, classics, and history? A historically derived cultural mission. 'A hundred, fifty, even twenty years ago', J.H. Plumb (1964a: 7) tells us, 'a tradition of culture, based on the Classics, on Scripture, on History and Literature, bound the governing classes together and projected the image of a gentleman.' In the scribbling classes not much has changed. British university fiction gives us a secularized version of this 'curious mixture of humanistic principles and national pride' (Plumb 1964a: 7): a celebration of English aristocratic culture rooted in once-monastic Oxford and Cambridge. Cambridge had strength in the humanities, but abnormally strong science. In Oxford strong humanities interests faced a weaker challenge from science. That is one important reason why Oxford is the preponderant setting for British university fiction. Thirty years out of our period, the Duke of Dorset had explained to Zuleika Dobson that the Second Division inter-collegiate boat races were rowed at 4.30, the First Division at 6.00. '"Isn't this rather an odd arrangement?"' she enquired. '"No doubt,"' the duke replied. '"But Oxford never pretended to be strong in mathematics"' (Beerbohm 1911: 58).

Writing from his Cambridge history chair, Plumb's essay forms the introduction to a mildly leftist collection of chapters on *Crisis in the Humanities*. Other contributors embroider this doom-laden title with evidence from particular humane disciplines. Moses Finlay (1964: 13) tells us that it used to be believed that 'one went to [classics] for education in its fullest sense, to learn how to live and what to live for': but Latin and Greek have been dethroned. They are not even compulsory university qualifying subjects any longer. History, Plumb (1964b: 30) tells us, 'is a dream world made up of actual events'. Crucified on the dilemma between scientific methodology and the impossibility of historical objectivity, 'it invents the past, and projects lies about the future'. Theology has lost its medieval position as queen of the sciences: since the seventeenth century 'its influence as a subject of supreme or commanding interest has been in a slow but sure decline, both in the academic world and in cultivated society'. Today, an interest in theology is regarded 'as a hobby, like bird-watching or chess' (Vidler 1964: 82, 83). With the erosion of the old Christian-humanist ideal 'the inherited pattern of literary education has fallen into a dismal confusion' (Hough 1964: 97). Finally, in the book's outstanding essay, Ernest Gellner goes for Oxford philosophy's jugular vein. He argues that philosophy should be at the apex of the human sciences, but that its English practit-ioners' professional blindness prevents them from seeing the fact. More important for our purposes, however, is his list of 'the symptoms of this curious phenomenon, contemporary philosophy':

> timelessness; the willingness to embrace a doctrine, or even a succession of doctrines, which only make sense if one is wholly oblivious of the social and intellectual transform-ations of the past four centuries or so; an affectation of imperturbability, a willingness to dispense with generality; ... a curious tendency to prepare elaborate defences along frontiers where virtually no enemy is in sight; a desire to return to the uncoordinated 'common sense' of the possibly educated but unspecialised man, and the tacit assumption of the existence of an allegedly viable and well tried form of life.
> (Gellner 1964: 69)

Gellner's focus is on Oxford philosophy, with its own specificities ('a sense of a lurking abyss of Nonsense at one's feet'); but otherwise his account is eerily familiar. The assertion of timeless verities walled up in a citadel besieged by enemies visible only to the defenders; the celebration of generalism within a complacently taken for granted world; the privileging of particular experience over general statements (vilified as 'theory'): Gellner could have been reading lots of indifferent university novels.

But he hasn't, of course. His list seems familiar because it is nourished by the same springs that water British university fiction's Oxbridge-centred dominant discourse. Those springs kept flowing, but the water carried different flotsam in 1869 and in 1964. When Arnold urged in *Culture and Anarchy* that the university could be culture's castle, he saw the keep in that castle to be classics. But classics' position as the central humane discipline slowly withered. In the early twentieth century several disciplines struggled for supremacy, with history having the strongest claim. A string of studies (Palmer 1965; Baldick 1983; Eagleton 1983: 17–53; Doyle 1986) describes how English literature captured the position, aided by anti-foreign sentiment in the First World War. English as the cultural heart of England: that, we have seen, is what modern British university novels urge on us. That is also the claim at the heart of twentieth-century English 'concealed sociology', social criticism masquerading as literary criticism in the work of T.S.Eliot, I.A. Richards, F.R. Leavis, and Raymond Williams. At this stage in our argument the most interesting of these men is the cantankerous Sage of Downing College, F.R. Leavis.

In 1943 Leavis sought, in *Education and the University*, to do one of the things that Arnold had done in *Culture and Anarchy*: assure the ancient English universities that they had a continuing vital function.

> The universities are recognised symbols of cultural tradition – of cultural tradition still conceived as a directing force, representing a wisdom older than modern civilization and having an authority that should check and control the blind drive onward of material and mechanical development, with its human consequences. The [English] ancient universities are more than symbols; they, at any rate, may fairly be called foci of such a force, capable, by reason of their prestige and their part in the life of the country, of exercising an enormous influence. Much has been compromised there; there, too, unconsciousness gains – it both spreads and deepens; but they are still in more than form representatives of humane tradition.
>
> (F.R. Leavis 1943:16–17)

He returned to universities' responsibility for culture many times in later decades, most notably in the attack on Snow's 'Two Cultures' lecture (F.R. Leavis 1962), in *English Literature In our Time and the University* (1969), and in the late essays collected in *Nor Shall My Sword* (1972). The language grew less temperate as the years passed, but the underlying message never shifted. Full and rich human experience must be rooted in membership of an organic community nourished by cultural continuity. Sturt's *The Wheelwright's Shop* shows what that once looked like, but it has gone:

there is no question of trying to reverse, or halt, the advance
of technology. There can be no restoring the wheelwright's
shop or the conditions of production that integrated work
organically with a living culture and associated it in a major
way with the creative human response.

(F.R. Leavis 1969: 58)

The enemies of culture gather: that complex of science, industrial
mass production, and utilitarianism that he came to call
'technologico-Benthamism'; foreigners, notably the assertedly
unhappy, massified Americans whose debased methods and
artefacts flood England; Marxism. The soul of England must be
defended against these threats, an icon to be preserved and
carried forward to nourish future generations. What is that soul?

English literature, magnificent and matchless in diversity and
range, and so full and profound in its registration of
changing life, gives us a continuity that is not yet dead. There
is no other; no other access to anything approaching a full
continuity of mind, spirit and sensibility – which is what we
desperately need.

(F.R. Leavis 1969: 60)

And where should this icon be protected? 'The "university" is the
inevitable, the inescapable, answer to the question: What would
provision of the kind needed be like? There is no other that could
be seriously proposed' (F.R. Leavis 1969: 2).

A vocabulary of necessity justifies the university, and locates 'the
centre of a university in a vital English School' (F.R. Leavis 1962:
29). English has a 'recognised position as chief of the humanities',
and a consequent 'key responsibility for education' (F.R. Leavis
1943: 33). Already a Good Thing, it

trains, in a way no other discipline can, intelligence and
sensibility together, cultivating a sensitiveness and precision
of response and a delicate integrity of intelligence. . . . It can,
in its peculiar preoccupation with the concrete, provide an
incomparably inward and subtle initiation into the nature
and significance of tradition.

(F.R Leavis 1943: 35)

But a Good Thing can be made better. A properly constituted
English School could become 'a real humane focus in a university,

pre-eminently representative of the Idea, and capable of discharging the function of the university in the matter of liberal education' (F.R Leavis 1943: 32). His example of what that liberal education might look like – a study of the seventeenth century – shows what this would imply: an English *lebensraum*. Controlled by the litterateur,

> Such a study would have the necessary comprehensiveness, complexity and unity: it would be a study in concrete terms of the relations between the economic, the political, the moral, the spiritual, religion, art and literature, and would involve a critical pondering of standards and key-concepts – order, community, culture, civilisation and so on.
>
> (F.R. Leavis 1943: 49)

If that is the means, what is the end? A familiar one.

> The aim is to produce a mind that will approach the problems of modern civilization with an understanding of their origins, a maturity of outlook, and, not a nostalgic addiction to the past, but a sense of human possibilities, difficult of achievement, that traditional cultures bear witness to and that it would be disastrous, in a breach of continuity, to lose sight of for good.
>
> (F.R. Leavis 1943: 56)

Leavis clearly wishes to set up an alien shell factory: the debts to Arnold reek from every page. But some emphases have changed. Arnold's unwavering support for state primary and secondary education flowed from his conviction that culture's survival required that an educated public be created. Leavis follows the form of this argument (1972: 109), but he has a very different sense of where that public should be manufactured. It is the reconstructed university English School's task to create an educated public, not mass state education. Aliens are to be turned out like widgets, but from a much smaller plant: the scope of the 'public' has contracted violently. Nor is this all. Where, we may ask, is the English School to be established? In every British institution of higher and further education? No fear. In every British university? Not likely. 'I'm not supposing that English Schools such as I have described are likely to be realised in all, or half, or even a quarter of the universities' (F.R. Leavis 1972: 132). As the numbers tumble, we arrive at a conception of the civilizing power of English that looks uncommonly like a defence of Oxbridge humanities: 'The British university as represented by Oxford and Cambridge was a distinct and strongly positive organic life, rooted in history' (F.R. Leavis 1972: 206). Arnold's concern to create an educated public has become an urge to build a private coterie.

There are other differences. Arnold put classics at the heart of culture, with English literature occupying a rather less exalted position. Leavis gives massive primacy to English. Much of Arnold's effectiveness lies in the geniality of his style (R. Chapman 1968: 222), flowing from his unchallenged location in the Victorian leisured classes. *Culture and Anarchy* defends an aristocratic Oxford from within its walls. Leavis's acerbity is rooted in his marginality. He constructs a flattering, a dream Arnoldian Cambridge, hoping that it will be his ticket to the enclosure that he takes to be the 'real' Cambridge. Not to put too fine a point on it, he grovels: 'the foundation at Cambridge towards the close of the first world war of the English Tripos was an important event in history' (F.R. Leavis 1969: 11). The shift from hunter-gathering to settled agriculture, Alaric's Roman holiday, the fall of Constantinople, the Black Death, Watt's separate condenser, Verdun, the Cambridge English Tripos: one sees his claim's sad bathos. But much of his plan for a new humane citadel meshes nicely with conservative Oxbridge assumptions; an uninterrogated notion of Englishness (F. R. Leavis 1943: 11; 1972: 35, 185), support for collegiate interdisciplinarity rather than a university built around departments (1962: 28-9), hostility to science (1969: 42) and to Marxism (1943: 30), the denial that ex-CATs and the Open University are 'real' universities (1969: 2).

> Only at Cambridge could *Scrutiny* have been conceived, launched and carried on. It was the justifying product of the English Tripos, and, in being the kind of enterprise it was, it implicitly insisted on a conscious realization that Cambridge English was pre-eminently the representative of a distinctive Cambridge tradition, to vindicate which in modern terms was to assert, re-conceived in relation to a rapidly changing world, the Idea of the University.
>
> (F.R. Leavis 1969: 18–19)

But *Scrutiny*, the magazine produced by F.R. and Q.D. Leavis with a group of fellow-believers (Mulhern 1979), exposes the plight in which F.R. Leavis found himself at Cambridge. He was both outside and inside the English literary establishment, both inside and outside 'real' Cambridge. 'I myself have no impulse, or reason, to see a model in Cambridge as I have known it,' he said in an ambiguously untruthful statement (F.R. Leavis 1972: 183). Ten years earlier he had recollected tilting against official Cambridge windmills: 'I will only say that the academic is the enemy and that the academic *can* be beaten, as we who ran *Scrutiny* for twenty years proved. We were, and knew we were, Cambridge – the essential Cambridge in spite of Cambridge' (F.R. Leavis 1962: 29). Here, and not here alone, Leavis is a pathetic figure, believing himself the victim of closure and shouting through his tears that he doesn't care. But he does care. 'His whole life has been a passionate wooing of Cambridge – he was even born there – but his ardour has been only grudgingly returned, and returned late,' Corke (1963) tells us in his comment on the Snow–Leavis fracas.

> He was forty-five before he achieved a Fellowship. He was never a Professor. Who kept him out? They did. And who's They? The Establishment, of course – and that is precisely the bogey that the unlucky Sir Charles [Snow] has been picked, almost fortuitously, in his single person to represent.
>
> (Corke 1963: 22)

Corke almost gets there. For Leavis (1972: 149-50, 164–8) Snow, Lionel Robbins, Alexander Todd, and Noel Annan were corrosive technologico-Benthams who must be outfaced. That explains some of his spleen. The rest is rooted in the fact that all were, or soon would be, peers; and that Annan, Snow, and Todd were Cambridge men. Believing himself unjustly excluded, Leavis attacked Snow as the embodiment of encrusted Cambridge; the embodiment of Leavis's, and therefore culture's, enemies. The personal is political.

Leavis believed that the humanities, with English at their heart, were fighting the last battle: 'the educated and cultivated have, in general, given in – have surrendered to the climate of the technological age' (F.R. Leavis 1972: 139). But he is determined not to give in without a fight. The point of dispatching aliens from the English School is to construct a body of educated opinion 'checking the confident destructive follies of enlightened statesmen, intellectuals, bureaucrats, educational reformers, Provosts of Kings College' (1972: 159), controlling the climate 'in which politicians, bureaucrats, Vice-Chancellors' committees and Ministers of Education had to do their planning, negotiating and performing' (1972: 125). The members of this veto group, united in their high moral seriousness, their delight in Lawrence's dark inwardness and their regret for the lost wheelwright's shop, will ensure that public and university authorities keep the cultural faith in the uttermost hour. It sounds like a secularized (or, rather, a differently mystical) C.S. Lewis fairy tale. It certainly sounds an implausible political programme. As is the way in Britain, however, the implausible happened.

In March 1969 a slim pamphlet slipped into print. It was published by the Critical Quarterly Society, a body better known for producing a literary critical journal. *Critical Quarterly* had been founded in 1958 to carry forward the torch of *Scrutiny*, extinguished five years earlier (C.B. Cox 1984: 5). Written by twenty authors, the pamphlet bore a combative title: *Fight for Education.* Few today will recognize that title. Many more will recognize the subtitle: *A Black Paper. Fight for Education* was the first of five Black Papers. The first three appeared in two years, edited by *Critical Quarterly*'s editors: C.B. Cox, Professor of English at Manchester University, and a Senior Lecturer in English at the University of East Anglia, A.E. Dyson. The fourth and fifth, published in 1975 and 1977, were edited by Cox and Rhodes Boyson, a headmaster turned Conservative MP. Very rapidly an attitude to these pamphlets came to predict attitudes on a range of other issues. Gervase Fen, Professor of English Language and Literature at Oxford University and Fellow of St Christopher's College, stares distastefully at an adolescent hunt saboteuse who has accused his friend of being a male chauvinist mouse: 'her package of progressive *idées reçues* was already a bit out of date, not to say rather blurrily cross-referenced. What would it be next, he wondered? Namibia? The perennial CIA? Chile again? The Black Papers on Education?' (Crispin 1977: 216).

Looking back over twenty-five years of *Critical Quarterly*, C.B. Cox (1984: 12) makes it clear that the Black Papers had no coherent party political location. Some authors were Labour supporters, others were not. This was to be a disinterested defence of education; very Arnoldian. He recounts (1984: 14) Dyson's

224

attempt to persuade Margaret Thatcher, by then Secretary of State for Education, not to turn an educational crusade into material for party politics. It is a touching story. We admire the attempt to keep culture's defence aloof from the Westminster bear-garden. We sigh at the naivety of men who believed that political pitch would not defile once the Butskellite cross-party accord on education had been broached.

Looking back over the first three pamphlets, Cox and Dyson (1971b: 16–17) identified four major themes: progressive methods of teaching, comprehensive schools, private education, and student revolt. It was clear enough that contributors were united in celebrating the third and attacking the others. But the initial impetus for the movement was firmly located in the last, in worries about university life.

> The first Black Paper was mainly concerned to combat left-wing student interference with traditional academic freedoms. When we thought up the idea of the Black Paper, on a walk on Hampstead Heath in summer, 1968, we were chiefly concerned with the threat to universities. But we realized that universities cannot be considered apart from primary and secondary schools, and that the crisis extended to education as a whole.
>
> (Cox and Dyson 1971b: 9–10)

Leavis had a similarly jaundiced view of student activism, expressed in less cautious language. In a letter to *The Times* (quoted in F.R. Leavis 1972: 103–4) he made it one of several manifestations of civilization's sickness. Others were 'violence, wanton destructiveness, the drug menace, adolescent promiscuity, permissiveness, the enlightened praise of the young for their "candour" about sex'. One is reminded of Antonia Fraser's motive for an Oxford murder: the hatred of the old for the young.

Like Leavis, Black Paper writers believed that progressive educational *nostra* had produced a generation of students unprepared for university study. 'No one should be admitted to read English at any university who isn't of university quality and hasn't a positive bent for literary study,' Leavis tells us (1972: 113). As early as 1954 Kingsley Amis believed that this pass had been sold, and not only in English. Indeed, the Professor of English in Jim Dixon's appalling minor redbrick, 'a youngish ex-Fellow of a

Cambridge college' known to his colleagues as Fred Karno, is alone in trying to maintain academic standards. 'No Firsts this year for us, four Thirds, and forty-five per cent of the first-year people failed,' Beesley tells Jim Dixon; 'that's the way to deal with 'em' (Amis 1954: 169). Dixon/Amis concurs:

> It's the same everywhere you look; not only this place, but all the provincial universities are going the same way. Not London, I suppose, and not the Scottish ones. But my God, go to most places and try and get someone turfed out merely because he's too stupid to pass his exams – it'd be easier to sack a prof.
>
> (Amis 1954: 170)

It is a short distance from this to Kingsley Amis's famous dictum that more [students] would mean worse [standards]: a phrase that became identified with the Black Papers. He himself tolled the bell.

> As a consequence of irresponsible expansionism, the universities today are full of students who do not understand what study is about, and who are painfully bewildered by the whole business and purpose of university life; more has meant worse. Student unrest has several causes, but here and now the prime one seems to me to be the presence in our universities of an academically-unfit majority, or large minority.
>
> (Amis 1968: 10)

University entrance procedures should set the agenda for all education, despite the fact that a small proportion of any cohort would darken a university's doors. This happened in the good old days, but progressive education has brought decay. British state schools' rottenness is reflected in the rottenness of many current undergraduates' preparation. Bryan Wilson (1968) echoed Amis's famous complaint.

> More *has* meant worse. This has not been so much a matter of admitting people with less intellectual capacity, but of admitting people who were less committed, had less self-control, and who were less adequately socialised for the university experience.
>
> (B. Wilson 1968: 73)

Preparation, we see, is about more than encouraging school-children's intellectual development. What more? Mowat gives us his answer:

> We forget at our peril the medieval origin of universities as guilds analogous to the craftsmen's guilds, in which the masters, journeymen and apprentices were all brethren but not equal. The apprentice had to serve his terms and learn the mystery before he could work on his own, and only the masters could judge a masterpiece and admit its maker to become one of themselves. The future of the craft, its standards, its ethics, were in their hands. Equally, today's professors and lecturers in the universities cannot abdicate from the duty laid upon them by their calling.
>
> (Mowat 1968: 13)

Students are like apprentices. Members of the university's organic community, they are to be inducted into the academic mystery by their masters. We may take it that as with any guild, the number of apprentices must be strictly controlled to maintain the masters' strong market position. This analogy is instructive, allowing us to construct the framework of implicit terms that holds up the Black Papers' account of British universities. Mowat's analogy between university and guild implies (1) that universities should govern themselves, and (2) have sovereign control over admitting a small flow of new recruits to their mystery; (3) that the mystery is stable, a codified body of knowledge that the apprentice must learn; (4) that the sole purpose of university education is to reproduce academics; and (5) that hierarchy in an inevitable and desirable feature of university life. Laid out like that, the programme loses its naturalness. Historically, state control of universities has been normal in Europe; only in England has 'donnish dominion' (Halsey 1982a) been fetishized around the example of Oxford and Cambridge. The notion of undergraduate education as the induction of a narrow stream of apprentices is central to idealized accounts of the Oxbridge tutorial system. A stable mystery makes the business of universities the conservation of knowledge rather than its creation. This puts the humanities at the centre of university life by definition. Everything else, from quantum mechanics to nursing studies, has to plead for admission. The notion that universities exist to reproduce academics reinforces

227

metropolitan conceptions, and denies legitimacy to competing definitions of the institutions' task. How can a not-Oxbridge university make strong connections with local firms and professional groups – to say nothing of community groups – if its sole mission is to create a free-floating intelligentsia? Finally, students' deference to their teachers mirrors a necessary hierarchy among universities. A Great Chain of Being links the most exalted universities (Oxford and Cambridge) to the most humble (ex-CATs) and, beyond the pale, to polytechnics. The world's goods go to each kind of place in different measure, but this is natural. Glittering Oxbridge is no better or worse than the most miserable ex-CAT. It is just different, occupying a separate niche in the God-given division of labour. Mowat's analogy, and with it the Black Papers' analysis of what is wrong with British universities, makes sense only if one assumes that Oxbridge is the template for the British university system, and that the university's heart is a sacred notion of Englishness walled up in the humanities. None of this is inconsistent with Leavis's views; in *Nor Shall My Sword* he joined the Black Papers in asserting that British universities in the 1960s and 1970s no longer met any of Mowat's criteria.

We are told that universities should govern and regulate their own affairs. But *Fight for Education* (Cox and Dyson 1968) tells us that this is no longer possible. The London School of Economics, like all British universities and university colleges, suffered strong government pressure to expand student and staff numbers, at least until a sterling crisis emptied the fiscal barrel (Watt 1968: 33–4). Nor was it simply a matter of numbers. External pressure from government merged with internal disaffection from radical – code for 'leftist' – students and junior staff, in urging 'relevance' on universities: 'the university should expand but with controlled costs and to socially useful ends, producing the relevant courses at the right price' ('B' 1968: 61). To fall prey to this naked utilitarianism, this technologico-Benthamism, was to install Dracula in the blood-bank. 'The student who is himself looking for relevance is looking for vocational training, a harmless desire in itself, though anti-academic and therefore not to be indulged at a university: the teacher who wants to import it is an enemy of culture' (Amis 1968: 10). The reticent 'B' expands the point:

The last few years have, of course, seen many significant

attempts at new modes of teaching, new views of disciplines, new forms of academic and social structure within the university community; but this activity conceals, I think, a seriously diminished confidence in the ideal of university education itself among many university teachers, and that decline is a manifest signal of the unhappy fortunes of that belief in culture, civilization and disinterested criticism that the university has particularly stood for in English society.

('B' 1968: 60)

We find ourselves on familiar territory. Bewailing the state control consequent on British universities' partly inadvertent whoring after state funds, Black Paper authors join Leavis in raising a blue-tinged wraith of Matthew Arnold.

They were not alone. *Fight for Education* appeared in the same year as a collection of essays on current difficulties in British universities. John Sparrow, Warden of All Souls, Oxford, had a fulminating piece in each volume. D.C. Watt deplored the consequences of expansion at the London School of Economics in the first Black Paper; the other collection was firmly centred in LSE. The most substantial essay in *Fight for Education* was by a sociologist of religion, Bryan Wilson. The other book was edited by another sociologist of religion, David Martin. Its title? *Anarchy and Culture.* Arnold is evoked explicitly, but with a suggestion that anarchy is no longer a looming threat. The lunatics are running the asylum.

Anarchy and Culture is not *Fight for Education.* The authors in Martin's collection hold more diverse views, and there is a higher ratio of analysis to vituperation. Some essays – notably yet another episode in Ernest Gellner's (1969) guerilla war against Oxford philosophy – have an intellectual distinction quite alien to Cox and Dyson's pamphlet. Yet the underlying discourse is not dissimilar: revolting students are to be understood so that they can better be resisted. Student revolt threatens the university's structure and values.

What is this structure? What are these values? It is an editor's job to specify a book's leading themes. David Martin's introduction is extraordinary. Theological language organizes the argument: subheadings are 'the end of the monks', 'ritual and the priesthood of all believers', 'sin', and 'the end of man'. Within this is set an

229

allegory of the way in which humanities and social science teachers in their universities ('monks' and 'friars' in 'monasteries') were suborned by utilitarianism (by 'technocrats' in 'the Great City'), and persuaded to allow a disastrously increased flow of students. Culture has been suborned by utilitarianism. More has meant worse. Back to the Black Papers.

Back to the Black Papers also in Martin's insistence on the monastic origins of British universities. Housed in overcrowded office blocks off Aldwych, LSE (and, we are to take it, all other British universities) looks back to Oxford's cloistered clerks. Oxbridge exemplifies the whole British university sector. This does not mean that LSE is Oxford. John Sparrow distinguishes sharply between two kinds of universities. The first 'exists solely to train its students for degrees, and regards them simply as citizen academic workers with whom it acknowledges no personal relationship and for whom it takes no responsibility outside the lecture-room'. The second kind of university

> interests itself in the whole being and welfare of its junior members, encourages human relations between them and their seniors, counts mutual trust and loyalty as academic virtues, asks for a decent standard of behaviour from its students and treats disruptive activity as an academic offence.
>
> (Sparrow 1969b: 182)

The difference between the two? The first is non-collegiate, the second collegiate. A warmly supportive judgement on the variously college-based universities of Durham, Kent, Lancaster, London, St Andrews, Wales, and York, one might think. But of course this is not at all what Sparrow means. 'Collegiate' means Oxbridge.

> What is the lesson, then, that Oxford – 'and when I say Oxford I mean Cambridge' – should learn from what has happened? . . . [I]t must not abandon the character of a collegiate university, a community interested in the whole range of its students' lives, and not merely in training them for a degree.
>
> (Sparrow 1969b: 183)

A sharp distinction between Oxbridge and not-Oxbridge controls judgements. Oxbridge educates gentlemen, not-Oxbridge trains citizen academic workers. Oxbridge is cultured, not-Oxbridge is utilitarian. Oxbridge is saved, not-Oxbridge is damned.

> In Essex the other day three young students, having drunk two bottles of whisky (Grants whisky, one may presume), stripped and brutally attacked a young girl; convicted of criminal assault, they pleaded 'the pressure of exams' and were taken back by the University. That is a good example of a non-collegiate university in action.
>
> (Sparrow 1969b: 182)

Hence Simon Raven's (1976: 284) paraphrase of the story: Robert Constable's disreputable readmission of undergraduates convicted of smashing up the college chapel as a trade for leftist fellows' acquiescence in his peerage shows that Lancaster, and with it all Cambridge, has become not-Oxbridge.

Sparrow's brutal arrogance is revealing. In his *Fight for Education* essay Warden Sparrow, head of the ultra-Oxonian All Souls College, connects the discourse of British university fiction with that of academic politics.

> 'Are you in favour of an academic *élite?*' The question was put to me in the course of an evening's discussion with undergraduates and young graduates in Oxford the other day. . . . My instinctive reaction was to reply 'Yes, of course' . . . The enemies of an *élite* are in a fair way to denying the very concept of academic value, and with it the whole purpose of education.
>
> (Sparrow 1968: 64, 66)

Privilege is nothing to be ashamed of:

> if an academic institution is able to offer those it educates superior conditions, whether in its style of life or in the quality of the instruction it provides, it should not abandon or modify those advantages simply in order to avoid the reproach involved in being regarded as an *élitiste* establishment. Excellence may not be a matter for pride; it is never something to be ashamed of. Universities and schools that cast away their inheritance not because they have ceased to believe in its value but out of deference to egalitarian

231

pressures are betraying an intellectual trust and becoming parties to the most recent manifestation of *la trahison des clercs*.

(Sparrow 1968: 66)

Slipping easily from academic prestige to social prestige, Sparrow rules out the possibility of any challenge to Oxbridge privilege from other British universities, 'the "mushrooms of mediocrity"' (F.R. Leavis 1972: 209). To challenge Oxford's self-asserted position at the pinnacle of British university life is to challenge 'the whole purpose of education', to become treasonable clerks. *Hubris* rides again, safely wrapped in clouds of hegemony.

The defence of a certain kind of university against others becomes a defence of a certain kind of subject against others. Amis and Conquest's cod educational dictionary counterposes two disciplines. On one hand we have '*Classics*. Dead languages, formerly the basis of education. Objectionable because a) irrelevant, b) difficult.' On the other hand we have '*Sociology*. 1) An academic, bourgeois, irrelevant (qq.v.) study of society and its institutions now largely outmoded by 2) a polysyllabic briefing on the decadence of western society and the means to overthrow it' (Amis and Conquest 1971: 216, 222). Sociology stands for all that has rotted British universities. Not inherently evil, it has been corrupted:

Sociology is the bastion of this barbarism. There is, indeed, a genuine sociology. It is concerned with social philosophy, not claiming the quantisation of science; or it is an investigation into a rigorously limited and definable set of facts, which can really be treated with numerical rigour. The 'sociology' more usually met with nowadays consists of seeking support for preconceived notions, usually of a notably shallow type, from selected or invented material.

(Conquest 1968: 17)

Conquest makes modern sociology intellectually dishonest, a simple fraud. Amis is more charitable. For him it is nugatory, 'a non-subject . . . thrown to alleviate the burden of concentrating on a real subject' (Amis 1968: 10). One might think that none of this would threaten universities very seriously. The usual methods of peer control would expel fraudulent sociologists in short order,

232

and non-subjects would wither rapidly. But this will not happen. Sociology is not one rotten apple in a barrel of healthy fruit. A better analogy makes it a systemic weedkiller, working its way up the trunk of the academic enterprise:

> Rapid growth in some disciplines has led to the recruitment of junior staff who have themselves suffered all the inadequacies of the expanding universities: they cannot transmit university values because they never really received them. So the deficiencies in communication and socialisation have grown. Many of those who have been prominent in recent disturbances in Britain, as elsewhere, have been junior lecturers and students in sociology, a subject that has grown at a rate unprecedented for any discipline in British academic history. Large numbers of young men, appointed before they had completed their apprenticeship either to the subject or to academic life, felt that the promised land of opportunity had become a desert, as the inevitable competition with too many colleagues of equal status began to make its demands. High aspirations, sufficient achievement to give a taste of success, and competition that made further success difficult – were enough to cause some to displace their anger on to the system. The universities were rotten. Sociology, in particular, had a fund of theories that could be used as 'scientific' explanations of the corruptness of the system.
>
> (B. Wilson 1968: 73)

Sociologists could deny Amis's and Conquest's accounts as simple prejudice. What did they know about sociology? Wilson was a different matter: a distinguished sociologist of religion had to be taken seriously. But to take him seriously would mean confronting the complex of social, institutional, and educational philosophies in which his uncharitable judgement was entwined.

That complex was influencing opinion. Consider the published judgements of Professor John Rex. Once every decade his thoughts turn to the state of British sociology. In 1961 his *Key Problems in Sociological Theory* sought to insert a wedge of left-Weberian 'conflict theory' into a perceived Parsonian hegemony. His recollected self-image of this time was of a man 'in the vanguard of protest and reform' (1974: 1). But by 1974 things had been transformed. The 'miserably underdeveloped' sociology of the 1950s had blossomed into new paradigms: notably ethnomethodology and phenomenology, which 'it would be wrong to underestimate' and a Marxism which 'is a rich enough doctrine to contain within itself a wealth of different emphases' (1974: 5, 6). Ten years later, and things look different again. Much of his 1983 paper reads like a recycling of the 1974 argument, but with the judgements reversed. British sociology in the 1950s now was not miserably underdeveloped. Instead, it formed the groundwork for an indigenous sociology which a rising group of LSE-sourced Young Turks, Rex among them, could have used to build a new national sociology.

The chance of building an authentic English sociology was ruined by foreign invasion. Rex's view of phenomenology is more guarded in 1983 than it was nine years earlier. His view of Marxism is acidulous. No longer a rich and diverse doctrine, it has been reduced to an Althusserian structuralism which, he argues, expanded 'at the expense of sociology' (1983: 1,003). The sorry consequence is that

> What most young sociologists were receiving by the early seventies was a sociology based on a political critique of capitalism on the one hand and an understanding of deviance on the other. The teaching rarely reached any profound depths and was packaged to meet the understanding of the young socially mobile but frustrated students of their own political condition. There was little place in this for the study of Weber and Durkheim. If they were prepared to make some obeisance to theory they did so by quoting half understood themes from Giddens, Althusser, Garfinkel, or Habermas.
>
> (Rex 1983: 1,006)

This reads like a parody. It could come from any Black Paper. It could come from any of the less temperate university novels: a reader given this passage blind might well place it in *The History Man*. Rex's 'Elijah manner' (Eldridge 1980: 160) remains from earlier years, but there is not much left of the man memorably apostrophized by Ronnie Frankenberg as 'The kind of Marxist who likes his friends to call him a Marxist'. The Young Turk has become an old fogey. To his tired but enlightened eyes the only hope for British sociology is 'to recall the discipline to its traditional vocation' (Rex 1983: 1,007): back to Durkheim and Weber (but less Marx); back to that submerged English sociological tradition that he had castigated nine years earlier. 'Tradition', 'English' are the new buzz-words; their antonyms are 'young', 'radical', 'socially mobile' (Heaven help us), and 'provincial'. After this, it is no surprise that Rex should devote a fair proportion of a brief essay on the state of British sociology to an account of the discipline's establishment in Oxford and Cambridge. The reverential tone of this account contrasts quaintly with a more measured judgement from within Oxford (Heath and Edmondson 1981) which Rex ignores. He puts his money for sociology's survival on accommodation to the general intellectual culture: xenophobic, hierarchical, seeking to restrict higher education to a tiny elite.

He is not alone. In his *Fight For Education* essay Bryan Wilson gave us a conservative sociological account of British culture in the 1960s. Like Max Weber in his time and place, Wilson is disenchanted with the modern world, depressed at bureaucracy's tightening grip; but Wilson's Weber is integrated with Durkheim in Parsons's (1937) conservative synthesis of European social theory as structural functionalism. Like Parsons, Wilson believes that order is rooted in commonly accepted central values. But the times are out of joint.

> Declining consensus about values in Britain has been reflected in universities. Intellect, untempered by taste, character, disposition or even commitment to academic work, has been elevated as the sole criterion of admission of candidates, even though we know that universities do not live by brain alone. Reliance on intellect for admission has accompanied reliance on business-management procedures in the running of universities. Lecturers so disposed could thus abandon moral obligation to care about students, since this should now be the concern of specialist welfare officers.
>
> (B. Wilson 1968: 76)

Universities, we learn, are not solely about intellect and hard work. They are also about inculcating taste, character and disposition: making gentlemen. The taint of trade – business-management procedures – has polluted sacred purlieus. University teachers have abandoned their moral obligations towards students. Writing from Sparrow's All Souls, Wilson – like almost any university novelist, like Leavis – collapses 'university' into a right-Arnoldian dream of Oxbridge. This dream generates his hostility to what he takes to be utilitarian tendencies in British university life: 'these ideas have seriously weakened those traditional academic values that were far more effective in eliciting student commitment – that education is for the enrichment of the individual, and that from such individuals an important, but latent, social benefit accrues' (B. Wilson 1968: 74). This celebration of an asserted lost traditional virtue then leads him to a revealing historical comparison: 'The mass university, like the mass factory of the nineteenth century, is an amorphous and bewildering world, and one which, to many of those involved, has lost coherent meaning and stable values' (B. Wilson 1968: 75). Technologico-Benthamism has triumphed. The right-Arnoldian aristocratic mass society line becomes explicit.

Leavis saw himself as culture's champion against 'an elite of the progressive intelligentsia' (1972: 168), against establishment barbarians. The Black Papers identified the same enemy within the citadel.

> Many of the foundations whose patronage of higher education is most trumpeted . . . are far too keen to be in with the establishment, far too chary of acknowledging their own debts to the spirit of private enterprise, far too concerned with another knighthood or another life-peerage, or simply far too frequently advised by what I have come to think of as the 'pink mafia', those tame academics beloved of the powers-that-be who man all those committees and commissions, who make all those speeches in the House of Lords and whose business it is to conceal what every teacher knows to be true: the high price in quality we have paid for the form educational expansion has taken in this country in the last quarter century.
>
> (Beloff 1977: 116)

'Piece by piece,' Bryan Wilson (1968: 77–80) tells us, 'the [egalitarian] legislation of the last decade or two has rent the fabric of the known social order, and has unwittingly destroyed the premises on which social decencies rested.' An earlier essay by Max

Beloff spelt out where these decencies once rested. 'Oxford thus suffers from a double dose of the fashionable egalitarianism of the day', he asserts (1969: 136). Externally it is under pressure to become more like not-Oxbridge universities. Internally there is pressure (most notably following the Franks Committee's report) to centralize university government and to equalize resources among the colleges (1969: 134, 136). These measures merely widen a breach in Oxford's walls. The real issue was lost years ago, over

> qualifications for admission, where the scientists have won a long battle to demote Latin, largely on grounds that modern languages were more 'useful' and equally good mental training, then proceeded to get rid of the two language requirement in its turn. A preceding generation of scientists (and not only in Oxford) would hardly have subscribed to the view that the best guarantee of numeracy is illiteracy; but philistinism of this kind is considered the advanced thing; also, the democratic thing.
>
> For there is an obvious connection between the philistinism of the anti-classical lobby and the passion for measures designed to promote some non-academic values that some people believe important. What people have been sensitive to is the charge that Oxford has been an elitist University in admitting undergraduates from too limited a number of schools, and too restricted a social class.
>
> (Beloff 1969: 135)

Red Rudi and Lord Snow ride together against crumbling Oxbridge. To borrow the English Civil War analogy employed by Antony Price (1976) in his novel about contemporary cultural struggle, Colonel Rainborough leads his levellers in a last charge against culture's ruined keep.

The dispirited Cavaliers man the walls once more. Against the egalitarian establishment's New Model Army they can set only old, decrepit weapons.

> We are in favour of major expansion in higher education, but we want this to be based on realism, not Utopian fantasy. There is a need for a hierarchical system, in which many students read for some kind of general degree, in a variety of

institutions, and only a few study specialist Honours courses
. . . . But, above all, standards of excellence must be
maintained.

(Cox and Dyson 1971b: 33)

Early skirmishes go badly, as the egalitarians lay down confusing
smoke screens (Amis and Conquest 1969), and try to discredit
brave officers: 'the nastiest feature of the reaction to Black Paper
Two was the personal attack on Professor Burt' (Cox and Dyson
1971b: 14). Enemies claimed that Sir Cyril Burt's article relied on
fabricated evidence: an outrageous charge to lay against a
distinguished psychologist. What a pity that careful later work
would show that Burt's whole academic reputation rested on
systematically fabricated evidence (Kamin 1974; Hearnshaw 1979;
Fancher 1985: 213–16).

Slowly the battle turned.

When Black Paper Three was published in November, 1970,
it was a sign of the change in the consensus of opinion that it
was treated far more rationally than the previous two, and
even achieved enthusiastic reviews in *New Society* and the
Economist. Since Black Paper Two, Mrs Thatcher had taken
over as Secretary of State . . . . The Black Papers had figured
quite largely in the debates in the House of Commons that
followed the General Election, and Mrs Thatcher's
withdrawal of circular 10/65, which had enforced
comprehensive education on local authorities.

(Cox and Dyson 1971b: 16)

By 1971 the Black Papers had 'broken the fashionable left-wing
consensus on education' (Cox and Dyson 1971b: 11). The election
of the Conservative government in 1979 was expected to solve all
problems. The Prime Minister, Margaret Thatcher, was a woman
and originally a chemist; but she was an Oxford graduate. Even
better news concerned her second Secretary of State for Education
and Science, Sir Keith Joseph: a man with an Oxford First in
Greats, a fellow of All Souls. These, indeed, were safe hands.

Pressure was maintained against culture's enemies. A
movement that started from a liberal defence of 'traditional
academic freedoms' in universities soon turned to witch-hunting.
The space under every bed was scoured for reds. When discovered,

238

they all seemed to be social scientists working in lowly institutions. *Rape of Reason* (Jacka *et al.* 1975) claimed a strong Marxist bias in North London Polytechnic. One author, Caroline Cox, was head of the sociology department in that polytechnic. They widened the attack in the last Black Paper:

> Nowadays in the academies of Britain – the institutions of higher education – there is continual and fundamental conflict. Superficially the academies are quiet; they seldom make the headlines as they did a few years ago in the time of large-scale student occupation. But conflict now, especially among members of the teaching staff, is just as intense and more deeply grounded than at that time. . . . Two groups are opposed in the conflict; we shall distinguish them as Academics and Marxists. 'Academics' because their way of thought and procedure (mode) has been gradually articulated and more or less established in the academies of Western Europe over a long period. 'Marxists' because they follow the doctrines of Karl Marx, and because many are members of Marxist political parties.
>
> (Cox *et al.* 1977: 117)

The hunt was now on in earnest. In May 1976 Caroline Cox claimed that an Open University course on *Patterns of Inequality* displayed Marxist bias (*THES* 14 May 1976). Seven months later Hugh Freeman, a psychiatrist (like Cox's husband) with connections to Salford and Manchester Universities, claimed to detect similar deformations in Open University courses on *Language and Social Reality*, and on *Politics, Work and Occupation* (*The Times* 10 December 1976). Two more months saw Julius Gould, Professor of Sociology at Nottingham University, identifying Marxist bias in yet another course, *Schooling and Capitalism* (*TES* 4 February 1977). The Open University was forced to mount a major investigation. All claims were found to be untrue, but the investigating committee proposed that future courses 'should be written in a manner sensitive to public opinion' (*THES* 30 September 1977). To its credit, the university's academic board threw out this disgraceful suggestion.

Caroline Cox and her friends had got it wrong. They diverted attention from this embarrassment by making another claim. In September 1977 Julius Gould's pamphlet *The Attack on Higher*

Education hit the news-stands. Published by a right-wing think-tank, the Institute for the Study of Conflict, it claimed to identify a conspiracy (rooted – incredibly – in the Communist Party of Great Britain; a sclerotic body incapable even of running a newspaper, as events would shortly show) to undermine Britain's universities. The absurdity of the scenario was matched by the paucity of the evidence, which relied mainly on critical exegesis of Marxisant social science literature rather than direct evidence of highly trained King Street moles' deadly work. More interesting was the membership of the working party that drew up the allegations. It had ten members. Three were ICS staffers. Some others we have met: Julius Gould, a professor of sociology who had endorsed Robert Conquest's vilification of sociology almost a decade earlier (*Observer* 23 March 1969) and had attacked the Open University; Caroline Cox, who had been flailing wildly for some years; and David Martin, editor of *Anarchy and Culture.* The four remaining members were Anthony Flew, Professor of Philosophy at Reading University, Kenneth Minogue from the Government Department at LSE, Edward Shils of Peterhouse, Cambridge, and D.K. Watkins of the Politics Department at Sheffield University. Advice was taken from Brunel University's John Vaizey, LSE's Stephen Haseler, Birmingham's C.B. Cox, and from Rhodes Boyson. In the same year C.B. Cox and Boyson edited the last Black Paper. The *Times Higher Education Supplement*'s leader tied Gould's pamphlet back to the Black Papers' origin:

> The real target of *The Attack on Higher Education* is not the Marxists who are doing the attacking but the 'soft centre' which allegedly is making such a mess of defending liberal values. Here perhaps Professor Gould has found a germ of truth. It is the decay of the centre which has allowed more radical ideologies to thrive. But it is also the disastrous decline in the self-confidence of the centre that has allowed bodies such as the right-wing Institute for the Study of Conflict to be taken more seriously.
>
> (*THES* 23 September 1977)

Sir Keith Joseph proved to be a mite less than perfect as education secretary. On the negative side, he had developed a bad case of businessman's Bernalism, believing that Britain's future lay unequivocally with commercially exploitable applied science. This

240

was alarming. More comforting was the strict limits that he placed on a definition of science, which ruled out his – and the Black Papers' – *bête noire*, sociology. His belief that social science was not real science led him to cut the state-funded Social Science Research Committee's funds disproportionately. More radically it led him to propose simply abolishing the council. Persuaded that abolition by ministerial fiat might be interpreted as prejudice, he adopted a well-tried Whitehall tactic. A hanging judge would be employed to conduct an impartial investigation of the doomed body. The Judge Jeffreys employed on this occasion was Lord Rothschild, author of a then-recent report on other government research councils which had proposed that funding should be based on a contract between the customer and the researcher. It was confidently expected that social science could not handle this utilitarian criterion, since a single end user could rarely be identified for social science research. Joseph and his advisers sat back to wait for Rothschild's report, quietly confident that they had set a creeping decision in motion. Imagine the shock, then, when Rothschild declined to wield the stiletto. He gave a clean bill of health to SSRC, apart from a token section attacking sociology. *THES* revealed his sources:

In his inner cabinet were his daughter, Professor Emma Rothschild, Dr Roger Scruton, author of a recent book on Conservatism, Sir Peter Swinnerton-Dyer, master of St Catherine's Cambridge, providing analysis of post-graduate education, and Mr Leonard Hoffman, a barrister. He consulted one politician, Shirley Williams, and she because of her previous job at the Department of Education. Other friends included Lord Flowers and Professor Bernard Williams. . . . For his comments on sociology he used Gary Runciman, Professor [sic] Jean Floud, principal of Newham [sic] College, Cambridge, and Sir Stuart Hampshire, warden of Wadham College, Oxford.

(*THES* 28 May 1982)

A tiny group of Rothschild's friends and relatives, men and women largely innocent of social science training and experience, hoisted Joseph with his own petard. Thrown the merest crumb of comfort on sociology – based on comments drawn exclusively from inhabitants of those Oxford and Cambridge universities where the subject

241

never had been taken seriously – he had to back down. He granted SSRC a three-year stay of execution. A year later, he changed the verdict to a conditional discharge: after 1985 SSRC – now renamed the Economic and Social Research Council to remove the implication that it had anything to do with science – would be funded similarly to all other research councils (*THES* 21 October 1983). Given government policy towards research funding this meant slow starvation, but at least ESRC was not to be hanged, drawn, and quartered.

In 1983 a senior lecturer at the Polytechnic of North London retired early after a prolonged period of sick leave. Once out, she sent Sir Keith Joseph a dossier alleging systematic left-wing bias in sociology and applied social studies courses in the polytechnic (*THES* 18 March 1983; 30 September 1983). Joseph ordered Her Majesty's Inspectors for Education to investigate. The inspectors' report criticized the applied social studies courses. Staff 'spoon-fed a narrowed down syllabus to students, many with non-traditional entry qualifications, encouraged a casual atmosphere and made it almost imposssible for anyone to fail a degree' (*THES* 7 October 1983). To this the two heads of the stigmatized department replied that the inspectors made their investigations during bank holidays and revision periods; that the courses criticized were on the point of being replaced with new courses which had just been validated by the Council for National Academic Awards after the usual lengthy and exhaustive screening process; that the four-person investigating team contained only one individual who would have the remotest idea of what was going on in the courses (the others were two historians and a biologist); and that the inspectors 'failed to understand the circumstances and development of mature students'. If all this was true, then it was clear that HMI had put together a model Black Paper team. As that week's *Times Higher Education Supplement* leader put it,

> If at first you don't succeed. . . . Having failed to persuade the CNAA to bring in a verdict of guilty against the Polytechnic of North London's sociology and applied social studies degrees, Sir Keith Joseph has had better luck with HM Inspectorate.
>
> (*THES* 7 October 1983)

Not for long. Inspectors from the Inner London Education

Authority were called in to adjudicate between the discrepant accounts of the HMIs and the department's heads. They accepted the heads' argument on every point, exonerating the form and content of courses while denying each HMI criticism (*THES* 9 March 1984). Keith Joseph's response, 'backed by senior ministers across a number of departments', was to threaten 'a short-sharp inquiry into the quality and validity of polytechnic and college degree courses' (*THES* 30 March 1984). More broadly the ILEA inspectors' report merely stiffened the Thatcher government's resolve to abolish the authority.

In 1981 a new champion thundered into the lists from the right-hand end. David Marsland, a sociologist at Brunel University, produced a little-noticed echo of Caroline Cox's and Julius Gould's fulminations about the condition of higher education:

> In the common rooms and on the committees where, sadly, too many fundamental decisions about higher education are taken, honest and able lecturers find themselves persistently defeated by a peculiarly unpleasant pincer movement. On the one hand phony supporters of genuine education whose real purpose is communism or some variant of socialism indistinguishable from communism except by initiates. [Reference to *Rape of Reason* and *The Attack on Higher Education*, which had asserted the existence of this group, but failed to persuade disinterested observers that it existed.] On the other hand uncomprehending philistines who would as willingly reduce education to its condition in an Orwellian people's democracy, if by a different route from the revolutionaries.
>
> (Marsland 1981: 44)

As with Julius Gould and Caroline Cox, the debt to right-Arnoldianism is very clear here. Four years later, Marsland sharpened his target, attacking all other British sociologists in a pamphlet published by yet another right-wing think-tank, the Institute for European Defence and Strategic Studies. University-based sociologists abuse their privileged position, he claimed, to force their anti-Nato and unilateralist views down students' throats. Unlike Julius Gould eleven years before, he could show us no identifiable group masterminding this devilish plot, the Communist Party of Great Britain having crumbled to miniscule warring factions in the years between. Perhaps it was Michael Innes's mischievous Martians up to new tricks, hypnotizing British sociology into a mind-set which rejects economic reality, denigrates liberal democracy, and has a naive faith in the state and in internationalism? Marsland quotes little evidence, so it might as well be the Martians. Certainly he fails to explain why, if sociology is so utterly corrupted by the left, right-wing sociologists – David Martin, Bryan Wilson, Caroline Cox, Julius Gould, Marsland himself – were so prominent in the Black Paper movement and its progeny.

There are two things worth doing with Marsland's argument. The first is to wonder why on earth anybody thinks his ideas worth considering; why attacks on sociology are as much an accepted and perennially recurring part of English culture as that first cuckoo which they resemble so closely. To contemplate that puzzle, gentle reader, is one of the purposes of the book which you hold in your hand. The second interesting thing about Marsland comes from turning him on his head and thus discovering what he holds dear: British (or, rather, English) nationalism, a strong British defence posture organized around military alliances, an uninterrogated faith in his own definition of liberal democracy, a desire to roll back the state through an 'economic reality' which corresponds remarkably closely with the Thatcher government's rhetoric (if not always with its policies). David Marsland is quite at liberty to identify others' ideological motes. It would be nice if he could come to recognize the beam in his own eye, which continues to inhibit vision in his recent work. *Bias Against Business* (1987) and *Seeds of Bankruptcy* (1988) use the same form of argument as the earlier pamphlet, claiming to be able to identify a systematic anti-business ideology in British sociology textbooks. From his perspective this is no doubt true: as a born-again convert to Hayekian economic liberalism he would find some passages in Smith's *Wealth of Nations* suspiciously anti-capitalist. And since sociology crystallized in critical response to the inhumanities of unbridled competition in British industrialization as well as to the threats to political and social order represented by the French Revolution – propositions amply established by the conservative Robert Nisbet (1967) – most of its practitioners have a professional tendency to look askance at the red-in-tooth-and-claw capitalism uncritically celebrated by Marsland. He marches off the parade ground, determinedly out of step. But he is in step with others: his allegations are congruent with those against PNL sociologists, and similarly difficult to disprove. In North London sociologists were required to demonstrate an absence of bias; to prove a negative. Marsland wants to extend this to the whole discipline. All British sociologists are to be forced to take a logically impossible test: 'Sociologists should be obliged to provide persuasive evidence in the next two years that their teaching, courses, reading lists and examination papers are free from bias' (*THES* 1 April 1988) When did David Marsland stop beating his wife?

If Black-Paper-inspired assaults on sociology enjoyed mixed fortune, then the overall war was going well. We saw earlier that *Fight for Education* was conceived as a right-Arnoldian defensive action against the corruption of British universities. As the political climate steadily improved, so defence gave way to agenda-setting attack. In 1971 C.B. Cox and Dyson still had supported continuing expansion in British higher education, if it was constrained by proper protection for hierarchy. The demands hardened as the years passed. In 1977 Cox and Boyson urged an end to increasing student numbers, and much else:

> In higher education research facilities should be increasingly concentrated in certain specified universities.... There should be no further significant university expansion. Polytechnics should return to the purpose for which they were originally intended: first degree institutions for vocations in science, engineering, the professions and business. Their arts and social science departments should be cut back. With the present shortage of money a system of student loans rather than grants seems inevitable.
>
> (Cox and Boyson 1977b: 9–10)

Six years later Max Beloff produced a plan for an overhauled higher education system. State grants to universities would be replaced by endowments. World-class centres of excellence would be created in some universities: others would decline to be mere teaching factories. The binary policy would be abolished along with the Council for National Academic Awards, reducing polytechnics to superior technical colleges. The UGC would be reformed, removing it from donnish dominion (*THES* 1 April 1983). This agenda was firmly rooted in a right-Arnoldian view of

245

the world. Research concentration would build a strengthened hierarchy among institutions. Not-university higher education would be restricted to its proper utilitarian function, leaving universities as the site for liberal education. The scandalously egalitarian notion that, as citizens, students should have a study grant by right would be replaced by a more proper loans scheme, under which cultural capital could be garnered by the children of nice people. It all seemed thoroughly Utopian.

By 1988 much of the agenda had been achieved. The most savage round of state funding cuts in British university history was announced in 1981, and implemented over the next three years. Cuts bore unevenly on different institutions, but sought to distribute state funds on a common basis. The principle of equal provision between universities, which Black Paper writers had denounced, still prevailed. University staff were assured that the sunlit uplands of level funding would be enjoyed once this exercise was completed. The government reneged. A second round of real cuts followed in 1985. In the following year the University Grants Committee produced a Beloffian blueprint for dividing British universities into different categories. All would be funded to teach undergraduates. Universities in the bottom tier would do no more than this: these would be that interesting animal, a teaching-only university. Second-tier institutions would be supported to do research in some disciplines but not others. Only top-tier universities would combine teaching with research across the whole range of disciplines. This rearrangement could be expected to have gratifying results as good staff and the best students gravitated to the top-tier institutions like negative-weight phlogiston floating upwards from a bowl of hot soup. Hierarchy would be strengthened with a vengeance, and not only in the research field.

Other things were going well. Advocacy of student loans rather than grants had moved from the wildest New Right shores to the centre of the agenda. In November 1988 a discussion paper by Robert Jackson, Higher Education Minister and former Fellow of All Souls, leaked into the public prints. Jackson proposed a state-funded voucher scheme in which the number of vouchers provided for each academic discipline would be determined by state manpower planning criteria, in which the value of a student's voucher would be determined by A level scores, and in which rich students would be able to buy entry outside the voucher scheme to a small number of universities (*Observer* 6 November 1988). With its combination of the old Right (returning Oxford and Cambridge to their pre-war status as havens for the wealthy but stupid), the meritocratic (making A level results mean real money), the utilitarian (providing more vouchers for chemical engineers than for philosophers), and the new Right (the Black Papers' voucher scheme, laughed out of court as ultramarine Utopianism when first proposed by Rhodes Boyson) this *mélange* of contradictory elements explains why critics have found it so difficult to get a line on Thatcherism: it is syncretic, an intellectual mess (Barker 1985). Jackson's proposal was leaked in the week before the Education Secretary, Kenneth Baker, unveiled his proposals for a scheme of student support that would replace existing grants. It came almost as a relief to find Baker proposing a move to student loans (*Guardian* 10 November 1988). Jackson's leaked paper had done its work.

University student numbers continued to climb throughout the 1980s, but the number of applicants climbed faster. This meant that a satisfactorily increasing proportion of well-qualified candidates was excluded. More would mean worse no longer. Those admitted came from a satisfactorily nice class of people: between 1971 and 1986 the proportion of British university students from working-class and lower middle-class backgrounds fell from 27 to 21 per cent (*THES* 29 January 1988). Research showed that Oxbridge continued to attract a nicer class of person than other universities (*THES* 6 May 1988). The Playful Giant was well under control.

New converts scrambled aboard the bandwagon set rolling by the Black Papers. Some of these were surprising people: notably two eminent members of Beloff's 'pink mafia', men who had seemed to Leavis the exemplification of technologico-Benthamism. Alexander Todd was reported telling a conference organized by the Centre for Policy Studies, the pre-eminent Thatcherite think-tank, that

> there were too many 'so-called' universities, that most should be more akin to polytechnics and that both should then be 'training people for useful things'. Traditional university

education, . . . which was of a very high standard, was never designed for so many people.

(*THES* 29 January 1988)

One could not ask for a more cogent distillation of Black Paper philosophy. Yet more surprising was the other apostate. Noel Annan was a former Provost of King's College, Cambridge, the reputed model for Simon Raven's Provost of Lancaster College, second demon to Charles Show in F.R. Leavis's pantomime. Distilling arguments that he had put to a conference the previous year (Annan 1987), he now spoke welcome words. He still believed that the Robbins Committee had been right to urge expansion of the British university sector; but, he claimed, the committee was wrong to recommend parity of esteem among universities. 'We need change. The great institutions must be treated differently to [sic] other universities and polytechnics and we mustn't feel guilty about this' (*THES* 29 January 1988). Warden Sparrow smiles encouragement.

The conference at which these two noble lords spoke their new minds was called to discuss a pamphlet written by Elie Kedourie from LSE. Its title? *Diamonds into Glass: The Government and the Universities*. Its major policy proposal? That the government should provide each university with a lump sum equivalent to ten to fifteen years' central funding, then withdraw completely from the university sector. If the proposal is *echt*-Black Paper, the pamphlet's title tells us that not everything in the Black Paper garden was lovely. Sublimely ignorant of science as he was, Sir Keith Joseph's businessman's Bernalism led him to see science as a panacea. One purpose of the 1981 round of university cuts was to redirect resources from the humanities and social sciences to applied sciences where a quick buck for private capital might be nurtured. When redirection proved difficult, he provided funds to purchase additional bodies for proper areas: the 'new blood' scheme. Most of the succulent virgins thus introduced were in two sexy fields: information technology and biotechnology. Few philosophers, historians, classicists, or literary critics. This was emphatically not what Joseph had been encouraged by Black Paper writers to do. His successor as education secretary, Kenneth Baker, gestated GERBIL, a mammoth education bill. Most of it was to Black Paperers' taste, but some proposals concerning higher education were not. Polytechnics were to be removed from local education authority control and given autonomy under their own central body. This looked like a rerun of the circumstances that led to comprehensivization of secondary education: low-status institutions getting uppity. Secondary modern schools had demolished intellectual justifications for tripartite educational apartheid when they started successfully entering pupils for the state examinations which only grammar school and public school children were supposed to be able to pass. The same grim history might be repeated in higher education as the binary system's cordon sanitaire was ruptured. Some polytechnics already had the temerity to call senior staff 'professors': a few were threatening to follow the former CATs and seek a university charter. This was dreadful news, though some comfort could be drawn from the likely merging of teaching-only universities with these aggressive polytechnics in a dismal swamp of low-status training institutions. Lord Todd's 'great institutions' would be able to sail on sublimely indifferent to the fate of lesser places, dispensing education to meritocrats (and, if the sale of entry were reinstated, to the wealthily born).

But the central worry over GERBIL concerned university autonomy. The Black Papers always had a schizoid attitude to state control. Government should abolish nasty things like sociology, but it must leave nice things alone. Chief among these nice things was donnish dominion. In the comfortable state-funding arrangement evolved since 1918, gentlemen in the government used gentlemen in the University Grants Committee to disburse money to gentlemen in the universities. Shared urbane understandings ensured that everything went smoothly without assumptions having to be spelt out. But Thatcher was no gentleman. Despite her Oxford education, she had become an iron-clad right-wing populist. Genteel accommodations hatched in the Athenaeum and ratified in the UGC's offices could not survive against a philistine Prime Minister with a whim of iron. The central Thatcherite slogan – There Is No Alternative – boded ill for anybody who got on her wrong side.

The university sector could not avoid getting on her wrong side, since a massive proportion of its capital and recurrent income came from state funds. Thatcherite policy was to save money. Thatcherite rhetoric, though not always Thatcherite practice, sought to roll back the state. This was seen to be a good thing in its own right: 'the Nanny State' was a major symptom of the British disease. It was also admirable because the money thus saved could be put to better use fortifying remote south Atlantic islands.

If state funds were to go to universities, then they would go on the government's terms. The 1981 cuts did not achieve the desired redistribution of resources towards commercially exploitable forms of research and learning because the UGC could not order autonomous universities to do this and not do that. Very well, things must change. Universities' internal culture must be transformed. The Jarratt Committee reported on institutional management, recommending that universities should be run like private companies. The vice-chancellor should become a chief executive, decisions be taken by a few small committees rather than a vast senate; academics take such an awfully long time to make a decision because they insist on *discussing* things. The state's funding whip must ensure that business-like managing practices are adopted. The whip must be brandished by a resolute hand. UGC's resolve must be stiffened; it must move from inviting suggestions to directing action. The attempt was made: before 1979 the research selectivity exercise of 1985–6 would have been seen as unacceptably *dirigiste*. It was not enough. The Croham Committee investigated the UGC, and GERBIL duly proposed a new body. The UGC had been dominated by academics. Its replacement would be dominated by industrialists and merchant bankers, men able to cut through academic clap-trap to make universities do what the government thought had to be done. Just to clarify the point, the new body had a new name: the University Funding Committee. No nonsense any more about grants, with their implication of qualified entitlement. UFC would adopt Rothschild's principle, contracting with each university to produce x biotechnologists and y classicists. It would be only reasonable to expect x to be significantly greater than y.

A 1986 survey undertaken for the Standing Conference of Arts and Social Sciences in Universities (Delamont and Read 1988) showed the consequences of seven years of Thatcherism. Student numbers in all arts and social science disciplines increased by 10 per cent between 1980 and 1986. The increase for social studies (the group of subjects clustered around sociology) was 6 per cent, for languages (including English) 7 per cent and for other humanities 14 per cent. This looks admirable, with sociologists losing out relative to humane disciplines as a government rhetorically committed to market principles directs student numbers: demand for entry to sociology courses rose by more than 30 per cent in 1986 and again in 1987, with negligible increases in available places. But evidence on staff numbers shows a different picture. Total numbers fell by 9 per cent between 1980 and 1986. Losses in languages (18 per cent) and humanities (8 per cent) exceeded those in social studies (7 per cent). Two social studies departments were closed. Three language departments and seven humanities departments were closed. Other evidence confirmed this picture. A 1984 survey by the History at the Universities Defence Group showed that the 1981 cuts round had meant the loss of eighty-seven permanent full-time jobs, with a serious loss of specialist skill in early modern, American and Asian history (*THES* 11 January 1985). The number of philosophers in British universities fell by almost a third in ten years after 1979. By 1988 twelve universities out of forty-seven had no philosophy department (*Observer* 20 November 1988). A UGC working party proposed that twelve out of thirty-one university classics departments should close (*THES* 15 January 1988).

The wrong subjects were being attacked. The wrong sort of department was being closed. 'Those of us who opposed student anarchy in the sixties,' said David Martin (1983: 183), 'find our critique has been taken up in a philistine and narrowly utilitarian way.' The Black Papers were about defending culture by defending the humanities. Thatcher's government had looked like their streetcar named desire. Now it was trundling quite in the wrong direction, and the driver appeared impervious to argument on this issue as on all others. Crisis time.

The empirical trace of crisis appears in university fiction. 'At the small provincial university where Henry Babbacombe performed the duties of Lecturer in English and Drama in the Department of Extra-Mural Studies, they were cutting almost everything' (Bradbury 1987: 40). The departments of Classics and English have been abolished. The department of Snooker Studies has been established. The library has been transformed into the Centre for Overseas Students. Babbacombe is the only worthy member of his department, but he has to be sacked if Extra-Mural Studies is to meet new staff limits. One colleague is incompetent, but he has seven children. Another has endless nervous breakdowns and perpetual agoraphobia, but she is a woman. The third colleague is the professor, entrusted with the decision about who gets the bullet. Babbacombe is shot. Krippendorf has lost his teaching job at another anonymous not-Oxbridge university; 'but that hardly counts as an impediment these days, now that they teach nothing but commercial arithmetic and fisheries science' (Parkin 1985: 46). A similar place used to be 'a comfortable backwater of quiet learning and modest scholarship' (Parkin 1987: 13). Then it was privatized. The Professor of Jurisprudence now advises the mafia, the Professor of Politics a string of military dictators. The Khomeini Centre for the Propagation of Islam has brought its funds to this campus, pipping Oxford. All staff wear identity disks. Teaching staff have to clock in. They are not paid outside teaching terms. Professor McGinty, DSc, FRS, FBA, OBE, has to ask the vice-chancellor to suspend his boilerhouse duties so that he can accept an honorary doctorate from Harvard. The departments of Classics, Mathematics, and English have been abolished. Philosophy is set to go the same way, but the department's two remaining members are offered a lifeline. If they can market philosophy successfully, then they can stay. Door-to-door selling having failed, The Mind Shop is opened off-campus. Unfortunately mind rapidly gives way to body: reorganized as The Mind and Body Shop, it becomes a haven for men in Lord Longford raincoats. Philosophy/sex, mind/body, culture/anarchy: Frank Parkin's scatological farce rests on parallel dualist foundations. A last dichotomy looms ever clearer for not-Oxbridge universities. Life faces death, with the latter gaining strength.

The once-new Lowlands University

> had survived the first round of cuts when other places had been hacked to pieces, but only through a bewilderingly Machiavellian restructuring plan and some highly creative accounting. But the second round of cuts was looming up already, and that would take something extra.
>
> (A. Davies 1986: 148)

Ernest Hemmingway, the *echt*-Oxbridge vice-chancellor, knows what that must be. Following the tenets of Thatcherite enterprise culture, Lowlands will have a Science Park, 'a dense concentration of high-technology research and development labs'. The inscrutable interpreter at last understands what he means. '"Ah, we see now. . . . In Japan we call that Industrial Estate or Row of Factories"' (A. Davies 1986: 159). Despite his good intentions, Hemmingway cannot cut the mustard. Sufficiently devious but insufficiently ruthless, failing even to evict the Lowlands women from their only hall of residence so that it can be occupied by a Japanese corporation, he is sacked. The university is merged with the Hendon Police College.

But this does not last: the police find their campus colleagues unpalatable. Lowlands needs a saviour. He proves to be Jack Daniels, the new American vice-chancellor. He believes what Hemmingway had merely mouthed, and resolutely sets to boosting applied science while decimating humanities. Little more than two years into his reign,

> Half a mile away down the hill, behind the high security fence with its barbed wire and observation posts, behind the inner fence with its electroacoustic warning and counter-insurgency system, behind the blank windowless concrete walls, three floors below ground level, Jack Daniels is walking down a long quiet carpeted corridor banked with main-frames which glow and flicker in an endlessly changing pattern of light, and hum and chatter to him softly. The one he likes best is right at the end of the corridor. He calls it Ronnie, and he likes to touch base with Ronnie every morning right after moving his bowels.
>
> (A. Davies 1988: 263)

Sweetness and light have darkened and soured. The university has become a fortified research establishment. Despite – perhaps because of – his Reagan complex, Daniels has won. But he never was a saviour. Jock McCannon, follower of Ronnie Laing, perennially collecting material for his monumental work on *The Sick University*, identified the new vice-chancellor as the anti-Christ in a single glance. C.S. Lewis's *That Hideous Strength* (1945) is conjured once more. The forces of good and evil skirmish before clashing in a final apocalypse. Good loses, utterly. McCannon dies in the last battle. '"Oh God,"' says Stephen Daker, '"It could have been such a good place, you know?"' (A. Davies 1988: 263). Like J.I.M. Stewart in *The Naylors* (1985), Andrew Davies can offer no way forward. Daker emigrates to Poland. *Solidarnosc* offers hope for a better future. Hope is dead in Thatcher's Britain.

Malcolm Bradbury's *Cuts*. Frank Parkin's *Krippendorf's Tribe* and *The Mind and Body Shop*. Andrew Davies's *A Very Peculiar Practice* and *A Very Peculiar Practice: The New Frontier*. Five novels published between 1985 and 1988. Five novels written by men who were full-time university teachers in 1980. By 1988 all had gone; Bradbury to a part-time appointment allowing him to write more; Davis and Parkin to be full-time writers. Five novels with a very similar theme: the collapse of not-Oxbridge university life under Visigoth government policy. Five novels with a similar tone: baffled rage. There are differences. Parkin owes more to Tom Sharpe than do the others, particularly in the scatological excess of his second book. Davies suggests to the reader that he cares much more about the demolition of British university culture than does Bradbury. But all share Hilda Naylor's doomed passivity: there is no recourse under Thatcher but to lie still and think of what England used to be. The promise of a government that would reverse the implicit egalitarianism of cross-party Butskellism, and the supposed aggressive levelling of Harold Wilson, has evaporated. Culture's grail was placed in safe hands, and those hands have melted it down for scrap. The guiding metaphor of the university as cultural citadel has produced disastrously illiberal results. But there is no other available metaphor: English culture had staked its shirt on a rightist interpretation of Matthew Arnold.

The most subtle examination of not-Oxbridge troubles goes to the root of the problem. *Nice Work* (1988) was written by another man who has pulled out from university teaching to write full-time, David Lodge. Philip Swallow still runs the Rummidge English department, but he is ailing, growing hard of hearing. His decline matches that of his institution. Swingeing cuts have made the heady days of *Small World* (1984), of Swallow as globe-trotting conference-going academic, of the world as conference, merely a hazily rosy memory. As the benignly ineffectual Dean of Arts at Rummidge, Swallow has a Dean's Relief for a fixed-term three-year period. The lot falls on Robyn Penrose.

Penrose is academically marginal. She is a woman; she is Australian-born; she took a first degree at Sussex before doing a doctorate in Cambridge; she is a feminist and post-structuralist literary critic; she is a fixed-term lecturer. Thus the dramatic effect is greatly heightened when she becomes culture's ancient, its standard-bearer. Rummidge's vice-chancellor has enthusiastically endorsed a proposal from CRUM – the Confederation of Rummidge Manufacturers – for an Industry Year Shadow Scheme, under which an academic will follow a senior manager around for one day each week for ten weeks in order to learn something about the real world. The vice-chancellor orders Swallow to find a shadow. Swallow loses the letter. Pressed for a nomination, he coerces Robyn Penrose to take on the task. Oppressed by her marginality, she has no alternative but to accept.

Since her field is the nineteenth-century industrial novel, she is an admirable choice. But she knows nothing about industry. Able to talk for hours about Mrs Gaskell's response to the industrial north, she is bewildered and horrified by her first visit to a Rummidge foundry. Penrose is to shadow Vic Wilcox, the thrusting managing director of a rundown local metal-bashing company. He is an engineer, a graduate not of Balliol-by-the-Sea and Cambridge, but of the local CAT before it was elevated to university status. His politics are utilitarian new Right, hers are a fuzzy liberalism. If Penrose, a specialist on the industrial novel, knows nothing of industry then he, a graduate, knows nothing of universities. Driving past the major redbrick Rummidge University every morning on his way to work, he looks at the place:

> With its massive architecture and landscaped grounds, guarded at every entrance by watchful security staff, the University seems to Vic rather like a small city-state, an academic Vatican, from which he keeps his distance, both intimidated by and disapproving of its air of privileged detachment from the vulgar, bustling industrial city in which it is embedded.
>
> (Lodge 1988: 14)

Lodge called his novel *Nice Work*. 'If you can get it / And you can get it if you try' – Tebbitt's Bike – remains implicit. But 'it' is sex as well as work. This is a novel about mating. The central characters' names tell us what is to be brought together: Vic[torian values] Wilcox, masculine utilitarian determination, faces Robyn Penrose, softly and ambiguously feminine letters. Initially the two worlds slide across each other. Wilcox's resolutely profit-centred meetings

– 'I'm proposing a new slogan. *If it's profitable, Pringle's will make it*' (Lodge 1988: 47) – are intercut with Penrose's careful seminar dissection of Dickens's objections to utilitarianism in *Hard Times*. Slowly, over her ten weeks, Penrose comes to appreciate Wilcox's difficulties and responsibilities. In return, his hostility melts as he sees dimly that culture might have a point. Wilcox and Penrose mate physically on a trip to buy a moulding machine at a European exhibition: Arnoldian liberalism and utilitarianism, hitherto sealed in different Rummidge boxes, interpenetrate. But they do not fuse. This sexual act is an episode for Penrose, a revelation for Wilcox. His appetite whetted, he pursues her relentlessly. A reverse shadow scheme is constructed: Wilcox spends one day each week in Penrose's classes.

How will this all end? Will David Lodge, the brightest and the best of British university novelists still writing, be able to find a new synthesis to solve the old problems that defeated Dickens, Carlyle and Arnold? Will Penrose fuse with Wilcox? Will there be a new way to save culture from utilitarian rape? Well, no. Wilcox's firm is merged with a competitor: he is sacked. The second round of UGC cuts having hit Rummidge less severely than the jeremiahs had predicted, Swallow hints to Penrose the possibility of continued employment. Wilcox repeats Rummidge industrial history, setting up his own company. The funding for this company forms the only link between the two worlds: Penrose's legacy from that tired old *deus ex machina*, a long-forgotten and unexpectedly wealthy Australian uncle. Lodge restates the Victorian debate about culture and utility, but ends with each still in its own box. Better mutual understanding is all for which we can hope. 'Only connect', as Morgan Forster used to say in King's, Cambridge.

English covert sociology, for so long a ready help in times of need, offers no solution: literary theory wallows helplessly on a lee shore (Eagleton 1983: 194–217). Consider Rodney Wainwright's sad plight in David Lodge's previous, marvellous novel. Wainwright teaches English in tropical Australia, in the University of North Queensland. His plan for escaping to somewhere less dreadful centres on a paper for Morris Zapp's Jerusalem conference on The Future of Criticism. He plunges his sticky fingers down on his typewriter's sticky keys:

The question is, therefore, how can literary criticism maintain its Arnoldian function of identifying the best which has been thought and said, when literary discourse itself has been decentred by deconstructing the traditional concept of the author, of authority?

(Lodge 1984: 84)

He gets no further. New drafts founder on the same rock. Even when he stands up at the conference to read his paper, the text breaks off at the same point. He is saved from humiliation only by rumours about an outbreak of Legionnaire's Disease in the conference hotel; rumours which surface just when he has got to his crunch question. For the point, of course, is that the question has no answer. Arnold assumed an authoritative elite that would warrant what was good, what constituted culture, what constituted truth. Post-structuralism denies the possibility of that privileged (in two senses) access to truth (Gilmour 1987; Welch 1987). Jack's discourse is as good as his master's. We celebrate diversity, wit, puns. Who cares if the centre does not hold; we no longer recognize that the centre ever existed.

For the crisis is not limited to not-Oxbridge universities: the centre also feels threatened. In 1986 Oxford University's vice-chancellor predicted an annual financial shortfall of £10 million within four years. To remedy the deficiency would mean losing one in ten academic posts. This 'was equivalent to wiping out all clinical medicine, engineering and metallurgy, and most of chemistry; or . . . dropping all history, theology, philosophy, English, Oriental studies, modern languages and preclinical study' (*THES* 5 December 1986). (A leader noted that this was a crisis for the university rather than the colleges. Relentlessly utilitarian government modernizers would strengthen the archaic at the expense of the modern part of the institution: *THES* 24 October 1986.) Once again, the crisis is refracted in fiction. The minister in charge of British intelligence operations under Thatcher had scraped a third-class Cambridge degree in Land Economy. He holds less than fond memories of those who taught him.

Wyman is a typical example. . . . Spends other people's money as if there's no tomorrow. Dons are like that. They live

257

too damned well, that's what it's all about. They sit in the lap
of collegiate luxury like medieval barons, and when you pull
them out into the real world they expect to carry on as usual.
They're out of date, Owen, completely out of date.

(Cook 1985: 166)

We are told that the Thatcher government had two principal
targets for cost-cutting exercises. One was the civil service.

The other target was education, in particular the Old
Universities. In the Chancellor's opinion, these
establishments fostered a brand of elitism that retarded the
progress of the New Right. The Chancellor was a New
Conservative. He fervently believed that all hope for the
future of his country lay with the dynamic middle classes. The
aristocracy of Oxbridge dinosaurs was a brake upon his
party's ideological progress. They would have to go.

(Cook 1985: 9–10)

A dreadful light breaks. The Conservative Party is in the hands not
of decent old Right county buffers but adamantine new Right
money-shufflers. With Dracula in the bloodbank, the only
novelistic recourse is nostalgia: a pretence that aristocratic
Oxbridge is alive and well (Fraser 1985; Lejeune 1987), a lovingly
knowing reincarnation of Oxford undergraduate experience
distanced by having the action set in the years between 1929 and
1931 (Wain 1988). The only practical recourse is to break with
tradition and refuse an Oxford-educated Prime Minister an
honorary Oxford degree. A noble gesture, but one which is likely
to have nasty consequences given this Prime Minister's celebrated
magnanimity. The rest is silence.

Chapter Eleven

HOW TO BE AN ALIEN

The interlarded discourses of English university fiction and the Black Papers promised to be a sure guide in need, but they have brought us to a quicksand. History has sprung a dreadful trap. In resisting the march of what they took to be illiberal barbarians, novelists and educational reformers have delivered British universities, and the culture that they assert to be cherished in those places, into the hands of a barbarous government. Thatcher's morally stunted economic liberalism is radically different from, inimical to, that liberal humanism which university novelists thought they were defending. Hence the baffled rage of recent novels. Hence Malcolm Bradbury's introduction to Laurie Taylor's *Professor Lapping Sends His Apologies* (1986); an essay in which he reverses the judgements of *The History Man.* In 1975 Bradbury had vilified sociology. In 1986 he celebrates Taylor's blackly perceptive applied sociology of collapsing British higher education. In 1975 Bradbury claimed to see a leftist assault on university culture, a pre-echo of Julius Gould's absurd conspiracy. In 1986 he rails at the rightist 're-barbarization of British culture and educational achievement. A country once famous for arts, learning and scholarship is quite simply dismantling a good part of its competence and power in these fields' (Bradbury 1986: 3).

What, then, is to be done? If British higher education lies ruined – to an extent not widely appreciated outside Britain: Wolfgang Weiss's recent book on English and American university fiction quite fails to connect with current difficulties because he is unable to conceive of a society which does not value world-class universities – then what routes can we find for crawling from the wreckage?

One of Raymond Williams's last essays bore the title 'Crawling from the wreckage' (1987). Williams is a useful guide, largely because of his marginality. Until his death in 1988 he was the last standard- bearer, the last ancient, for left-Arnoldian cultural theory. Strongly influenced by F.R. Leavis, Williams sought to root his defence of culture in the lived experience of working-class Britons rather than a dream of blended aristocratic and merit-ocratic Cambridge. Leavis celebrated social closure on his own terms. Williams consistently resisted social closure in all its forms. That alone makes him important for our purposes; but there is more. He spent his working life teaching in Oxford and Cam-bridge universities, but he distanced himself from some features of those institutions. His one university novel, *Second Generation* (1964), was unparalleled until John Wain's *Where the Rivers Meet* (1988) in making the Cowley car factories equally central to Oxford life as the university and colleges. Williams's origin in the Welsh Marches allowed him to avoid a routine genuflection to Englishness. A small group of Welsh-language novels (Dafydd 1975; Elis 1953; Miles 1979; Rowlands 1978), all written by people who attended the University College of North Wales, Bangor, makes Anglicization the fungus that is rotting Welsh university life. Raymond Williams was sensitive to the possibilities and dangers of nationalist strategies – in his novel *The Volunteers* (1978), for instance – but as an English-speaking Welshman from a skilled working-class background he gave a higher priority to class analysis. In *Border Country* (1960) he produced an account of the southern Marches and Cambridge as not only two countries but also two class cultures. Fred Inglis (*THES* 5 February 1988) quotes Williams's account of his first reaction to Cambridge: 'What really shocked me, much more than the luxury, the snobbery, the fan-tastically different scale of money-values, was the use of literature, the use of learning in general, to ratify just this economic and social system, and its way of life'. In the introduction to his masterly critical study of *The Country and the City* (1973) Williams sits in his study near Cambridge, looking over the rich, flat farmlands; seeing them as the result of centuries of labour by nameless men and women, not as the natural backdrop to the university city. He confides that he had no stomach for Jesus College's ritual paternalistic dinners for its tenant farmers.

In 'Crawling from the wreckage' (1987) Williams asserts the

importance of Victorian arguments about university life for thinking through current difficulties. Then as now, opinions divided sharply between humanist 'traditionalists' and utilitarian 'modernisers'. But all Victorian sages insisted 'that there were no simple and reliable lines of transfer between new kinds of knowledge and skill and their actual realization in any complex general society'.

> Decisions of every kind, about economic demand, about political directions, about social and cultural policy, about relations with other peoples, were increasingly passing, if more indirectly than directly, into general public hands. Therefore only a much better educated society – not only sectors within it but their complex interactions in an inevitable practical whole – could now succeed. This consideration was not only for the general good but also for the best intentions of old humanists and industrial trainers alike.
>
> (R. Williams 1987)

This is the great Victorian truth that has been obscured by British university novelists' obsession with social closure. Williams's assertion of the value of general education for humanists' sectoral interests is warranted by American experience. In Britain novel-writing university humanists have dug their disciplines' graves by seeking to define and defend an ever-shrinking laager. 'I suggest', says the historian Keith Thomas (1988), 'that the original rationale for the study of the humanities has largely collapsed.' The rubble should be used to construct educational experiences which

> enlarge our experience, enhance our self-consciousness, widen our sense of what is humanly possible, and most important of all, enable us to step outside the assumptions of our own day and to escape the tyranny of present-mindedness, so that we can view our own times with some sense of detachment.
>
> (K. Thomas 1988)

This looks back towards *Culture and Anarchy*, but it is consistent with Raymond Williams's notion – also ultimately grounded in a reading of Arnold – that universities' central task is the creation of a critically literate citizenry. There would be a widespread welcome for this idea in many parts of the university. Looking outwards with confidence, looking to strengthen connections with humane academics in other disciplines, would strengthen the humanities' now seriously eroded political and intellectual position. It would also be a small step to countering a looming tyranny.

For there are wider issues at stake. The Black Papers and British university fiction's dominant discourse helped open the road to Thatcher's iron rule. That rule is riddled with contradictions: between populist rhetoric and viciously defended loyalty to the Leader's person; between Friedmanite economic liberalism and increasingly authoritarian social policies; between affluence in the home counties and squalor in remote provinces that consistently reject Thatcherite candidates in elections. This, too, is significant. If Raymond Williams celebrated the Matthew Arnold who valued continental countries' state-sponsored education systems, then he also developed a version of Arnold's mass society line. Universities are important places because they are bastions against tyranny. Arnold was a thoroughgoing aristocratic mass society theorist; for him the threat came from 'the Playful Giant', the proletariat. Raymond Williams was the most distinguished modern democratic mass society theorist. In his view the dreadful threat posed by the Thatcher governments lay not in their desire to open the British elite to mass pressure, but in their determined assault on institutions inhibiting the full and direct mobilization of the mass of British people by their leaders. The politicization of the civil service; the destruction of local government's relative autonomy; the assault on trade unions and other working-class institutions; the neutering of public broadcasting: these are the actions of an elected tyranny determined to destroy all potential sites of resistance. What defensible forts remain in England? The established Church, the monarchy and the universities: not the institutions that a left-Arnoldian would choose to garrison. Bolshie bishops and a pugnacious Prince of Wales might cause Thatcher's *chelas* local difficulties, but universities form the main remaining defence against tyranny. As the *Times Higher Education Supplement*'s leader writer noted, commenting on the successful campaign to enshrine a definition of academic freedom in GERBIL against Kenneth Baker's wishes, 'There are few independent institutions in Britain today with the power and the nerve to force Mrs Thatcher's government to back down' (*THES* 26 February 1988).

Culture and Anarchy is back on the agenda, but with an urgency that Arnold never foresaw. Aliens must be made, and in unprecedented numbers. The survival of those values that used to be celebrated as quintessentially English – tolerance, decency, moderation, democracy; the values that British university novelists and Black Paper writers thought they were defending, but helped to subvert – requires the creation of an educated public through a massively expanded university system. This will involve hard choices: no publicly funded system could achieve participation rates comparable with those in the United States of America – and that must the aim – if it took Oxbridge's personal socialization model of university education as its guide. Where are we to look for a guide?

One possibility might be to seek out renegades. Starting with T.H. Green, an Oxford Hegelian, a stream of Oxford and Cambridge academics has sought to think through what an anti-thesis to Oxbridge hegemony might look like. This has produced very distinguished work deriving from notions of equality (R.H. Tawney) and citizenship (T.H. Marshall 1950). Once again we see that Oxford and Cambridge universities contain more varied people than fiction would suggest. But this effort, for all its earnestness and good-heartedness, has its problems. The contributors to Finch and Rustin's collection *A Degree of Choice* (1986) – few of them based in Oxford or Cambridge – look towards a British higher education system built around equality and citizenship rights, but they can provide no clear route-map for getting from here to there. The obstacles lie less in party politics than in cultural politics. When the most distinguished modern follower of William Morris can anathematise structuralists for bringing foreign ideas to England (Thompson 1978), when Inglis's *Radical Earnestness* (1982) swallows Oxbridge hegemony whole while celebrating T.H. Green's intellectual children, then we need to rethink the relationship between culture and the university if a claim for radically widened access is not to be interpreted simply as barbarians beating on the gates.

*

When times get tough, turn to fantasy: the Hollywood maxim. The team that enjoyed *The Purple Rose of Cairo* brings you a fairy story. Like any proper fairy story, we begin once upon a time; but not very long ago and not so far away.

Once upon a time there was a country which had come down in the world. Formerly the centre of a mighty empire, it had fallen on hard times. Now it was a shabby, decent sort of place governed by shabby, decent sorts of people.

Then, one day, a frightful woman appeared. She had once been a reasonable sort of person herself, but her mind had been captured by two warlocks. One was the crazed central European, Hyjack. The other was an American, Fraudperson; he was an honoured citizen of a town otherwise known only for its gangsters.

Once under these men's spell, the woman turned from being shabby and decent to being crisp and indecent. Although loved by far fewer than half of the people in the country, she crowned herself Black Queen. (Since this is an anti-racist fairy story we must make it clear that her blackness lay in her heart, not her skin – which was a repulsive putty colour rather than a proper, glorious, ebony). *Although pretending to bend the knee to a woman who had been White Queen for many years, the Black Queen became the country's real ruler. She spoke words of freedom, but practised tyranny. She pandered to the basest human instincts. Under her guidance greed became a virtue, compassion a vice. When poor people told her that they had no bread, she told them to eat cake: she HATED poor people. When muttering against her grew rather loud, she killed many young men and women in a crusade against funny foreigners: she didn't much like young people, and she HATED foreigners.*

Indeed, she hated anybody who was not like her, who had not been reconstructed by Hyjack and Fraudperson. 'Madam,' a few brave courtiers told her, 'your cruelty is not what we expect from a queen.' These people were called 'wets', because the Black Queen had them drowned in a butt of Malmsey. 'Madam,' her civil servants told her, 'under your policies the rich are getting richer and the poor poorer; the rich are living much longer and the poor scarcely any longer; the money-shufflers in the parishes around your castle are floating in lager while the people who used to make things elsewhere in your realm have no work. Surely this is a mistake?' To show just how much of a mistake this was, the Black Queen neutered her civil servants with a blunt knife. 'Madam,' the sheriffs of cities and shires told her, 'we wish to continue to serve the people in our bailliewicks as best we can.' 'So you shall,' said the Black Queen, and cut off their heads.

'Madam,' said the bishops, 'you act immorally'. 'Yah, boo, sucks,' said the Black Queen. 'How many morals to the groat?' (She could not manage a more civilized response than this, partly because she was such an uncivilized person, and partly because – occasional delusions notwithstanding – she was not God.)

The Black Queen's vicious reign caused much rending of garments and gnashing of teeth in the country's secular monasteries, which she had savaged with the rest. Her ravaging cuts were bad enough. Far, far worse was the knowledge that some of the monks once had supported her, not seeing that she would use their quaint arguments, developed to defend the monasteries, against them as part of her evil strategy. After five years of her reign Marplan (yes, they have a fairy branch) surveyed the monasteries, and found that only one monk in five loved the Black Queen. The other four-fifths suggested all sorts of imaginative things that should be done with her. These usually involved stakes through the heart or boiling oil; though being kindly folk at bottom – and cowards – the monks did not mention these things to her face.

The monks did NOT love the Black Queen. But they could do little. They propped a claret-sodden champion in his saddle and sent him to fight the Gerbil in the Lords lists. Sir Woy did manage to cut off the Gerbil's nose – or another part of its anatomy – but few believed that it would not grow a new one. This small victory apart, the monks were helpless. 'Give us a sign,' they cried, reverting to their pre-secular habits; 'give us a pillar of smoke by day, of fire by night. Show us a way out of the Black Queen's thraldom.' But no sign came. Nobody could suggest a way out.

Life in the monasteries grew more and more miserable. The Black Queen demanded that more and more effort be devoted to producing lager-style Benedictine in monastery cellars, less and less to those contemplative and educational purposes for which the places had been founded. 'Contemplation butters no parsnips,' she snapped. 'And as for education, it only encourages Grantham grocers' daughters. Think of the awful consequences.' The monks thought, and saw that she was right about Grantham grocers' daughters, though they believed that the rest of what she said was hogwash.

Then, one day, an old monk was scouring through hogwash. Part of a lager-style Benedictine production brigade, he had been sent to the piggery because it once had been the monastery's library. (With contemplation and education declared redundant, there was now no need for a library.) 'The market for Benedictine is flooded,' his production brigade chief had told him. 'You're so old that you were taught to read; go and look *for a recipe for lager-style Strega.' He did as he was bidden, though he knew that it was a hopeless quest. Most of the books had been eaten by generations of pigs. Only the most indigestible works remained: books on monastic history. Thumbing through one of these, the old monk found himself reading about a time and place where things had been different. Far, far to the north, and many, many years before, monasteries had been cherished by the people, and had welcomed any men – and, after a struggle, any women – within their doors. They had combined contemplation, education and Benedictine-distilling in a way quite different from the monasteries with which the old monk was familiar. He realized that he had found his pillar of fire.*

The old monk hurried back to his brothers. 'The Black Queen has lied,' he shouted. 'She keeps telling us that THERE IS NO ALTERNATIVE: but there is one. I have read about it. It once existed, and we can make something like it happen again. It will not be easy to rebuild our monastery on the new plan – which, like all new plans, really is a very old plan – but it is worth trying. I will tell you about it this evening.'

He never did tell them about it. He was run down in the monastery cloister by Tebbitt's Bike. A pure accident, of course, as the rider menacingly explained to the other monks. Briefly flickering hope extinguished, the monks returned to their cellars.

Tyrants fear books: that is why pigs are set to eat them. But the Black Queen failed to destroy all copies of the book which the old monk found. One copy remains. Through the dung and cobwebs, we just can read the writing on its spine: R.D. Anderson, *Education and Opportunity in Victorian Scotland* (1983). Open its pages, and we discover a conception of what universities were for, and whom they should serve, that disrupts English university fiction's dominant discourse. Things once were different in a different part of Britain.

The 1707 Act of Union explicitly protected the key institutions of Scottish civil society: the Roman-based Scots law, the Presbyterian kirk, and the Scottish education system. That system was much better developed than the corresponding English system. The ancient Scottish universities taught science and medicine when these were ignored in Oxford and Cambridge, yet science in Scottish university education was blended in general, liberal education (R.D. Anderson 1988: 14). The key discipline – the one that made sense of all the others – was moral philosophy, combining what we now call sociology, economics, psychology, politics, and philosophy. The Scottish Enlightenment was an efflorescence of moral philosophy; but social theory and analysis, classics, and natural philosophy – the local name for physics – were less divorced from practical matters than in England. Divisions between 'pure' and 'applied', between 'culture' and 'science' resonated very differently in nineteenth-century Aberdeen, Edinburgh, Glasgow and St Andrews on the one hand and nineteenth-century Oxford and Cambridge on the other, the result of significantly different conceptions of what a university should be. Table 4 displays this contrast, focusing on notions of the university as an agent of moral education. We see that each 'system' has a moral justification, but that these justifications are mutually exclusive.

We see that British novels' conception of Oxbridge liberal education is an artefact of time and place, not an eternal verity. A feasible alternative, just as well grounded in moral concerns, existed north of the border. Scottish universities challenged other features of the Oxbridge model. Their supporters castigated the southern universities' pedagogic inefficiency, taking them to be more concerned with turning louts into gentlemen than teaching anything very systematically. Two justifying myths grappled: the Oxbridge genteel amateur and the generally educated Scottish lad of parts (McPherson 1972; R.D. Anderson 1985). Nineteenth-century controversies set the Oxbridge 'tutorial system' against the Scottish 'professorial system', by no means always to the former's advantage. Thus the English nonconformist Walter Bagehot denigrated Oxbridge education, 'designed to teach men to write essays and articles', comparing it unfavourably with the Scottish 'education of speculation, the training and philosophical application of the reasoning faculties' (quoted in Wright 1979: 91). A degree of control over Scottish universities came from public authorities: Edinburgh University was founded by the Town Council, which retained appointment rights well into the nineteenth century. Nor did public obligations disappear then. As late as 1910 Scottish universities received between a third and a half of their funds from the state (R.D. Anderson 1983: 289). Once again, Scotland stands in sharp contrast to Oxbridge. The notion that a university should be autonomous, that state funding was an aberration to be ditched at the earliest opportunity, was quite foreign in Scotland – as in continental countries to this day (Neave

1982–3) – until her universities were fully assimilated in the British system after the Second World War.

Table 4 Two kinds of university

	'ancient Scottish'	*'ancient English'*
student intake relative to population	high and heterogenous	low and homogenous
resources per student	low	high
residence	lodgings/home	hall
teaching	lecture	tutorial
student/staff contact	low	high
student/student contact	low	high
locus of extra-curricular student life	outwith university	within university
student role	'customer'	'member'
student 'wastage'	high, but not seen as 'wastage'	low
typical product	heterogenous (variable numbers of class tickets or 'credits': few graduates)	homogenous (the graduate)
indicative moral purpose	'The Scottish student prizes his independence . . . the habits of self control which are called forth in the student who lives as his own master in lodgings, and there commences in earnest to fight the battle of life are perhaps the most valuable results of his university life' (Grant 1884)	'So long as students live at home or in lodgings and merely travel backwards and forwards to attend university classes, it is difficult to develop that community life which is perhaps the most educative thing that the university has to offer' (H.C. Barnard 1947)

Source: Burnhill and McPherson 1983: 265

The obverse of public control was strong public support for Scottish universities, and a clear purpose. Universities were not for the education of a tiny elite, but for all men – and, after a struggle – for all women. This noble ideal was never fully achieved, but nineteenth-century Scottish university students were drawn from an unusually wide social spectrum in a European perspective. In the 1860s some 20 per cent of students came from manual workers' homes (McPherson 1973: 169); though Robert Anderson (1983: 318) shows that they were drawn predominantly from the skilled working class. Detailed work on Aberdeen (R. D. Anderson 1988) shows that lower-class participation rates rose sharply in the early twentieth century in response to increased demand for schoolteachers. Cunningham (1984) argues strongly that this democratic ethos extended beyond injuries of class: women formed a significantly higher proportion of Scottish university students than was true for England. Compared with Oxford and Cambridge, Scottish universities seemed positively Jacobin in declining to make education a mechanism of social closure. When Professor Prothero suggests that the minor English redbrick Buriton University should be 'Open to anyone who wants to come, without examination qualifications', the other Senators see this as no more than his usual New Left ravings: Prothero is a sociologist, 'a bearded man with a Northern accent whose speeches made his colleagues groan at their own folly in having appointed him' (Mann 1975: 9–10). But the ultra-conservative professors of King's College, Aberdeen, opposed the 1826 Royal Commission on Scottish Universities' suggestion that an entrance examination should be introduced, identifying it as 'part of a "system of exclusion" which would deprive the common people of their rights'. The Edinburgh professors declared that an entrance examination would destroy the University's nature as a 'free and public school' (R. D. Anderson 1983: 47–8).

The determinedly democratic nature of Scottish university entrance did not mean the triumph of culture's enemies. Consider the position of classical languages, the touchstone of culture for Arnold and for many of his more recent rightist followers. In nineteenth-century Oxford and Cambridge the privileging of Latin and Greek in entry requirements served to close those universities to all but a minute proportion of the population. The same prescription applied in Scotland, but with very different consequences. A firm grounding in Latin formed the foundation of an Arts degree, but knowledge of ancient languages was not limited to a tiny elite. Scholars in Scottish parochial schools who aimed for university study sat alongside those with more modest ambitions. Students – of many ages – were prepared for study in the most democratic of all the universities, King's and Marischal in

Aberdeen (united in 1860), by a network of well-trained parish schoolmasters spread throughout the region and supported by the Dick Bequest. 'Significantly, the great *individual* benefactions in Scotland have been made to education,' Andrew McPherson (1973: 160) notes, 'and, unlike England, have been made to the *public* system'. Classics provided a common groundwork on which the arts curriculum constructed a philosophically centred education. In the almost continuous nineteenth-century controversy over Scottish university reform the relationship of culture to science, and of culture to utilitarianism, were running subtexts. Discussion and struggle eventually produced a compromise between collectivist and individualist emphases, in the distinctively Scottish idea of democratic elitism (Davie 1962, 1986). While J.H. Newman's *University Sketches* (1856) were ignored, Matthew Arnold's *Culture and Anarchy* (1869) was read widely in Scotland; but it became a rather different argument when read against the local democratic ethos. Arnold's defence of aristocratic Oxford coloured English interpretations; his enthusiasm for European state-sponsored secondary education coloured readings in Scotland, where state support for schools and universities had existed for centuries. Arnold's debate with Huxley also struck a sympathetic chord. Towards the end of the nineteenth century Lyon Playfair, an Edinburgh University chemist and a strong defender of the democratic tradition in Scottish education, paraphrased the debate's conclusion when he urged a radical combination of university arts and science teaching as a remedy for the inefficiency of British technical education (F.S.L. Lyons 1983: 126). In England this suggestion sounded like a barbarian trumpet-call; in Scotland it was little more than an assertion of what had been common practice. Had it been implemented throughout Britain then we might have been spared Snow's 'Two Cultures' lecture; and, with luck, his novels.

But by Playfair's day the Scottish alternative was already beginning to dissolve. The mid-century Northcote-Trevelyan civil service reforms forced belated reform in Oxford and Cambridge, but they applied English assumptions on a British scale. The marking scheme for early examinations was intended to give graduates from all universities an equal chance, but it gave high marks for knowledge of English history and literature, and privileged an Oxbridge classics-centred education over a Scottish philosophy-centred one (R. D. Anderson 1983: 63–4). This, together with the steady drip of agitation from Edinburgh lawyers impressed with Oxbridge social prestige (McPherson 1973: 172), forced a drastic modification of Scottish university education. Honours degrees were introduced. The arts curriculum became more specialized, with the consequent decentring of philosophy (Davie 1962). Assimilation with English models was not uncontested. A rearguard action for Scottish 'democratic intellectualism' was fought between 1917 and 1927. It failed:

> the debate of the twenties resulted in a disruption of the Scottish educational system in which the universities turned their backs on the S[cottish] E[ducation] D[epartment] and the Scottish schools in order to join themselves, in due course, with the system of schools and universities in England, under the auspices of the Department of Education and Science.
>
> (Davie 1986: ii)

Another chance appeared in the 1970s, when Scottish universities had an opportunity to renew a connection with their particular and distinguished past, and move towards different futures, by throwing their weight behind the movement for political devolution. They declined, preferring the security blanket of the British UGC. What a splendid decision that looks, with hindsight. The difficult birth of a Scottish Committee of the new University Funding Committee may herald less awful things, though one should not be too sanguine about this prospect in the current British political climate.

This history is both effect and cause of the steady, century-long assimilation of Scottish universities to an English hierarchy. Explanations differ – the application of unthinking Englishness to a once proudly independent Scotland for George Davie, conflict between a professional and a commercial bourgeoisie within Scotland for Robert Anderson – but there is no dispute over the main outlines of the process. The Oxbridge-focused dominant discourse of British public policy for universities once faced a real competitor. That competitor was suppressed. Scottish universities were integrated in a British system as English redbricks; exactly what happens to St Andrews in the single significant post-war university novel set north of the border (Walker 1959). The most resolute nineteenth-century bastion of Scottish democratic intellectualism, Aberdeen University, was the seventh hardest hit British university in the 1981 cuts round. Further serious reductions in state support have been applied in later years. There is a real possibility that Aberdeen University will not survive to celebrate the five hundredth anniversary of its foundation in 1495. Those are the wages of accommodation to the English hierarchy. All attempts to construct Scottish-type universities in England as a conscious challenge to Oxbridge hegemony – the 'Godless' University College, London (Bellot 1929: 8; New 1961: 378) and the forerunner of major redbrick Manchester (Fiddes 1937) in the nineteenth century; Sandy Lindsay's Keele, the result of his many years' exasperation with Oxford fogeyism as Master of Balliol, in the twentieth century (Gallie 1960) – have failed, as the institutions were subsumed in the English hierarchy.

There is an obvious response to all this. The Scottish university system was dismantled, it might be argued, because it could not work under modern conditions. Moral philosophy was a splendid educational integument in the days of Adam Smith, David Hume, and William Robertson, but as separate disciplines crystallized – first economics, then psychology, political science, and sociology – so they left the merest rump, concerned with what one should do if one saw somebody fall into a canal. As its central organizing focus withered, so the Scottish vision of liberal education crumbled. The Scottish universities are simply the victims of modernization (McPherson 1973: 175–7). Assimilation could have been less crassly Anglocentric, but it was inevitable.

Not true. Scottish models had wider influence outside than inside Britain. Wherever Scots wandered, they took their view of a university with them: Dalhousie University is a distinguished Canadian example (Reid 1989). These places steadily became syncretic institutions, combining Scottish ancestry with adaptation to local beliefs and practices.

Only in one place did the Scottish model spawn an entire university system. The nineteenth-century Otago Settlement was organized from Edinburgh. When Scottish settlers arrived in this comfortingly cold region of New Zealand, they soon set about organizing a copy of Edinburgh University. Otago University, founded in 1869, was the first in the colony. As other provinces began to think of founding a university college, they copied the first. A Scottish university system was constructed at the uttermost end of the earth.

The Scottish pattern was not followed in New Zealand out of Caledonian pride. Otago was the only province organized by Scots. English ideas prevailed elsewhere. The most famous of these ideas, the Wakefield settlements in different parts of the country, was inspired by a George Eliotish vision of rural England recreated at the end of the earth, with ties of happy deference uniting landowners, tenant farmers, and landless labourers. Just the sort of society to produce a proper Oxbridge university system.

It did not happen, because the firm social constraint necessary to hold the English dream together could not be combined with an open land frontier. Men could not be held to wage labouring for others' profit when they could occupy what they, but not Maori people, took to be unclaimed land. In place of deference, colonial New Zealand generated a ruggedly democratic ethos. Big landowners in rich pastoral areas – the squattocracy – could mitigate this by shipping their sons off to Oxford or Cambridge for a spit and polish (Eldred-Grigg 1980: 158–9); other groups set to building a university system better adapted to local circumstances. These circumstances – a democratic culture, poor communications between different districts – had marked pre-modern Scotland. Small wonder, then, that the Scottish university system proved admirably suited to their needs.

Indeed, like other imported practices (Carter 1986: 42), the Scottish university model flourished better in New Zealand than in its native country. In Scotland, relentless anglicizing pressure forced change and dilution: increasing specialization, increasingly restrictive entry qualifications. In New Zealand the Scottish university faced no competition, and changed little. In the early 1980s the structure would have been familiar to a mid-nineteenth-century Aberdeen Doctor: local rather than national universities, with the country divided into zones and students from each zone required to go to the local university unless they could show need to study a subject not offered there; admission to a faculty rather than a department or college; a strong, though weakening, body of part-time students; education built around lectures rather than tutorials; formal public control of the curriculum; classified Honours degrees mostly still awarded at the postgraduate level (this marks the system as mid-Victorian Scottish rather than late-

Victorian Scottish); small bursaries, paid to any student, which were valid for up to five years and sufficient to pay the university's negligible tuition fees and make a modest contribution to living costs; effective open entry to university. 'This', our Aberdeen Doctor would sigh, 'is what a university should look like'. And this vision would not be bought at the expense of quality. Those who know the country might think Ninian Smart's description of New Zealand universities as the world's finest (*THES* 29 April 1977) a mite extravagant, but an authoritative recent international comparison (Watts 1987) showed teaching and research to be well up to scratch.

But there was a tension in the New Zealand university system. Scottish by structure, it was staffed by people who took their conception of what a proper university looked like from England. There are many indications of this. Otago University's original architecture is stern Scottish baronial. When Auckland came to erect its symbolic building in the 1920s, it chose to employ an architect who had trained under Frank Lloyd Wright. What did he build? A fake-Tudor block surmounted by a detumescent Tom Tower. New Zealand university novels show us struggles for the Rhodes Scholarship, for the right to be groomed in culture's citadel. There are departments which still encourage their best graduates to go to Oxford or Cambridge for postgraduate work. This may benefit the reputation of New Zealand academics, but it impoverishes the country. It is said that a lower proportion of New Zealand Rhodes Scholars returns from Oxford than is the case for any other country. Novelists – M.K. Joseph, Dan Davin, Karl Stead, Wayne Innes – construct New Zealand universities as not-Oxbridge English universities, pale and feeble imitations of Oxbridge glories. English university novelists bear guilt for preparing the ground for Thatcherite higher education policy. New Zealand university novelists bear a heavier guilt: focusing on English culture rather than Scottish structure, they failed to assert the difference of the New Zealand university system, a difference that should have made it less simple for new-Right barbarism to be transferred from Whitehall to Wellington.

For the transfer did take place. British initiatives were conned. The Jarratt Report spawned its New Zealand imitator, equally concerned to apply business management methods to education and scholarship. Universities in New Zealand as in Britain were to play M'Choakumchild to private capital's Bounderby. Embarrassed by a distinguished international committee's endorsement of New Zealand universities' quality, and consequent recommendations that the system should be doubled at state expense (Watts 1987), the Labour government commissioned a second report from a team led by a local academic with a taste for Thatcherite remedies (Hawke 1988). Bereft of evidence (and, some would say, of rational argument) though it is, the government chose to base policy proposals on this second report (New Zealand 1989). Lunatic pressure to raise the already mountainous entry barriers to British universities, the Black Papers' legacy, was copied in New Zealand's very different circumstances. Saddled with a Scottish university system whose chief glory was formal open entry, local politicians and educational administrators set about destroying their heritage. Declining state funding forced entry restrictions in more and more disciplines. The last to succumb will be arts faculties, the heart of liberal education for Scots as for the English: but in time they, too, will fall. Together with the threatened replacement of universal small bursaries by student loans, the imminent demise of open entry in New Zealand universities means that the last Scottish university system, the last evidence that Oxbridge-centred hierarchy was not the only British model for a university system, will collapse.

Events at the other end of the earth prevent us from following the example of Stuart Evans's university novel (1984: 300–2), and conjuring Macaulay's New Zealander smugly contemplating the ruins of English civilization. But we will end in Britain. The Black Papers broke the non-partisan Butskellite accord on education. In defence of culture, education became a political football. In 1970 the corporatist Edward Short was replaced as education secretary by Margaret Thatcher. In 1979 Thatcher formed a government which identified consultation with corporatist evil. Earlier comfortable accommodations over education, and much else, were ruled off the political agenda. They will not easily be put back. Should the present abrasive government eventually be replaced by one with a softer touch, then British universities can scarcely expect a less barbarous policy. Labour properly suspects university elitism, and less properly spins neo-Thatcherite economic policies. Not much hope there. The old liberal-social democratic Alliance, very much the university party, has imploded in claret-swigging acrimony. These are hard times for university education elsewhere but, Neave (1982–3: 14) tells us, 'nowhere have the vexations that universities in Western Europe face, attained such a suicidal level as in Britain.' In no other country is the governing political rhetoric so mean-spirited, so 'lacking at the heart' (Hoggart 1984). The prospect of progress in British university life has slammed against TINA's buffers.

There Is No Alternative is a totalitarian doctrine, reflecting the profound social authoritarianism that is blended with free market economics in Thatcherite policy. Alternatives always exist; they are ruled out not by logic but by terror. When Black Paper writers asserted – and Thatcher's education secretaries concurred – that Britain could not afford to maintain fifty universities funded at the level of Oxford and Cambridge they meant (a) that tax cuts were a more urgent political priority than creating an educated citizenry; and (b) that the UGC-mediated levelling up of standards among British universities was ideologically unacceptable. These are not self-evident truths, but political choices. Other choices always exist, suppressed by the discourse.

The Scottish alternative, tenuous though it is in the country of its birth, remains available. While congruent with much English concealed sociology concerned to justify liberal education, it challenges other conventional English ideas. Universities, it asserts, should seek to educate the largest possible proportion of the population. As Robert Anderson said,

> in the post-Robbins era the Scottish universities may invoke their past traditions to assert that their social mission is not to be defined only by the needs of school leavers, and that they have a duty to place their resources of science and scholarship at the service of the whole community rather than of a specially selected elite.
>
> (R.D. Anderson 1983: 344)

Three cheers for that. Social closure through education is bad for culture and bad for democracy. If present trends continue, if reduced state support encourages enhanced difference among

British universities, then Thatcherite policy will penalize all but a few universities. Oxford, and to a rather lesser extent Cambridge, will cash cultural capital, moving ever closer to becoming completely private universities. Some major not-Oxbridge universities will form a second division, with strength over a wide range. All other places will decline relatively, some absolutely. Some may die. At the turn of 1989 Britain's Secretary of State for Education and Science, Kenneth Baker, laid out a blueprint for the next generation in higher education. He looked towards massively expanded access to universities and polytechnics, but at significantly reduced cost to the state. Thatcherite contradictions could scarcely be better expressed. Rhetorical references to the United States as the model for this marvel are punctured by American universities' massive, if partially concealed, dependence on state funds. Starved of those funds through the Grantham grocer's daughter's insistence on managing the economy as if it were her housekeeping money, the British university system will indeed come to look much more like the American; but without the United States' high age participation rates and its emphasis on contest mobility. English conceptions of sponsored mobility, the obsession with social closure through education, will ensure that Thatcher's TINA bequeaths the worst of all possible worlds to her vassals and successors.

Self-proclaimed ancient of Victorian Values, Thatcher's education policies – and her policies in many other areas – would have been damned as crassly utilitarian by eminent Victorians from Carlyle and Arnold to Dickens. Today those policies must be damned, and resisted, on precisely the same grounds. This means taking culture seriously, and taking universities to be important bastions of culture. But the notion of what constitutes culture must be transformed from that typical of British university fiction. As Raymond Williams said thirty years ago,

> The attachment to culture which disparages science; the attachment which writes off politics as a narrow and squalid misdirection of energy; the attachment which appears to criticize manners by the priggish intonation of a word: all these, of which Arnold and his successors have at times been guilty, serve to nourish and extend an opposition which is

277

**already formidable enough. The idea of culture is too
important to be surrendered to this kind of failing.**

(R. Williams 1958: 127)

APPENDIX: BRITISH UNIVERSITY FICTION 1945–88 (WITH SELECTED EARLIER NOVELS)

DATE	AUTHOR	TITLE	SETTING
1933	Masterman, J. C.	*An Oxford Tragedy*	Oxford
1935	Sayers, D.L.	*Gaudy Night*	Oxford
1936	'Innes, M.'	*Death at the President's Lodging*	Oxford
1937	Cole, G.D.H. and Cole, M.	*Disgrace to the College*	Oxford
1938	Cole, G.D.H. and Cole, M.	*Off With her Head!*	Oxford
1939	'Innes, M.'	*Stop Press*	Oxford
1942	Cole, G.D.H. and Cole, M.	*A Knife in the Dark*	Minor redbrick
1943	Cole, G.D.H. and Cole, M.	*The Oxford Mystery*	Oxford
1944	'Crispin, E.'	*The Case of the Gilded Fly*	Oxford
1944	'Innes, M.'	*The Weight of the Evidence*	Major redbrick
1945	'Campbell, R.T.'	*Unholy Dying*	Redbrick
1945	Lewis, C. S.	*That Hideous Strength*	Oxford
1945	Murray, D. L.	*Folly Bridge*	Oxford
1945	'Rees, D.'	*The Cambridge Murders*	Cambridge
1945	Waugh, E.	*Brideshead Revisited*	Oxford
1946	'Crispin, E.'	*The Moving Toyshop*	Oxford
1946	Harrison, P.	*Oxford Marmalade*	Oxford
1946	Hartley, L. P.	*The Sixth Heaven*	Oxford

279

1946	Larkin, P	*Jill*	Oxford
1947	'Crispin, E.'	*Swan Song*	Oxford
1947	'Gray, J.'	*Untimely Slain*	Oxford
1947	Snow, C. P.	*The Light and the Dark*	Cambridge
1948	Kennington, A.	*Pastures New*	Oxford
1948	Liddell, R.	*The Last Enchantments*	Oxford
1948	MacInnes, H.	*Friends and Lovers*	Oxford
1948	Morgan, W. G. C.	*An Oxford Romance*	Oxford
1949	Mais, S. P. B.	*Who Dies?*	Oxford
1950	Wilson, A.	'Totentanz'	Scottish
1951	'Innes, M.'	*Operation Pax*	Oxford
1951	Powell, A.	*A Question of Upbringing*	Oxford
1951	Snow, C. P.	*The Masters*	Cambridge
1952	Atiyah, E.	*Black Vanguard*	Oxford
1952	Balsdon, J.P.V.D.	*Freshman's Folly: An Oxford Comedy*	Oxford
1952	'Cooper, W.'	*The Struggles of Albert Woods*	Oxford
1952	Hsuing, D.	*Flowering Exile*	Oxford
1952	Masterman, J. C.	*To Teach the Senators Wisdom*	Oxford
1952	Vulliamy, C. E.	*Don Among the Dead Men*	Oxford
1953	Elis, I. F.	*Cysgod y Cryman*	Wales
1953	Postgate, R.	*The Ledger is Kept*	Oxford
1954	Amis, K.	*Lucky Jim*	Minor redbrick
1954	Stewart, J. I. M.	*Mark Lambert's Supper*	Oxford
1954	Trickett, R.	*The Course of Love*	Minor redbrick
1955	Farrer, K.	*The Missing Link*	Oxford
1955	Hale, J.	'A backward glance'	Oxford
1955	Pym, B.	*Less than Angels*	London
1955	Stewart, J. I. M.	*The Guardians*	Oxford
1955	Pym, B.	*Less Than Angels*	London
1956	'Innes, M.'	*Old Hall, New Hall*	Minor redbrick
1956	McIntosh, L.	*Oxford Folly*	Oxford

1956	Robinson, R.	*Landscape with Dead Dons*	Oxford
1957	Avery, G.	*The Warden's Niece*	Oxford
1957	Farrer, K.	*Gownsman's Gallows*	Oxford
1957	'Hocking, A.'	*The Simple Way of Poison*	Oxford
1957	Humphreys, E.	*A Man's Estate*	Cambridge
1957	Jameson, M. S.	*A Cup of Tea for Mr Thorgill*	Oxford
1957	Kelly, M.	*Dead Man's Riddle*	Scottish
1957	Masterman, J.C.	*The Case of the Four Friends*	Oxford
1958	'Cooper, W.'	*Young People*	Minor redbrick
1958	Goodman, G. L. W.	*A Time for Paris*	Oxford
1958	Jones, D. A. N.	*Parade in Pairs*	Oxford
1958	Sayers, D. L.	*'A murder at Pentecost'*	Oxford
1959	Bradbury, M.	*Eating People is Wrong*	Minor redbrick
1959	Sinclair, A.	*My Friend Judas*	Cambridge
1959	Walker, J. K.	*Running on the Spot*	Scottish
1960	Avery, G.	*The Elephant War*	Oxford
1960	Butler, G.	*Death Lives Next Door*	Oxford
1960	Raven, S.	*Doctors Wear Scarlet*	Cambridge
1960	Ross, J.M.	*Until the Day She Dies*	Oxford
1960	Snow, C. P.	*The Affair*	Cambridge
1961	Balsdon, J.P.V.D.	*The Day They Burned Miss Termag*	Oxford
1961	Buchan, S. C.	*A Stone in the Pool*	Oxford
1961	Day, L.	*The Looker In*	Oxford
1961	Mitchell, J.	*Imaginary Toys*	Oxford
1961	Robinson, T.	*When Scholars Fall*	Oxford
1961	Spencer, P.	*Full Term*	Oxford
1961	Stewart, J. I. M.	*The Man Who Won the Pools*	Oxford
1961	Vulliamy, C.E.	*Tea at the Abbey*	Minor redbrick
1962	'Nash, S.'	*Death of a Counterplot*	London
1962	Smith, M. L.	*No Easy Answer*	Oxford
1963	Cooper, B.	*A Path to the Bridge*	Cambridge
1963	Kennaway, J.	*The Mind Benders*	Oxford

Year	Author	Title	University
1963	Stewart, J. I. M.	*The Last Tresillians*	Oxford
1963	Waugh, A.	*The Path of Dalliance*	Oxford
1964	Forster, M.	*Dames' Delight*	Oxford
1964	Turner, J.	*The Long Avenues*	Oxford
1964	Williams, R.	*Second Generation*	Oxford
1965	Fleming, J.	*Nothing is the Number When You Die*	Oxford
1965	Gray, S.	*Simple People*	Cambridge
1965	Lodge, D.	*The British Museum is Falling Down*	London
1965	Mosley, N.	*Accident*	Oxford
1966	'Cooper, W.'	*Memoirs of a New Man*	Oxford
1966	Devine, D.M.	*Devil at your Elbow*	Minor redbrick
1966	Stewart, J. I. M.	*The Aylwins*	Oxford
1966	Trickett, R.	*The Elders*	Oxford
1967	'Bernard, R.'	*Death Takes the Last Train*	Oxford
1967	Clinton-Baddeley, V.C.	*Death's Bright Dart*	Cambridge
1967	'Peters, E.'	*Black is the Colour of my True Love's Heart*	Minor redbrick
1967	Sheed, W.	*A Middle-Class Education*	Oxford
1967	Stewart, J. I. M.	*Vanderlyn's Kingdom*	Oxford
1968	'Malloch, P.'	*Murder of a Student*	Minor redbrick
1968	Priestley, J. B.	*Out of Town*	Ex-CAT
1968	Priestley, J. B.	*London End*	Ex-CAT
1968	Snow, C. P.	*The Sleep of Reason*	Ex-CAT Cambridge
1969	Devine, D.M.	*Death is my Bridegroom*	Minor redbrick
1969	'Innes, M.'	*A Family Affair*	Oxford
1969	Thomas, A.E.W.	*The Professor*	Oxford
1970	Lait, R.	*Switched Out*	Cambridge
1970	'Melville, J.'	*A New Kind of Killer, an Old Kind of Death*	New
1970	Raven, S.	*Places Where They Sing*	Cambridge

1971	'Candy, E.'	*Words for Murder, Perhaps*	Minor redbrick
1971	Hoyle, F. and Hoyle, G.	*The Molecule Men*	Cambridge
1971	Hoyle, F. and Hoyle, G.	*The Monster of Loch Ness*	Scottish
1971	White, R.J.	*A Second-Hand Tomb*	Major redbrick
1972	'Ashford, J.'	*A Man Will Be Kidnapped Tomorrow*	Minor redbrick New
1972	'Bell, J.'	*Death of a Poison Tongue*	Minor redbrick
1972	Davin, D.	*Brides of Price*	Oxford
1972	James, P. D.	*An Unsuitable Job for a Woman*	Cambridge
1972	Price, A.	*Colonel Butler's Wolf*	Oxford New
1972	Storey, D.	*Pasmore*	London
1973	Butler, G.	*A Coffin for Pandora*	Oxford
1973	Hosegood, L.	*A Time-Torn Man*	New
1973	'Innes, M.'	*Appleby's Answer*	Oxford
1973	Mann, J.	*The Only Security*	Minor redbrick
1973	Stewart, J. I. M.	*Mungo's Dream*	Oxford
1973	'Yorke, M.'	*Grave Matters*	Oxford
1974	Evans, S.	*Meritocrats*	Oxford
1974	Mann, J.	*The Sticking Place*	New
1974	'Ruell, P.'	*Death Takes the Low Road*	Minor redbrick
1974	Sharpe, T.	*Porterhouse Blue*	Cambridge
1974	Stewart, J. I. M.	*The Gaudy*	Oxford
1975	Bradbury, M.	*The History Man*	New
1975	Dafydd, M.	*I'r Gad*	Wales
1975	Dexter, C.	*Last Bus to Woodstock*	Oxford
1975	Lodge, D.	*Changing Places*	Major redbrick
1975	Mann, J.	*Captive Audience*	Minor redbrick
1975	Stewart, J. I. M.	*Young Pattullo*	Oxford
1976	Archer, J.	*Not a Penny More, Not a Penny Less*	Oxford
1976	Clarke, A.	*The Deathless and the Dead*	Oxford
1976	'Davey, J.'	*A Treasury Alarm*	Oxford

1976	Lovesey, P.	*Swing, Swing Together*	Oxford
1976	Raphael, F.	*The Glittering Prizes*	Cambridge New
1976	Raven, S.	*The Survivors*	Oxford
1976	Rendell, R.	*A Demon in my View*	London
1976	Stewart, J. I. M.	*A Memorial Service*	Oxford
1976	'Yorke, M.'	*Cast for Death*	Oxford
1977	'Aird, C.'	*Parting Breath*	Minor redbrick
1977	Dexter, C.	*The Silent World of Nicholas Quinn*	Oxford
1977	Evans, S.	*The Caves of Alienation*	Oxford
1977	Stewart, J. I. M.	*The Madonna of the Astrolabe*	Oxford
1977	Williams, D.	*Treasure by Degrees*	Oxford
1978	Amis, K.	*Jake's Thing*	Oxford
1978	Collins, R.	*The Case of the Philosopher's Ring*	Oxford
1978	Evans, S.	*Centre of Ritual*	Oxford
1978	Rowlands, J.	*Tician Tician*	Wales
1978	Stewart, J. I. M.	*Full Term*	Oxford
1979	Barnard, R.	*Posthumous Papers*	Minor redbrick
1979	Evans, S.	*Occupational Debris*	Oxford
1979	Miles, G.	*Treffin*	Wales
1980	Fiske, D.	*Academic Murder*	Cambridge
1980	Gloag, J.	*Sleeping Dogs Lie*	Cambridge
1980	Raphael, F.	*Oxbridge Blues*	Cambridge
1980	Raven, S.	*An Inch of Fortune*	Cambridge
1981	'Bellingham, L.'	*Oxford: The Novel*	Oxford
1981	Shaw, H.	*Death of a Don*	Oxford
1981	Stewart, J. I. M.	'The time-bomb'	Oxford
1981	Stewart, J. I. M.	'The Chomsky file'	London
1983	Dexter, C.	*The Riddle of the Third Mile*	Oxford
1983	Jacobson, H.	*Coming from Behind*	Cambridge
1983	Stewart, J. I. M.	'The doctor's son'	Major redbrick Cambridge
1983	Stewart, J. I. M.	'Dining Limber'	Oxford
1983	Stewart, M.	*Monkey Shines*	Oxford
1984	Evans, S.	*Houses on the Site*	Oxford

1984	Lodge, D.	*Small World*	Major redbrick
			Oxford
			New
1985	Byatt, A. S.	*Still Life*	Cambridge
1985	Fraser, A.	*Oxford Blood*	Oxford
1985	Pym, B.	*Crampton Hodnet*	Oxford
1985	Stewart, J. I. M.	*The Naylors*	Oxford
1986	Davies, A.	*A Very Peculiar Practice*	New
1986	Evans, S.	*Seasonal Tribal Rituals*	Oxford
1986	Gethin, D.	*Dane's Testament*	Minor redbrick
1986	Hulland, J.R.	*Student Body*	Major redbrick
1986	Pym, B.	*An Academic Question*	Ex-CAT
1986	Stewart, J. I. M.	'The dyslexia factor'	Oxford
1986	Stewart, J. I. M.	'Two strings to his bow'	Oxford
1987	Bradbury, M.	*Cuts*	Major redbrick
			Minor redbrick
1987	Judd, A.	*The Noonday Devil*	Oxford
1987	'Lejeune, A.'	*Professor in Peril*	Oxford
1987	Middleton, S.	*After a Fashion*	Minor redbrick
1987	Murdoch, I.	*The Book and the Brotherhood*	Oxford
1987	Parkin, F.	*The Mind and Body Shop*	New
1987	Sutherland, N.S.	*Men Change Too*	New
			Oxford
1988	Davies, A.	*A Very Peculiar Practice: The New Frontier*	New
1988	Duffy, B.	*The World As I Found It*	Cambridge
1988	Lodge, D.	*Nice Work*	Major redbrick
1988	Myer, V. G.	*Culture Shock*	Cambridge
1988	Wain, J.	*Where the Rivers Meet*	Oxford
1988	Williams, D.	*Treasure in Oxford*	Oxford

BIBLIOGRAPHY

Abrams, P., Deem, R., Finch, J., and Rock, P. (eds) (1981) *Practice and Progress: British Sociology 1950–80*, London: Allen & Unwin.

Acker, S. and Piper, D.W. (eds) (1984) *World Yearbook of Education 1984: Women and Education*, London: Kogan Page.

'Aird, C.' (1977) *Parting Breath*, London: Collins.

Aitkin, D. (1977) *The Second Chair*, Sydney: Arkon, 1981.

Allott, K. (ed.) (1975) *Matthew Arnold*, London: Bell.

Amis, K. (1954) *Lucky Jim*, Harmondsworth: Penguin, 1961.

————(1967) 'Why Lucky Jim turned right', in Amis 1981: 200–10.

————(1968) 'Pernicious participation', in Cox and Dyson (eds) 1968: 9–10.

————(1978) *Jake's Thing*, London: Hutchinson.

————(1981) *What Became of Jane Austen?*, London: Cape.

Amis, K. and Conquest, R. (1969) 'The anti-sex, croquet-playing, statistic-snubbing, Boyle-baiting, Black fascist Paper', in Cox and Dyson (eds) 1969: 153–9.

————(1971) 'A short educational dictionary', in Cox and Dyson (eds) 1971: 215–23.

Amos, W. (1985) *The Originals: Who's Really Who in Fiction*, London: Cape.

Anderson, D., Lait, J., and Marsland, D. (1981) *Breaking the Spell of the Welfare State*, London: Social Affairs Unit.

Anderson, J.R.L. (1977) *Death in the Caribbean*, London: Gollancz.

————(1981) *Death in a High Latitude*, London: Gollancz.

Anderson, R.D. (1983) *Education and Opportunity in Victorian Scotland*, Oxford: Clarendon Press.

————(1985) 'In search of the "lad of parts": the mythical history of Scottish education', *History Workshop Journal* 19: 82–104.

————(1988) *The Student Community at Aberdeen, 1860–1939*, Aberdeen: Aberdeen University Press.

Annan, N. (1960–1) 'Peck-orders among universities', *Universities Quarterly*, 15: 351–9.

————(1987) 'The reform of higher education in 1986', *History of Education* 16: 217–26.

Archer, J. (1976) *Not a Penny More, Not a Penny Less*, London: Cape.

Ardener, S. (1984) 'Incorporation and exclusion: Oxford academic wives', in Callan and Ardener (eds) 1984: 27–49.

Arnold, M. (1867) *Friendship's Garland [Part I]*, in R.H. Super (ed.) 1965: 1–84.

————(1869) *Culture and Anarchy*, in R.H. Super (ed.) 1965: 85–256.

Ashe, R. (1976) *Moths*, London: Hutchinson.

'Ashford, J.' (1972) *A Man Will be Kidnapped Tomorrow*, London: John Long.

Atiyah, E. (1952) *Black Vanguard*, London: Davies.

Avery, G. (1957) *The Warden's Niece*, London: Collins.

————(1960) *The Elephant War*, London: Collins.

Axelrod, P. and Reid, J.G. (eds) (1989) *Youth, University and Canadian Society*, Kingston and Montreal: McGill-Queens University Press.

'B' (1968) 'Decline and fall of the university idea', in Cox and Dyson (eds) 1968: 60–2.

Baldick, C. (1983) *The Social Mission of English Criticism, 1848–1932*, Oxford: Clarendon Press.

Balsdon, J.P.V.D. (1952) *Freshman's Folly: an Oxford Comedy*, London: Eyre & Spottiswoode.

————(1961) *The Day They Burned Miss Termag*, London: Eyre & Spottiswoode.

Banks, J.R. (1985) 'Back to Bradbury Lodge', *Critical Quarterly* 27: 79–81.

Barker, R. (1985) 'Bespoke learning by the academic tailor', *Times Higher Education Supplement*, 4 October.

Barnard, H.C. (1947) *A History of English Education from 1760 to 1944*, London: University of London Press.

Barnard, R. (1974) *Death of an Old Goat*, London: Collins.

————(1979) *Posthumous Papers*, London: Collins.

————(1980) *Death in a Cold Climate*, London: Collins.

Barth, J. (1966) *Giles Goat-Boy*, London: Granada, 1981.

Beerbohm, M. (1911) *Zuleika Dobson*, Harmondsworth: Penguin, 1952.

'Bell, J.' (1972) *Death of a Poison Tongue*, New York: Day, 1981.

Bell, R.E. and Youngson, A.J. (eds) (1973) *Present and Future in Higher Education*, London: Tavistock.

'Bellingham, L.' (1981) *Oxford: The Novel*, London: Nold Jonson.

Bellot, H.H. (1929) *University College, London, 1826–1926*, London: no publisher stated.

Beloff, M. (1969) 'Oxford: a lost cause?', in Cox and Dyson (eds) 1969: 134–7.

————(1977) 'The University College at Buckingham', in Cox and Boyson (eds) 1977b: 114–17.

Berger, B. (1957) 'Sociology and the intellectuals', *Antioch Review* 17: 275–90.

'Bernard, R.' (1967) *Death Takes the Last Train*, London: Constable.

Blomfield, B.C. (1979) *Philip Larkin: A Bibliography 1933–1976*, London: Faber & Faber.

Bock, H. and Wertheim, A. (eds) (1986) *Essays on the Contemporary British Novel*, Munch: Huabar.

Boyle, T.E. and Brown, T. (1966–7) 'The serious side of Kingsley Amis', *Critique* 9: 100–7.

Bradbury, M. (1959) *Eating People is Wrong*, London: Arrow, 1978.

————(1960) *Phogey, or How to Have Class in a Classless Society* London: Parrish.

————(1962a) 'Iris Murdoch's *Under the Net*', *Critical Quarterly* 4: 47–54.

————(1962b) *All Dressed up and Nowhere to Go*, London: Parrish.

————(1965) *Stepping Westward*, London: Arrow, 1979.

————(1971) *The Social Context of Modern English Literature*, Oxford: Blackwell.

————(1975) *The History Man*, London: Arrow, 1977.

————(1976) *Who Do You Think You Are?* London: Secker & Warburg.

————(1984) 'Graduating from nostalgia to reality', *Times Higher Educational Supplement* 9, November: 13.

————(1986) 'Introduction', to L. Taylor 1986: 1–5.

————(1987) *Cuts*, London: Hutchinson.

Bradbury, M., Heading, B., and Hollis, M. (1972) 'The man and the mask', in J.A. Jackson (ed.) 1972: 41–64.

Breckling, G.J. (1955) *Walk in Beauty*, New York: Scribner.

'Broome, A.' (1929) *The Oxford Murders*, London: Bles.

————(1936) *The Cambridge Murders*, London: Bles.

Brown, R.K. (ed.) (1973) *Knowledge, Education and Cultural Change*, London: Tavistock.

Buchan, S.C. (1961) *A Stone in the Pool*, London: Duckworth.

Burgess, A. (1978) *1985*, London: Hutchinson.

Burnhill, P. and McPherson, A.F. (1983) 'The Scottish university and undergraduate expectations, 1971–1981', *New Universities Quarterly* 37: 253–70.

Butler, C. (1985) *Interpretation, Deconstruction and Ideology*, London: Macmillan.

Butler, D. and Halsey, A.H. (eds) (1978) *Policy and Politics: Essays in Honour of Norman Chester*, London: Macmillan.

Butler, G. (1960) *Death Lives Next Door*, London: Bles.

————(1962) *Coffin in Oxford*, London: Bles.

————(1973) *A Coffin for Pandora*, Harmondsworth: Penguin, 1978. See also Melville, J.

Byatt, A.S. (1985) *Still Life*, London: Chatto & Windus.

Callan, H. and Ardener, S. (eds) (1984) *The Incorporated Wife*, London: Croom Helm.

Campbell, R.T. (1945) *Unholy Dying*, no place of publication or publisher stated.

'Candy, E.' (1971) *Words for Murder, Perhaps*, London: Gollancz.

Carling, A. (1985) 'What a university is not', *Culture, Education and Society* 39: 335–7.

Carpenter, H. (1978) *The Inklings: C.S. Lewis, J.R.R. Tolkien, Charles Williams and their Friends*, London: Allen & Unwin.

Carr, J.D. (1951) *The Devil in Velvet*, London: Hamish Hamilton.

Carter, I. (1986) 'Most important industry: how the New Zealand state got interested in rural women, 1930–1944', *New Zealand Journal of History* 20: 27–43.

Caute, D. (1971) *The Occupation*, London: Deutsch.

Chapman, J.W. (ed.) (1983) *The Western University on Trial*, Berkeley: University of California Press.

Chapman, R. (1968) *The Victorian Debate: English Literature and Society, 1832–1901*, London: Weidenfeld & Nicolson. (See also Nash, S.)

Clarke, A. (1966) *The Deathless and the Dead*, London: Collins.

Clinton-Baddeley, V.C. (1967) *Death's Bright Dart*, London: Gollancz.

Cohen, S. (1977) 'Sociologists, history and the literary men', *Sociology* 11: 533–47.

Cole, G.D.H. and Cole, M. (1937) *Disgrace to the College*, London: Hodder & Stoughton.

————(1938) *Off With her Head!*, London: Collins.

————(1942) *A Knife in the Dark*, London: Collins.

————(1943) *The Oxford Mystery*, London: Todd.

Collins, R. (1978) *The Case of the Philosopher's Ring*, New York: Crown.

Colls, R. and Dodd, P. (eds) (1986) *Englishness: Politics and Culture*, London: Croom Helm.

Conn, G.K.T. (1960–1) 'Finishing or beginning school?', *Higher Education Quarterly* 15: 345–51.

Connington, J.J. (1947) *Common Sense is All You Need*, London: Hodder & Stoughton.

Conquest, R. (1968) 'Undotheboys Hall', in Cox and Dyson (eds) 1968: 17–20.

Cook, B. (1985) *Disorderly Elements*, London: Gollancz.

Cooper, B. (1963) *A Path to the Bridge*, London: Heinemann.

Cooper, S. (1970) *J.B. Priestley: Portrait of an Author*, London: Heinemann.

'Cooper, W.' (1950) *Scenes from Provincial Life*, London: Macmillan, 1969.

———(1952) *The Struggles of Albert Woods*, London: Cape.

———(1958) *Young People*, London: Macmillan.

———(1966) *Memoirs of a New Man*, London: Macmillan.

Coplestone, F. (1963) *A History of Philosophy*, volume 3, London: Burns & Oates.

Corbett, J.P. (1964) 'Opening the mind', in Daiches (ed.) 1964: 22–39.

Corke, H. (1963) 'The dog that didn't bite', in Cornelius and Vincent (eds) 1964: 22–7.

Cornelius, D.K. and Vincent, E.K. (eds) (1964) *Cultures in Conflict: Perspectives on the Snow–Leavis Controversy*, Chicago, Ill: Scott Foresman.

Cox, C., Jacka, K. and Marks, J. (1977) 'Marxism, knowledge and the academies', in Cox, C. and Boyson, K. (eds) 1977b: 117–26.

Cox, C.B. (1984) 'Critical Quarterly–Twenty-five years', *Critical Quarterly* 26, 1 and 2: 3–16.

Cox, C.B. and Boyson, R. (1977a) 'Letter to Members of Parliament', in Cox and Boyson (eds) 1977b: 5–10.

———(eds) (1977b) *Black Paper 1977*, London: Temple Smith.

Cox, C.B. and Dyson, A.E. (eds) (1968) *Fight for Education: A Black Paper*, London: Critical Quarterly Society.

———(eds) (1969) *Black Paper Two*, London: Critical Quarterly Society.

———(1971a) 'Introduction', to Cox and Dyson (eds) 1971b: 9–34.

———(eds) (1971b) *The Black Papers on Education*, London: Davis-Poynter.

'Crispin, E.' (1944) *The Case of the Gilded Fly*, New York: Walker, 1979.

———(1946) *The Moving Toyshop*, London: Gollancz.

———(1947) *Swan Song*, London: Gollancz.

———(1950) *Frequent Hearses*, New York: Walker, 1982.

———(1977) *The Glimpses of the Moon*, London: Gollancz.

'Cross, A.' (1983) *A Death in the Faculty*, London: Gollancz.

Cunningham, S. (1984) 'Women's access to higher education in Scotland', in Acker et al. (eds) 1984: 173–87.

'Dafydd, M.' (1975) *I'r Gad*, Talybont: y Lolfa.

Daiches, D. (ed.) (1964) *The Idea of a New University: An Experiment in Sussex*, London: Deutsch, 2nd edn, 1970.

Daniel, G. (1954) *Welcome Death*, London: Gollancz. See also Rees, D.

Darling, J. (1983) 'What were universities for?', in Jacques and Richardson (eds) 1983: 120–6.

'Davey, J.' (1960) *A Touch of Stage Fright*, Harmondsworth: Penguin, 1963.

————(1976) *A Treasury Alarm*, London: Chatto & Windus.

————(1982) *Murder in Paradise*, London: Chatto & Windus.

Davidoff, L. (1973) *The Best Circles: Society, Etiquette and the Season*, London: Croom Helm.

Davie, G.E. (1962) *The Democratic Intellect*, Edinburgh: Edinburgh University Press.

————(1986) *The Crisis of the Democratic Intellect: The Problem of Generalism and Specialism in Twentieth-Century Scotland*, Edinburgh: Polygon.

Davies, A. (1986) *A Very Peculiar Practice*, London: Methuen.

————(1988) *A Very Peculiar Practice: The New Frontier*, London: Methuen.

Davies, R. (1981) *The Rebel Angels*, Harmondsworth: Penguin, 1983.

Davin, D. (1970) *Not Here, Not Now*, London: Hale.

————(1972) *Brides of Price*, London: Hale.

Day, L. (1961) *The Looker In*, London: Cape.

Deighton, L. (1981) *XPD*, London: Hutchinson.

Delamont, S. and Read, M. (1988) 'The effects of the cuts, 1980–86: a SCASSU survey of British universities', Cardiff: Social Research Unit, University College Cardiff.

Devine, D.M. (1966) *Devil at Your Elbow*, London: Collins.

————(1969) *Death is my Bridegroom*, London: Collins.

Dexter, C. (1975) *Last Bus to Woodstock*, London: Macmillan.

————(1977) *The Silent World of Nicholas Quinn*, London: Macmillan.

————(1981) *The Dead of Jerico*, London: Macmillan.

————(1983) *The Riddle of the Third Mile*, London: Macmillan.

————(1986) *The Secret of Annexe 3*, London: Pan, 1987.

Dodd, P. (1986) 'Englishness and the national culture', in Colls and Dodd (eds) 1986: 1–28.

Doyle, B. (1986) 'The invention of English', in Colls and Dodd (eds) 1986: 89–115.

Drabble, M. (1977) *The Ice Age*, London: Weidenfeld and Nicolson.

Dudley, F. (1942) 'Matthew Arnold and science', *Proceedings of the Modern Languages Association*, 77: 275–94.

Duffy, B. (1988) *The World as I Found It*, London: Secker & Warburg.

Eagleton, T. (1983) *Literary Theory*, Oxford: Blackwell.

————(1988) 'The silences of David Lodge', *New Left Review* 172: 93–102.

Eco, U. (1984) *Reflections on 'The Name of the Rose'*, London: Secker & Warburg.

Eldred-Grigg, S. (1980) *A Southern Gentry*, Wellington: Reed.

Eldridge, J. (1980) *Modern British Sociology*, London: Macmillan.

Eliot, T.S. (1949) *Notes Towards the Definition of Culture*, London: Faber & Faber.

Elis, I.F. (1953) *Cysgod y Cryman*, Llandysul: Gomer, 1980.

Elkin, P.K. (1976) 'The university novel', *Times Higher Education Supplement*, 24 December.

Enright, D.J. (1955) *Academic Year*, Oxford: Oxford University Press, 1985.

Evans, S. (1974) *Meritocrats*, London: Hutchinson.

———(1977) *The Caves of Alienation*, London: Hutchinson.

———(1978) *Centre of Ritual*, London: Hutchinson.

———(1979) *Occupational Debris*, London: Hutchinson.

———(1984) *Houses on the Site*, London: Hutchinson.

———(1986) *Seasonal Tribal Rituals*, London: Hutchinson.

Fallis, R. (1977) '*Lucky Jim* and academic wishful thinking', *Studies in the Novel*, 9: 65–72.

Fancher, R.E. (1985) *The Intelligence Men: Makers of the IQ Controversy*, New York: Norton.

Farrer, K. (1955) *The Missing Link*, London: Collins.

———(1957) *Gownsman's Gallows*, London: Hodder & Stoughton.

Fiddes, E. (1937) *Chapters in the History of Owen's College and Manchester University, 1851–1914*, Manchester: Manchester University Press.

Finch, J. and Rustin, M. (eds) (1986) *A Degree of Choice: Higher Education and the Right to Learn*, Harmondsworth: Penguin.

Finlay, M. (1964) 'Crisis in the classics', in Plumb (ed.) 1964b: 11–23.

Fiske, D. (1980) *Academic Murder*, London: Cassell.

Flandrau, C.M. (1897) *Harvard Episodes*, Boston, Mass: Copeland & Day.

Fleming, J. (1965) *Nothing is the Number When You Die*, London: Collins.

Forster, M. (1964) *Dames' Delight*, London: Cape.

Fowler, G. (1985) 'A myriad woes' *Culture, Education and Society*, 39: 302–5.

Fraser, A. (1985) *Oxford Blood*, London: Weidenfeld & Nicolson.

Freeman, K. (1947) *Gown and Shroud*, London: Macdonald.

Fremlin, C. (1975) *The Long Shadow*, London: Gollancz.

Friedmann, M. (1986) 'Malcolm Bradbury's "plot of history"', in Bock and Wertheim (eds) 1986: 213–26.

Gallie, W.B. (1960) *A New University: A.D. Lindsay and the Keele Experiment*, London: Chatto & Windus.

Gellner, E. (1964) 'The crisis in the humanities and the mainstream of philosophy', in Plumb (ed.) 1964: 45–81.

———(1969) 'The panther and the dove: reflections on rebelliousness and its milieux', in Martin (ed.) 1969: 129–47.

Gethin, D. (1986) *Dane's Testament*, London: Gollancz.

Giddens, A. and Mackenzie, G. (eds) (1982) *Social Class and the Division of Labour: Essays in Honour of Ilya Neustadt*, Cambridge: Cambridge University Press.

Gilmour, R. (1987) 'The skilful subversive', *Times Higher Education*

Supplement, 20 February.

Giner, S. (1976) *Mass Society,* London: Martin Robertson.

Gloag, J. (1980) *Sleeping Dogs Lie,* London: Secker & Warburg.

Goller, N. (1979) *Tomorrow's Silence,* London: Macmillan.

Goodman, G.J.W. (1958) *A Time for Paris,* New York: Bantam.

Gordon, R. (1952) *Doctor in the House,* London: Joseph.

Gould, J. (1977) *The Attack on Higher Education,* London: Institute for the Study of Conflict.

Grant, A. (1884) *The Story of the University of Edinburgh During Its First Three Hundred Years,* London: Longman Green.

'Gray, J.' (1947) *Untimely Slain,* London: Hutchinson.

Gray, S. (1965) *Simple People,* London: Faber & Faber.

Green, M. (1963) 'A literary defence of "The Two Cultures"', in Cornelius and Vincent (eds) 1964: 31–7.

Green, V.H.H. (1957) *Oxford Common Room: A Study of Lincoln College and Mark Pattison,* London: Arnold.

Haffenden, J. (1985) *Novelists in Interview,* London: Methuen.

Haight, G.S. (ed.) (1971) *The Portable Victorian Reader,* Harmondsworth: Penguin, 1976.

Hale, J. (1955) 'A backward glance', *Twentieth Century* 157: 522–9.

Haley, S. (1984) *A Nest of Singing Birds,* Toronto: Paperjacks.

Halsey, A.H. (1961–2a) 'A pyramid of prestige', *Universities Quarterly* 15: 341–5.

———(1961–2b) 'University expansion and the collegial ideal', *Universities Quarterly* 16: 55–8.

——— (1968–9) 'The universities and the state', *Universities Quarterly* 23: 128–48.

———(1982a) 'The decline of donnish dominion?', *Oxford Review of Education* 8: 215–29.

———(1982b) 'Provincials and professionals: the British post-war sociologists' *European Journal of Sociology* 23: 150–75.

———(1985) 'The idea of a university', *Oxford Review of Education* 11: 115–32.

Halsey, A.H. and Trow, M.A. (1971) *The British Academics,* London: Faber & Faber.

Harrison, D. (1985) 'Universities: "excellent, fit for the purpose, and cost effective"?' *Culture, Education and Society* 39: 293–6.

Harrison, M. (1951) *Long Vacation,* London: Werner Laurie.

Harrison, P. (1946) *Oxford Marmalade,* London: Peter Davies.

Hartley, L.P. (1946) *The Sixth Heaven,* London: Putnam.

Harvey, A.D. (1976) 'Universities as subjects of academic study', *Higher Education Review* 9: 19–30.

Hawke, G.R. (1988) *Report of the Working Party on Post Compulsory Education and Training,* Wellington: Government Printer.

Hawthorne, N. (1828) *Fanshawe*, Boston, Mass: Marsh & Capen.

Hearnshaw, L.S. (1979) *Cyril Burt: Psychologist*, Ithaca, NY: Cornell University Press.

Heath, A. and Edmondson, R. (1981) 'Oxbridge sociology: the development of excellence?', in Abrams *et al* (eds) 1981: 39–52.

Herrick, R. (1926) *Chimes*, New York: Macmillan.

Hill, R. (1971) *An Advancement of Learning*, London: Fontana, 1974.

———(1977) 'The educator: the case of the screaming spires', in Winn (ed.) 1977: 470–2.

See also Ruell, P.

'Hinde, T.' (1968) *High*, New York: Walker.

Hobsbaum, P. (1964) 'University life in English fiction', *Twentieth Century* 173: 139–47.

Hobsbawm, E. and Ranger, T. (eds) (1983) *The Invention of Tradition*, Cambridge: Cambridge University Press.

'Hocking, A.' (1957) *The Simple Way of Poison*, London: W.H. Allen.

Hoggart, R. (1984) 'Lacking at the heart: the country under Thatcherism', *Culture, Education and Society*, 38: 283–99.

Honan, P. (1981) *Matthew Arnold: A Life*, London: Weidenfeld & Nicolson.

Hosegood, L. (1973) *A Time-Torn Man*, London: Heinemann.

Hough, G. (1964) 'Crisis in literary education', in Plumb (ed.) 1964b: 96–109.

Hoyle, F. (1959) *Ossian's Ride*, London: Heinemann.

Hoyle, F. and Hoyle, G. (1971a) *The Molecule Men*, London: Heinemann.

———(1971b) *The Monster of Loch Ness*, London: Heinemann.

Hsuing, D. (1952) *Flowering Exile*, London: Davies.

Hubbard, P.M. (1963) *Flush as May*, London: Michael Joseph.

Hulland, J.R. (1986) *Student Body*, London: Hodder & Stoughton.

Humes, W. and Patterson, H. (eds) (1983) *Scottish Culture and Scottish Education, 1800–1980*, Edinburgh: Donald.

Humphreys, E. (1957) *A Man's Estate*, London: Eyre & Spottiswoode.

Hutchings, W. (1977) 'Kingsley Amis' counterfeit world', *Critical Quarterly*, 19: 77–95.

Inglis, F. (1982) *Radical Earnestness: English Social Theory 1880–1980*, Oxford: Martin Robertson.

'Innes, M.' (1936) *Death at the President's Lodging*, London: Gollancz.

———(1937) *Hamlet, Revenge!* Harmondsworth: Penguin, 1961.

———(1938) *Lament for a Maker*, London: Four Square Books, 1964.

———(1939) *Stop Press*, London: Gollancz, 1971.

———(1940a) *There Came Both Mist and Snow*, London: Gollancz.

———(1940b) *The Secret Vanguard*, London: Gollancz.

———(1941) *Appleby on Ararat*, London: Gollancz, 1972.

———(1942) *The Daffodil Affair*, London: Gollancz.

————(1944) *The Weight of the Evidence*, Harmondsworth: Penguin, 1961.

————(1945) *Appleby's End*, London: Gollancz.

————(1946a) *From London Far*, London: Gollancz.

————(1946b) *What Happened at Hazelwood*, London: Gollancz.

————(1948) *A Night of Errors*, London: Gollancz.

————(1949) *The Journeying Boy*, London: Gollancz.

————(1951) *Operation Pax*, London: Gollancz.

————(1952) *A Private View*, London: Gollancz, 1974.

————(1953) *Christmas at Candleshoe*, Harmondsworth: Penguin, 1961.

————(1955) *The Man from the Sea*, Harmondsworth: Penguin, 1961.

————(1956a) *Appleby Plays Chicken*, London: Gollancz.

————(1956b) *Old Hall, New Hall*, Harmondsworth: Penguin, 1961.

————(1958) *The Long Farewell*, London: Gollancz.

————(1959) *Hare Sitting Up*, London: Hamlyn, 1981.

————(1966) *The Bloody Wood*, London: Gollancz.

————(1968) *Appleby at Allington*, London: Gollancz.

————(1969) *A Family Affair*, London: Gollancz.

————(1970) *Death at the Chase*, Harmondsworth: Penguin, 1971.

————(1972) *The Open House*, London: Gollancz.

————(1973) *Appleby's Answer*, London: Gollancz.

————(1975a) *Appleby's Other Story*, London: Gollancz.

————(1975b) *The Appleby File*, London: Gollancz.

————(1976) *The Gay Phoenix*, London: Gollancz.

————(1977) *Honeybath's Haven*, London: Gollancz.

————(1978) *The Ampersand Papers*, New York: Dodd, Mead.

————(1980) *Going it Alone*, London: Gollancz.

————(1981) *Lord Mullion's Secret*, London: Gollancz.

————(1982) *Sheiks and Adders*, New York: Dodd, Mead.

————(1983) *Appleby and Honeybath*, London: Gollancz.

————(1986) *Appleby and the Ospreys*, London: Gollancz.

See also Stewart, J.I.M.

Innes, W. (1983) *The Department*, Auckland: Lindon.

Isherwood, C. (1964) *A Single Man*, New York: Simon & Schuster.

Jacka, K., Cox, C., and Marks, J. (1975) *Rape of Reason: The Corruption of the Polytechnic of North London*, Enfield: Churchill Press.

Jackson, J.A. (ed.) (1972) *Role*, Cambridge: Cambridge University Press.

Jacobson, H. (1983) *Coming from Behind*, London: Black Swan, 1984.

————(1986) *Redback*, London: Bantam.

Jacobus, M. (1986) *Reading Women*, New York: Columbia University Press.

Jacques, D. and Richardson, J.T.E. (eds) (1983) *The Future for Higher Education*, Guildford: Society for Research into Higher Education and NFER-Nelson.

James, P.D. (1972) *An Unsuitable Job for a Woman*, London: Faber & Faber.

Jameson, M.S. (1957) *A Cup of Tea for Mr Thorgill*, London: Macmillan.

Jarrell, R. (1954) *Pictures from an Institution*, London: Faber & Faber.

'Jay, S.' (1968) *Sleepers Can Kill*, London: Collins.

Johnson, L. (1979) *The Cultural Critics: From Matthew Arnold to Raymond Williams*, London: Routledge & Kegan Paul.

Johnson, O.M. (1912) *Stover at Yale*, New York: Stokes.

Johnson, P.H. (1963) *Night and Silence, Who is There?*, New York: Scribner.

Jones, D.A.N. (1958) *Parade in Pairs*, London: Cape.

Joseph, M.K. (1962) *A Pound of Saffron*, London: Gollancz.

Judd, A. (1987) *The Noonday Devil*, London: Hutchinson.

Kamin, L.J. (1974) *The Science and Politics of IQ*, Harmondsworth: Penguin, 1977.

Kearney, H. (1973) 'Universities and society in historical perspective', in Bell and Youngson (eds) 1973: 1–12.

Keating, P. (1975) 'Arnold's social and political thought', in K. Allott (ed.) 1975: 207–35.

Kedourie, E. (1988) *Diamonds into Glass: The Government and the Universities*, London: Centre for Policy Studies.

Kelly, M. (1956) *A Cold Coming*, London: Secker & Warburg.

————(1957) *Dead Man's Riddle*, London: Secker & Warburg.

Keneally, T. (1969) *The Survivor*, Harmondsworth: Penguin, 1970.

Kennaway, J. (1963) *The Mind Benders*, London: Longman.

————(1969) *The Cost of Living Like This*, London: Longman.

Kenney, S. (1985) *Graves in Academe*, New York: Viking.

Kennington, A. (1948) *Pastures New*, London: Melrose.

Kenyon, M. (1967) *The Whole Hog*, London: Collins.

Kenyon, J.P. (1980) 'The business of university novels', *Encounter*, June 1980: 81–4.

Kerr, C. (1963) *The Uses of the University*, Cambridge, Mass: Harvard University Press.

Kiernan, V.G. (1969) *The Lords of Human Kind*, Harmondsworth: Penguin, 1972.

Kornhauser, A. (1959) *The Politics of Mass Society*, London: Routledge & Kegan Paul.

Kramer, J. (1979) 'Images of sociology and sociologists in fiction', *Contemporary Sociology* 8: 356–62.

————(1981a) *The American College Novel: An Annotated Bibliography*, New York: Garland.

————(1981b) 'College and university presidents in fiction', *Journal of Higher Education*, 52: 81–95.

Kramer, J. and Kramer, J. (1983) *College Mystery Novels: An Annotated Bibliography*, New York: Garland.

Lait, R. (1970) *Switched Out*, London: Macgibbon & Key.

Larkin, P. (1946) *Jill: A Novel*, London: Fortune Press.

———(1969) 'Couplet', in Cox and Dyson (eds) 1969: 133.

———(1983) *Required Writing: Miscellaneous Pieces 1955–1982*, London: Faber & Faber.

Lawler, J. (ed.) (1968) *The New University*, London: Routledge & Kegan Paul.

Leach, E.R. (1984) 'Glimpses of the unmentionable in the history of British social anthropology', *Annual Review of Anthropology* 13: 1–23.

Leavis, F.R. (1943) *Education and the University: A Sketch for an 'English School'*, London: Chatto & Windus.

———(1962) *Two Cultures?*, London: Chatto & Windus.

———(1969) *English Literature in our Time and the University*, London: Chatto & Windus.

———(1972) *Nor Shall My Sword: Discourses on Pluralism, Compassion, and Social Hope*, London: Chatto & Windus.

Leavis, Q.D. (1980–1) 'The Englishness of the English novel', *New Universities Quarterly* 35: 149–71.

'Lejeune, A.' (1987) *Professor in Peril*, London: Macmillan.

Lepenies, W. (1988) *Between Literature and Science: The Rise of Sociology*, Cambridge: Cambridge University Press.

Lewis, C.S. (1945) *That Hideous Strength*, London: Bodley Head.

Liddell, R. (1948) *The Last Enchantments*, London: Cape.

Linn, J.W. (1936) *This Was Life*, Indianapolis, Ind: Bobbs-Merrill.

Lodge, D. (1962) *Ginger, You're Barmy*, Harmondsworth: Penguin, 1984.

———(1965) *The British Museum is Falling Down*, London: Macgibbon & Key.

———(1975) *Changing Places*, Harmondsworth: Penguin, 1978.

———(1984) *Small World*, London: Secker & Warburg.

———(1986) *Write On: Occasional Essays '65–'85*, London: Secker & Warburg.

———(1988) *Nice Work*, London: Secker & Warburg.

Lovesey, P. (1976) *Swing, Swing Together*, London: Macmillan.

Lurie, A. (1962) *Love and Friendship*, Harmondsworth: Penguin.

———(1967) *Imaginary Friends*, London: Pan, 1970.

———(1974) *The War Between the Tates*, Harmondsworth: Penguin, 1977.

Lyall, F. (1987) *A Death in Time*, London: Collins.

Lyons, F.S.L. (1983) 'The idea of a university: Newman to Robbins', in Phillipson (ed.) 1983: 113–44.

Lyons, J. (1962) *The College Novel in America*, Carbondale, Ill: Southern Illinois University Press.

————(1974–5) 'The college novel in America, 1962–1974', *Critique* 16: 121–8.

McCall, R. (1983–4) 'The comic novels of Tom Sharpe', *Critique* 25: 57–65.

McCarthy, M. (1953) *The Groves of Academe*, London: Panther, 1964.

McDermott, J. (1985) 'Kingsley and the women', *Critical Quarterly* 27: 65–71.

MacInnes, H. (1948) *Friends and Lovers*, London: Harrap.

McIntosh, L. (1956) *Oxford Folly*, London: Johnson.

Mackenzie, W.J.M. (1960–1) 'Oxbridge myths – and others', *Universities Quarterly* 15: 337–41.

McPherson, A.F. (1972) *The Generally Educated Scot: An Old Ideal in a Changing University Structure*, Milton Keynes: Open University E 282, unit 15.

————(1973) 'Selections and survivals: a sociology of the ancient Scottish universities', in Brown (ed.) 1973: 163–202.

————(1983a) 'An angle on the Geist: persistence and change in the Scottish educational tradition', in Humes and Patterson (eds) 1983: 216–43.

————(1983b) 'Comments', in Phillipson (ed.) 1983: 285–96.

Mais, S.P.B. (1949) *Who Dies?*, London: Hutchinson.

Malamud, B. (1961) *A New Life*, London: Four Square, 1964.

'Malloch, P.' (1968) *Murder of a Student*, London: Long.

Mann, J. (1973) *The Only Security*, London: Macmillan.

————(1974) *The Sticking Place*, London: Macmillan.

————(1975) *Captive Audience*, London: Macmillan.

Marshall, T.H. (1950) *Citizenship and Social Class*, Cambridge: Cambridge University Press.

Marsland, D. (1981) 'Education – vast horizons, meagre vision', in D. Anderson, Lait, and Marsland (eds) 1981: 39–62.

————(1985) *Neglect and Betrayal: War and Violence in Modern Sociology*, London: Alliance Publishers for the Institute for European Defence and Strategic Studies.

————(1987) *Bias Against Business: Anti-Capitalist Inclinations in Modern Sociology*, Lancing: Gordon Pro-Print.

————(1988) *Seeds of Bankruptcy*, London: Claridge Press.

Marston, E.C. (1954) *Take the High Ground*, Boston, Mass: Little, Brown.

Martin, D. (ed.) (1969) *Anarchy and Culture: The Problem of the Contemporary University*, London: Routledge & Kegan Paul.

————(1983) 'Trends and standards in British higher education', in J.W. Chapman (ed.) 1983: 167–83.

Masterman, J.C. (1933) *An Oxford Tragedy*, Harmondsworth: Penguin, 1939.

————(1952) *To Teach the Senators Wisdom: An Oxford Guide-Book*,

London: Hodder & Stoughton.

————(1957) *The Case of the Four Friends*, London: Hodder & Stoughton.

'Melville, J.' (1970) *A New Kind of Killer, an Old Kind of Death*, London: Hodder & Stoughton.

Middleton, S. (1987) *After a Fashion*, London: Hutchinson.

Miers, E. (1933) *Big Ben*, Philadelphia, Pa: Westminster, 1942.

Miles, G. (1979) *Treffin*, Talybont: y Lolfa.

Miller, N. (1947) *The Merry Innocents*, New York: Harper.

Miner, V. (1982) *Murder in the English Department*, London: Women's Press.

Minogue, K.R. (1973) *The Concept of a University*, London: Weidenfeld & Nicolson.

Mitchell, G. (1958) *Spotted Hemlock*, Harmondsworth: Penguin, 1960.

Mitchell, J. (1961) *Imaginary Toys*, London: Hutchinson.

Moodie, G.C. and Eustace, R. (1974) *Power and Authority in British Universities*, London: Allen & Unwin.

Morgan, W.G.C. (1948) *An Oxford Romance*, Carmarthen: Druid Press.

Morrah, D.M.M. (1933) *The Mummy Case*, London: Faber & Faber.

Morris, C.R. (1960–1) 'The popularity of Oxford and Cambridge?', *Universities Quarterly* 15: 327–36.

————(1962) 'The function of universities today', in Niblett (ed.) 1962: 18–28.

Morrow, H.M.W. (1917) *Lydia of the Pines*, New York: Stokes.

Mosley, N. (1965) *Accident*, London: Hodder & Stoughton.

Mowat, C.L. (1968) 'A community of scholars', in Cox and Dyson (eds) 1968: 11–13.

Muir, D. (1948) *The Pilgrims Meet Murder*, London: Herbert Jenkins.

Muir, T. (1952) *Death under Virgo*, London: Hutchinson.

Mulhern, F. (1979) *The Moment of 'Scrutiny'*, London: New Left Books.

Murdoch, I. (1987) *The Book and the Brotherhood*, Harmondsworth: Penguin, 1988.

Murray, D.L. (1945) *Folly Bridge*, London: Hodder & Stoughton.

Myer, V.G. (1988) *Culture Shock*, London: Duckworth.

Nabokov, V. (1957) *Pnin*, Harmondsworth: Penguin, 1960.

————(1962) *Pale Fire*, New York: Berkeley Books, 1968.

Nash, S. (1962) *Death of a Counterplot*, London: Bles.

Neave, G. (1982–3) 'Cuts, constraints and vexations in European higher education', *Higher Education Review* 15: 5–19.

New, D.W. (1961) *The Life of Henry Brougham to 1830*, Oxford: Clarendon Press.

Newman, J.H. (1856) *University Sketches*, Dublin: Richview, n.d.

New Zealand (1989) *Learning for Life: Education and Training Beyond the Age of Fifteen*, Wellington: Government Printer.

Niblett, W.R. (ed.) (1962) *The Expanding University*, London: Faber & Faber.

Nisbet, R. (1967) *The Sociological Tradition*, London: Heinemann.

Oakley, A. (1974) *The Sociology of Housework*, London: Robertson.

Oliver, W.H. (1968) 'A society and its universities: the case of New Zealand', in Lawler (ed.) 1968: 157–95.

Palmer, D.J. (1965) *The Rise of English Studies*, London: Oxford University Press.

Parkin, F. (1979) *Marxism and Class Theory: A Bourgeois Critique*, New York: Columbia University Press.

————(1982) *Max Weber*, Chichester: Horwood.

————(1985) *Krippendorf's Tribe*, London: Fontana, 1986.

————(1987) *The Mind and Body Shop*, London: Fontana.

Parsons, T. (1937) *The Structure of Social Action*, New York: McGraw-Hill.

Pearson, B. (1952) 'Fretful sleepers', *Landfall* 3: 201–30.

Peter, J. (1967) *Take Hands at Winter*, New York: Doubleday.

'Peters, E.' (1967) *Black is the Colour of my True Love's Heart*, London: Collins.

Phillipson, N.T. (ed.) (1983) *Universities, Society and the Future*, Edinburgh: Edinburgh University Press.

Plumb, J.H. (1964a) 'Introduction', to Plumb (ed.) 1964b: 7–10.

————(ed.)(1964b) *Crisis in the Humanities*, Harmondsworth: Penguin.

Postgate, R. (1953) *The Ledger is Kept*, London: Michael Joseph.

Powell, A. (1951) *A Question of Upbringing*, London: Heinemann.

Price, A. (1972) *Colonel Butler's Wolf*, London: Gollancz.

————(1976) *War Game*, London: Gollancz.

————(1981) *Soldier No More*, London: Grafton.

Priestley, J.B. (1968a) *Out of Town*, London: Heinemann.

————(1968b) *London End*, London: Heinemann.

————(1984) *The Image Men*, London: Allison & Busby.

Proctor, M. (1957) *The English University Novel*, Berkeley: University of California Press.

Pym, B. (1955) *Less than Angels*, Bath: Chivers, 1971.

————(1980) *A Few Green Leaves*, London: Macmillan.

————(1982) *An Unsuitable Attachment*, London: Macmillan.

————(1985) *Crampton Hodnet*, New York: Dutton.

————(1986) *An Academic Question*, London: Macmillan.

Quinton, A.M. (1958) 'Oxford in fiction', *Oxford Magazine* 76: 212–18.

Ramanathan, S. (1978) *The Novels of C.P. Snow: A Critical Introduction*, London: Macmillan.

Raphael, F. (1976) *The Glittering Prizes*, Harmondsworth: Penguin.

————(1980) *Oxbridge Blues*, London: Cape.

Raven, S. (1960) *Doctors Wear Scarlet*, London: Blond.

————(1966) *The Sabre Squadron*, London: Blond.

————(1970) *Places Where They Sing*, London: Blond.

————(1976) *The Survivors*, London: Blond & Briggs.

————(1980) *An Inch of Fortune*, London: Blond & Briggs.

Reckwitz, E. (1987) 'Literaturprofessoren als Romanciers – die Romane von David Lodge und Malcolm Bradbury', *Germanisch-Romanische Monatsschrift*, 37: 199–217.

'Rees, D.' (1945) *The Cambridge Murders*, Harmondsworth: Penguin, 1952.

Reid, J. (1989) 'Beyond the democratic intellect: the Scottish example and university reform in Canada's Maritime Provinces, 1870–1933', in Axelrod and Reid (eds) 1989: 275–300.

Rendell, R. (1976) *A Demon in my View*, London: Hutchinson.

Rex, J. (1961) *Key Problems in Sociological Theory*, London: Routledge & Kegan Paul.

————(1974) *Sociology and the Demystification of the Modern World*, London: Routledge & Kegan Paul.

————(1983) 'British sociology 1960–1980', *Social Forces* 61: 999–1,009.

Roberts, G. (1974) *Chemical Eric*, St John's: Belvoir.

Robinson, R. (1956) *Landscape with Dead Dons*, Harmondsworth: Penguin, 1963.

Robinson, T. (1961) *When Scholars Fall*, London: Hutchinson.

Ross, J.M. (1960) *Until the Day She Dies*, London: Hamish Hamilton.

Rossen, J. (1987) *The World of Barbara Pym*, London: Macmillan.

Rothblatt, S. (1968) *The Revolution of the Dons*, London: Faber and Faber.

————(1988) 'An open mind looking down', *Times Higher Education Supplement* 22 April.

Rowlands, J. (1978) *Tician* Tician, Llandyssal, Gomer.

'Ruell, P.' (1974) *Death Takes the Low Road*, London: Hutchinson.

Ruthven, K.K. (1983) 'Male critics and feminist criticism', *Essays in Criticism* 33: 263–72.

Sanderson, M. (ed.) (1975) *The Universities in the Nineteenth Century*, London: Routledge & Kegan Paul.

Sayers, D.L. (1935) *Gaudy Night*, London: Gollancz, 1972.

————(1958a) 'A murder at Pentecost', in Sayers 1958b, 102–11.

————(1958b) *A Treasury of Sayers Stories*, London: Gollancz.

Schellenberger, J. (1981) 'Life after Lucky Jim', *Times Higher Education Supplement* 28 August.

————(1982a) 'Fiction and the first women students', *New Universities Quarterly* 36: 352–8.

————(1982b) 'University fiction and the university crisis', *Critical Quarterly* 24: 45–8.

————(1982–3) 'Life after Lucky Jim: the last thirty years of English university fiction', *Higher Education Review* 15: 69–76.

————(1984) 'Literature and society: after Raymond Williams', *Culture, Education and Society* 38: 347–57.

Schumann, K. (1983) 'Die Wirklichkeit der Fiktion; J.I.M. Stewarts Oxford Quintett', *Recent Novels on Society*, anglistik und englischunterricht 19: 43–63.

Sciama, S. (1984) 'Ambivalence and dedication: academic wives in Cambridge University, 1870–1970', in Callan and Ardener (eds) 1984: 50–66.

Scott, J. (1982) *The Upper Classes: Property and Privilege in Britain*, London: Macmillan.

Scott, P. (1984) *The Crisis of the University*, London: Croom Helm.

Sharpe, T. (1974) *Porterhouse Blue*, London: Pan, 1978.

————(1976) *Wilt*, London: Pan, 1978.

Shaw, H. (1981) *Death of a Don*, London: Hodder & Stoughton.

Sheed, W. (1967) *A Middle-Class Education*, London: Cassell.

Sheppard, R. (1989) 'Meetings and exchanges: images of academics', *Oxford Magazine* 41: 5–8.

Sinclair, A., (1959) *My Friend Judas*, London: Faber & Faber.

Smith, M.L. (1962) *No Easy Answer*, London: Hutchinson.

Snow, C.P. (1947) *The Light and the Dark*, Harmondsworth: Penguin, 1962.

————(1951) *The Masters*, London: Macmillan.

————(1954) *The New Men*, Harmondsworth: Penguin, 1959.

————(1959) *The Two Cultures and the Scientific Revolution*, Cambridge: Cambridge University Press.

————(1960) *The Affair*, London: Macmillan, 1972.

————(1968) *The Sleep of Reason*, Harmondsworth: Penguin, 1970.

————(1971) *Public Affairs*, London: Macmillan.

Sparrow, J. (1968) 'Egalitarianism and an academic elite', in C.B. Cox and A.E. Dyson (eds) 1968: 64–6.

————(1969a) 'Revolt and reform in Oxford, 1968–9', in C.B. Cox and A.E. Dyson (eds) 1969: 125–33.

————(1969b) 'Revolting students?', in D. Martin (ed.) 1969: 172–84.

Spencer, P. (1961) *Full Term*, London: Faber & Faber.

Stead, C.K. (1971) *Smith's Dream*, Auckland: Longman Paul.

————(1986) *The Death of the Body*, London: Collins.

Stewart, J.I.M. (1954) *Mark Lambert's Supper*, London: Gollancz.

————(1955) *The Guardians*, London: Gollancz.

————(1961) *The Man Who Won the Pools*, London: Gollancz.

————(1963) *The Last Tresillians*, Harmondsworth: Penguin, 1966.

————(1966) *The Aylwins*, London: Gollancz.

————(1967) *Vanderlyn's Kingdom*, London: Gollancz.

———(1971) *Avery's Mission*, New York: Norton.

———(1972) *A Palace of Art*, London: Gollancz.

———(1973) *Mungo's Dream*, London: Gollancz.

———(1974) *The Gaudy*, London: Gollancz.

———(1975) *Young Pattullo*, London: Gollancz.

———(1976) *A Memorial Service*, London: Gollancz.

———(1977) *The Madonna of the Astrolabe*, London: Gollancz.

———(1978) *Full Term*, London: Gollancz.

———(1979) *Our England is a Garden, and Other Stories*, London: Gollancz.

———(1981) *The Bridge at Arta and Other Stories*, London: Gollancz.

———(1982) *A Villa in France*, London: Gollancz.

———(1983) *My Aunt Christina, and Other Stories*, London: Gollancz.

———(1985) *The Naylors*, London: Gollancz.

———(1986) *Parlour 4, and Other Stories*, London: Gollancz.

———(1987) *Myself and Michael Innes*, London: Gollancz.

See also Innes, M.

Stewart, M. (1983) *Monkey Shines*, New York: Freundlich.

Storey, D. (1972) *Pasmore*, London: Longman.

Super, R.H. (ed.) (1965) *The Complete Prose Works of Matthew Arnold*, volume V, Ann Arbor, Mich: University of Michigan Press.

Sutherland, N.S. (1987) *Men Change Too*, London: Duckworth.

Swinden, P. (1984) *The English Novel of History and Society*, 1940–1980, London: Macmillan.

Symons, J. (1972) *Bloody Murder: From the Detective Story to the Crime Novel*, 1st edn, London: Faber & Faber.

———(1985) *Bloody Murder*, 2nd edn, Harmondsworth: Penguin.

Taylor, J.L. (1985) 'Beyond a utilitarian scenario', *Culture, Education and Society* 39: 306–9.

Taylor, L. (1986) *Professor Lapping Sends his Apologies*, Stoke-on-Trent: Trentham Books.

Thomas, A.E.W. (1969) *The Professor*, London: Gollancz.

Thomas, K. (1988) 'The past in a clearer light, a beacon on our future', *Times Higher Education Supplement* 2 December.

Thompson, E.P. (1978) *The Poverty of Theory*, London: Merlin.

Todd, R. (1981) 'Malcolm Bradbury's *The History Man*: the novelist as reluctant impresario', Dutch Quarterly Review of Anglo-American Letters 11: 162–82.

Trickett, R. (1954) *The Course of Love*, London: Constable.

———(1966) *The Elders*, London: Constable.

Trilling, L. (1962) 'Science, literature and culture: a comment on the Leavis–Snow controversy', in Cornelius and Vincent (eds) 1964: 37–54.

'Truscott, B.' (1943) *Redbrick University*, London: Faber & Faber.

Turck, S. (1967) *An Interpretation of C.P. Snow's 'The Masters'*, Frankfurt.

Turner, B.S. (1986) *Citizenship and Capitalism*, London: Allen & Unwin.

Turner, J. (1964) *The Long Avenues*, London: Cassell.

Usborne, R. (1976) *Wodehouse at Work to the End*, London: Barrie & Jenkins.

Vidler, A. (1964) 'The future of divinity', in J.H. Plumb (ed.) 1964b: 82–95.

Vogel, A. (1963) 'The academic world of C.P. Snow', *Twentieth Century Literature* 9: 143–52.

Vulliamy, C.E. (1952) *Don Among the Dead Men: A Satirical Thriller*, London: Michael Joseph.

————(1961) *Tea at the Abbey*, London: Michael Joseph.

Wain, J. (1988) *Where the Rivers Meet*, London: Hutchinson.

Walker, J.K. (1959) *Running on the Spot*, London: Hutchinson.

Watkin, L.E. (1940) *Geese in the Forum*, New York: Knopf.

Watson, G. (1978) 'Fictions of academe: dons and realities', *Encounter* 51, 5: 42–6.

Watt, D.C. (1968) 'Expansion at the London School of Economics,' in C.B. Cox and A.E. Dyson (eds) 1968: 32–5.

————(1969) 'The freedom of the universities: illusion and reality, 1962–69', in C.B. Cox and A.E. Dyson (eds) 1969: 119–25.

Watts, R.L. (1987) *New Zealand's Universities: Partners in National Development*, Wellington: New Zealand Vice-Chancellors' Committee.

Waugh, A (1963) *The Path of Dalliance*, London: Chapman and Hall.

Waugh, E. (1928) *Decline and Fall*, London: Chapman and Hall.

————(1945) *Brideshead Revisited*, Harmondsworth: Penguin, 1962.

Weiss, W. (1988) *Der Anglo-Amerikanische Universitatsroman: Eine Historische Skizze*, Darmstadt: Wissenschaftliche Buchgesellschaft.

Welch, R. (1987) 'Arnold's sofa and Derrida's gymnasium', *Times Higher Education Supplement* 23 January.

Wersky, G. (1978) *The Visible College: A Collective Biography of British Scientists and Socialists of the 1930s*, London: Allen Lane.

White, R.J. (1971) *A Second-Hand Tomb*, London: Macmillan.

Widdowson, P. (1984) 'The anti-history men: Malcolm Bradbury and David Lodge', *Critical Quarterly* 26, 4: 5–32.

Williams, D. (1977) *Treasure by Degrees*, London: Collins.

————(1988) *Treasure in Oxford*, London: Macmillan.

Williams, R. (1958) *Culture and Society, 1780–1950*, London: Chatto & Windus.

————(1960) *Border Country*, London: Chatto & Windus.

————(1964) *Second Generation*, London: Hogarth Press.

————(1973) *The Country and the City*, London: Chatto & Windus.

————(1978) *The Volunteers*, London: Hogarth Press, 1985.

————(1980) *Problems in Materialism and Culture: Selected Essays,* London: Verso.

————(1981) *Culture,* Glasgow: Fontana.

————(1987) 'Crawling from the wreckage', *Times Higher Education Supplement* 5 June.

Wilson, A. (1950a) 'Totentanz', in A. Wilson 1950b: 128–51.

————(1950b) *Such Darling Dodos and Other Stories,* Frogmore: Granada, 1980.

————(1958) *Anglo-Saxon Attitudes,* Harmondsworth: Penguin, 1963.

Wilson, B. (1968) 'Youth culture, the universities and student unrest', in C.B. Cox and A.E. Dyson (eds) 1968: 70–80.

Wilson, K. (1982) 'Jim, Jake and the years between: the will to stasis in the contemporary British novel', *Ariel* 13: 55–69.

Winn, D. (ed.) (1977) *Murder Ink,* New York: Workman.

Wister, O. (1903) *Philosophy Four: A Story of Harvard University,* New York: Macmillan.

Wodehouse, P.G. (1914a) 'Pots o' money', in Wodehouse 1914b: 162–75.

————(1914b) *The Man Upstairs, and Other Stories,* London: Barrie & Jenkins, 1980.

————(1934) *Thank You, Jeeves,* London: Barrie & Jenkins, 1975.

————(1963) *Stiff Upper Lip, Jeeves,* London: Herbert Jenkins.

Wright, C.J. (1979) 'Academics and their aims: English and Scottish approaches to university education in the nineteenth century', *History of Education* 2, 91–7.

'Yorke, M.' (1972) *Silent Witness,* London: Arrow Books.

————(1973) *Grave Matters,* Leicester: Ulverscroft, 1975.

————(1976) *Cast for Death,* London: Hutchinson.

————(1977) 'Oxford vs Cambridge: the Dark Blues Have the Most', in Winn (ed.) 1977: 264–6.

NAME INDEX

SUBJECT INDEX